Rethinking Environmental Protection

A Natural Approach to Nature

Phillip F. Cramer

LEXINGTON BOOKS
Lanham • Boulder • New York • Oxford

LEXINGTON BOOKS

Published in the United States of America
by Lexington Books
4720 Boston Way, Lanham, Maryland 20706

12 Hid's Copse Road
Cumnor Hill, Oxford OX2 9JJ, England

Copyright © 2000 by Lexington Books

All rights reserved. No part of this publication may be reproduced, stored in a retrieval system, or transmitted in any form or by any means, electronic, mechanical, photocopying, recording, or otherwise, without the prior permission of the publisher.

British Library Cataloguing in Publication Information Available

Library of Congress Cataloging-in-Publication Data

Cramer, Phillip F., 1975–
  Rethinking environmental protection : a natural approach to nature / Phillip F. Cramer.
     p. cm.
  Includes bibliographical references and index.
  ISBN 0-7391-0115-3 (cloth : alk. paper)
  1. Environmental protection. 2. Environmental degradation. 3. Environmental policy. 4. Local government. 5. Environmental protection—International cooperation. I. Title.
  TD170 .C73 2000
  363.7'056—dc21   00-020610

Printed in the United States of America

∞™ The paper used in this publication meets the minimum requirements of American National Standard for Information Sciences—Permanence of Paper for Printed Library Materials, ANSI/NISO Z39.48–1992.

To Anna

Contents

Preface	ix
Acknowledgments	xiii
1. The Groundwork	1
2. Environmental Insecurity	7
3. No Place, People, or Person Is Immune	25
4. A Natural Approach to Nature	47
5. Getting There Together	69
6. Creating Global Foundations	91
7. All Pollution Is Local	113
8. Everyone Else Is Doing It	135
9. Putting It All Together	167
10. Getting Past the Hurdles and Reaping the Rewards	183
11. Rewarding the New Century with a New Approach	207
Selected Bibliography	211
Index	217
About the Author	227

Preface

I can remember the first time I became seriously interested in environmental issues. Some of my fourth-grade classmates and I became concerned about land development around our school and neighborhoods. The woods and grasslands where we would play and discover nature were being plowed under as new homes were popping up in their place. As development continued, I can remember episodes when deer and other animals would find themselves wandering into our subdivision and hop fences as they traversed across our backyards. Even a ten-year-old could understand that the nearby developments were destroying habitats. In response, some fellow classmates and I started a group called CHASE, Children Helping Animals Survive Everywhere. We did not know much about habitats or environmental values, but we did have a sense that something was not right. Our teacher allowed us to discover why we felt the way we did. She allowed us to research and discover the value of wildlife. She also taught us about the need for new housing developments. By providing us with the resources and information, she urged us to form our own opinions and develop our own relationship with nature. As young schoolchildren, we could not understand all of the forces at work, but we did understand that a small change in the ecosystem creates waves throughout the entire environment much like a rock thrown into a pond sends ripples throughout the water. We discovered that the deer in our backyards, the silt in our local creek, and the loss of our woods were all related to the new developments. We never did stop the new housing development. But I did learn some very valuable lessons about both the environment and education. First, I discovered that an ecosystem consists of many interconnected parts. When one part is affected, the whole ecosystem is affected. Second, I learned that if we are to change individual outlooks on environmental issues, people must be able to discover the value of nature themselves. My teacher did not impose certain beliefs upon us; rather, she provided us with the information and resources we need to create our feelings toward environmental issues.

This book attempts to translate some of these simple lessons into a new approach to environmental protection. The book is the culmination of years of research and debate about approaches to environmental protection. It illustrates how environmental issues affect every place and every person in the world. Due to the cumulative effect of environmental degradation, environmental issues have risen to the forefront of both national and international agendas. Policymakers who once dismissed threats of environmental degradation are quickly taking notice as environmental degradation brings new security concerns. If policymakers are to craft a solution, they must recognize any approach to environmental degradation requires change at both the policy and personal levels. At the policy level, a solution should mirror the interconnected nature of the environment. Thus change must occur at all levels: the international, national, regional, and local. The utilization of a web of actors is best able to take a holistic approach to environmental protection. It is also able to effectuate change at the personal level. A workable and long-lasting solution requires changes in individual behavior and attitudes, which is necessary for the creation of ecologically sensitive legal, political, and social institutions. The following chapters explain, in detail, how we can forge such a solution that is able to reward the next century with a new approach to environmental protection.

Chapter 1 provides the theoretical background for the book's thesis. It introduces the problem of environmental degradation and the need for thoughtful and scientifically sound solutions. It sets forth the analytical framework and application that the book explores. Chapter 2 discusses how environmental degradation breaks down world order and international law. It traces the relationship between environmental issues and interstate and intrastate security issues. Chapter 3 provides case studies of states and peoples struggling with environmental degradation. It illustrates how environmental issues contribute to the collapse of legal, social, and political stability.

Chapter 4 introduces and explains the synergistic linkage paradigm and its scientific framework for environmental solutions. It proposes an integrated approach to solving environmental problems. The chapter discusses various case studies and the need for change in the current approach to environmental policy. Additionally, it argues that a change in ethics is needed in order to overcome these problems.

Chapter 5 introduces how within such an approach it is necessary to build global frameworks. It explains how environmental degradation can assist in the formulation of treaties and international agreements. Chapter 6 provides case studies of how international cooperation brings states and peoples together to solve environmental degradation. It explains the legal agreements resulting from such interaction and the success of international governing bodies to address various environmental problems.

Chapter 7 emphasizes the need for local action to complement international action. It introduces the concept of localism and explains the legal and philosophical roots of localism in Western thought. It illustrates the movement towards local solutions to address environmental problems and explores the evolution of legal institutions designed to accomplish the goals of this movement. Chapter 8 provides an in-depth and exhaustive survey of local solutions, both in the United States and abroad, to environmental problems. The chapter illustrates the relative success of local legal institutions to protect the environment.

Chapter 9 attempts to create a holistic approach for environmental protection that taps both international and local action. It illustrates how local action within global frameworks can realize the goals of international agreements while providing for innovation and involvement at the local level.

Chapter 10 highlights some of the barriers to an integrated approach such as North/South problems and ethical obstacles. It explains how a linkage approach that operates at both the policy and personal level can overcome these barriers and accomplish environmental protection. It also illustrates the tangential benefits an integrated approach can have on the overall well-being of society. Finally, chapter 11 provides a summary of the findings and proposed solutions set forth in this book. It argues that we have the structural frameworks already in place to carry out an integrated approach, but immediate and thoughtful action is required if we are to steer away from the current path of unsustainability.

Acknowledgments

There are many people to whom I owe tremendous gratitude. Without their support, help, and encouragement, this book would be but a few observations and theories jotted down on scrap paper. It is said that the trouble with the publishing business is that too many people who have half a mind to write a book do so. I have been very fortunate to have the valuable input of so many other minds to make up for the half I may be missing.

First and foremost, my wife, to whom this book is dedicated, deserves special recognition for her help through the years. She has given so much of her time and effort to help me refine and revise this book. Anna has been by my side since the first day of my research, and her support and encouragement have meant a lot. She also has the unique ability to be painfully honest and still help me through difficult times.

Two individuals to whom I would like to extend a very special thank you are Dr. John Outland of the political science department at the University of Richmond and Professor Jon Bruce of Vanderbilt University School of Law. Their help and support really made this book a reality. Dr. Outland was there for me at the conception of this project, reviewing drafts of papers that would later become the basis for the manuscript. Professor Bruce helped me turn a set of ideas and theories into the finished book before you today. He also undertook the painful task of reviewing early drafts of the completed manuscript. Throughout the entire process, each has been a wise mentor and a trusted friend.

Special thanks must also be extended to my family, for their support and encouragement; Nicholas Brown, for providing me with an opportunity to discuss my work and reviewing early chapters; Lisa Heller, for her help in initiating my research; David Spence and Wendi Wagner, for their invaluable recommendations and comments on the manuscript; Abigail Johnson, for her wonderful assistance and encouragement; and the great folks at Lexington Books, for everything they did to help bring this project to fruition. There are many more people, too numerous to mention, to whom I am also indebted. Hopefully, they know who they are and will accept my sincere thanks.

1

The Groundwork

Smog permeates our air. Storms ravage our coasts. Solid waste fills our land. Heavy metals pollute our water. Hazardous wastes seep into our groundwater. Human population reaches all time levels. Species biodiversity approaches all time lows. Tropical diseases emerge in temperate climates. Polar ice caps shed large fragments. Fisheries collapse. Pesticides poison thousands.[1] Are these the signs of an environmental crisis or just the precursors to even greater environmental degradation?[2] Unfortunately, there may be no way to tell. What we do know is that no region, state, community, or individual is immune from the far-reaching effects of environmental degradation.

It has been more than twenty-five years since the first U.N.-sponsored Conference on the Human Environment in Stockholm and the list of environmental problems requiring attention is longer than ever: climate change, ozone depletion, transboundary air pollution, deforestation, soil loss and contamination, desertification and drought, destruction of biological diversity, pollution of the oceans and seas, deterioration of fresh water resources, traffic in toxic and dangerous products and wastes, and so on.[3] While scientists may be able to describe where our path is headed, it is up to policymakers to alter our direction.

Environmental scientists have long recognized that humanity is on an unsustainable path that threatens the Earth's life-sustaining systems.[4] Unfortunately, such recognition has not been followed by communication with leaders and policymakers. However, for the first time these lines of communication are opening. Consequently, environmental issues are rising to the top of many international and national policy agendas.[5] The international community is increasingly focusing on the environment as an issue for diplomatic discourse and interaction.[6] Part of this heightened interest is due to the link between the environment and the international security agenda.[7] For example, Kofi Annan, the secretary general of the United Nations, observed that "[f]ailure to act now could endanger our plant irreversibly, unleashing a spiral of increased hunger, deprivation, disease, and squalor. Ultimately, we could face the destabilizing effects of conflict over vital natural resources."[8]

World leaders and policymakers are not the only ones interested in environmental issues. Numerous interest groups have taken up the cause. Our primary and secondary schools now teach our young about environmental ethics. Polls in both North America and Europe illustrate that a majority considers protection of the environment and fighting pollution as top priorities.[9] Additionally, similar surveys show parallel levels of concern in less-developed countries.[10]

As concern and education rise, people no longer view the Earth's ecological system as resilient and stable in the face of human intrusions.[11] Rather, they understand that living on the earth is a balancing act.[12] The prevailing notion is that the solution, if there is one, to such environmental problems is not to be found in individual actions. Rather, such problems require a concerted effort on the part of every individual, society, state, and civilization of the world.[13]

Humans possess the basic instinct of survival. This instinct is most apparent when we try to minimize war, chaos, and suffering while we attempt to maximize peace, harmony, and opulence. To that list, we now find ourselves adding environmental issues. More and more, environmental problems are finding themselves prominent on our scientific, policy, and public agendas.[14]

Global environmental problems are everyone's problems. The emergence of international law calls upon all states (and even peoples), of varying degrees of economic development and differing commitments to environmental action, to work together not only on environmental issues, but also on all issues that affect the global order. Differences in perception and capability are not easily overcome, but because no state can avoid the most serious of environmental problems, such as climate change and loss of biodiversity, the perception among both environmentalists and policymakers is that there is little choice other than consensus building and cooperative action.[15] Unfortunately, many see international law as the end rather than just the beginning.

With the end of the cold war, the prospects would appear promising for such international cooperation.[16] Environmental activism has attempted to fill the vacuum left by the collapse of communism by offering a new vision for an alternative world order.[17] This vision of environmental protection, however, is faltering in practice. International efforts are stripping local communities of their activism and innovation. Meanwhile, environmental policymakers ignore the interconnected nature of the environment degradation, opting for piecemeal solutions instead of a holistic approach. The task thus becomes to develop an approach to environmental protection that is capable of unifying the states, regions, peoples, *and* ecosystems of this world while solving for the root problems of environmental degradation. This entails developing an approach that can address environmental degradation at both the policy and personal levels.

The following chapters set forth such an approach. It begins by illustrating the need for a new approach to reverse the trend of environmental degradation. Environmental degradation has the ability to cause worldwide destruction and upset order and unity in the global community. Conflict and chaos follow such disturbances. Only a chance in how we approach environmental issues can overcome these problems. Such an approach needs to incorporate lessons learned in the fields of biology, ecology, chemistry, sociology, philosophy, political science, and international relations.

These lessons challenge our current notions and ideas of environmental protection and ecological understanding, but afford us the best opportunity to save ourselves and our environment. They teach us that global institutions are a vital part of any approach to environmental protection, but should be primarily used to assist local communities identify local instances of environmental abuse. These lessons show us that communities can mobilize quickly because of their closeness to the problem. As a result, local empowerment and realization changes human viewpoints and helps to overcome institutional inertia. National governments realize that local action relieves the state of costly obligations and increases governing efficiency. As communities respond to their individual problems, global institutions can monitor the overall health of the world ecosystem.

Notes

1. See, among others, Ranee K. L. Panjabi, *The Earth Summit at Rio: Politics, Economics, and the Environment* (Boston: Northeastern University Press, 1997), 9; John Last, "Redefining the Unacceptable," *The Lancet* 346, no. 8991 (December 23, 1995): 1642.

2. See, for example, Robert D. Kaplan, "The Coming Anarchy: How Scarcity, Crime, Overpopulation, Tribalism, and Disease Are Rapidly Destroying the Social Fabric of Our Planet," *The Atlantic Monthly* (Feb. 1994): 44-75. Five years ago, Robert Kaplan scared the world with his predictions of a coming anarchy. Kaplan described how severe environmental degradation and resource scarcities in many less-developed states are contributing to social collapse, anarchy, and conflict. Kaplan concluded that, given the current economic, political, and social trajectories of many developing states, the world can expect conflicts and crises of this nature to proliferate in the future.

3. Lawrence Susskind and Connie Ozawa, *The International Politics of the Environment*, ed. Andrew Hurrell and Benedict Kingsbury (Oxford: Clarendon Press, 1992).

4. See, among others, Gliberto C. Gallopin and Paul Raskin, "Windows on the Future: Global Scenarios and Sustainability," *Environment* 40, no. 3 (Apr. 1998): 6; John Brodribb, "Mission Earth," *New Scientist* (Dec. 13, 1997).

5. For example, towards the end of his tenure as secretary of state, Warren Christopher emphasized the need to take action on environmental issues. In one speech, Christopher remarked that "our ability to advance our global interests is inextricably linked to how we manage the Earth's natural resources." Richard Norton-Taylor, "Environment: CIA Turns Green," *The Guardian* (London), 11 Sept. 1996, 4. He explained that "as we move to the twenty-first century the nexus between security and environment will become even more important." Milton Viorst, "The Coming Instability," *The Washington Quarterly* 20, no. 4 (autumn 1997): 153. These speeches preceded a memorandum entitled "Memorandum to All Under and Assistant Secretaries: Integrating Environmental Issues into the Department's Core Foreign Policy Goals," in which Christopher wrote:

> Under the leadership of President Clinton and Vice President Gore, our administration has identified international environmental and resource issues as an important component of our long-term economic and political interests. . . . America's national interests are inextricably linked with the quality of the Earth's environment. . . . World-wide environmental decay threatens U.S. national prosperity. . . . Environmental and resource issues can also have an important effect on political stability in regions key to U.S. interests.

Gerald B. Thomas, "U.S. Environmental Security Policy: Broad Concern or Narrow Interests," *Journal of Environment and Development* 6, no. 4 (Dec. 1997): 397. However, Secretary Christopher's successor, Madeleine Albright, has yet to stress the theme even though global warming and deforestation have recently surfaced at the top of the U.S. policy agenda. Editorial, "Green Diplomacy," *The Washington Post*, 14 Mar. 1997, sec. A, p. 26 (F).

6. Brian R. Shaw, "When Are Environmental Issues Security Issues?" *Report of the Environmental Change and Security Project, The Woodrow Wilson Center*, Issue 2 (spring 1996): 39. Available from http://w3.pnl.gov:2080/ces/academic/ww_1shaw.htm; Internet. For a discussion on the sudden attention environmental degradation has received from the world community, see Thomas F. Homer-Dixon, "On the Threshold: Environmental Changes As Causes of Acute Conflict," *International Security* 16, no. 2 (fall 1991): 76. Available from http://utl.library.utoronto.ca/www/pcs/thresh/thresh1.htm; Internet.

7. Shin-wha Lee, "Not a One-Time Event: Environmental Change, Ethnic Rivalry, and Violent Conflict in the Third World," *Journal of Environment and Development* 6, no. 4 (Dec. 1997): 365.

8. Interview of Kofi Annan, "Gore Visits Earth Summit Plus Five," *All Things Considered, National Public Radio* (June 23, 1997), Transcript No. 97062314-212.

9. See, among others, "Europeans and the Environment in 1992," *Eurobarometer* (Brussels, Belgium, 1992).

10. R. E. Dunlap, G. H. Gallup, and A. M. Gallup, "Of Global Concern: Results of the Health of the Planet Survey, *Environment* 35, no. 9 (1993).

11. This is not to say that there are not skeptics (many of whom are supported by hard scientific data and research) who feel that environmental issues have been overclaimed. But the mere fact that they feel this way indicates that there is a predominant perception that environmental degradation deserves attention. One need only visit a local library or review congressional hearings; the amount of literature and attention environmental issues have produced is immense.

12. David Adamson, *Defending the World: The Politics and Diplomacy of the Environment*, (New York: I. B. Tauris & Co., 1990), 15.

13. Some question the mere existence of environmental crises. This book does not address that concern, but rather defers to the numerous titles, reports, and studies that illustrate the existence of environmental problems.

14. Thomas F. Homer-Dixon, "On the Threshold: Environmental Changes As Causes of Acute Conflict," *International Security* 16, no. 2 (fall 1991): 76. Available from http://utl.library.utoronto.ca/www/pcs/thresh/thresh1.htm; Internet. Two of the many trends that have emerged in the post–Cold War era are the acceptance of the free enterprise system and the emergence of international environmental law. Jang B Singh and Emily F. Carasco, "Business Ethics, Economic Development, and Protection of the Environment in the New World Order," *Journal of Business Ethics* 15, no. 3 (Mar. 1996): 297-307. With respect to the former, environmental issues synergize with the free market to produce a mutually dependent interaction. Uncontrolled business activity, in many cases, harms the environment, while at the same time a harmed environment hampers

most business activities. Udi Helman, "Sustainable Development: Strategies for Reconciling Environment and Economy in the Developing World," *The Washington Quarterly* 18, no. 4 (autumn 1995): 189. See also, Jeremy Breacher and Tim Costello, "Labor's Day: The Challenge Ahead," *The Nation* 267, no. 8 (Sept. 21, 1998): 11; Paul R. Ehrich et al., "No Middle Way on the Environment," *The Atlantic Monthly*, 280, no. 6 (Dec. 1997): 98. This spiraling interaction poses a special problem for environmental protection.

15. Jeffrey Stoub, "The Environment—A New Priority in International Relations, a Planetary Problem," *Business Mexico* (Jan./Feb. 1994).

16. But as Zhang Yunling observes, despite "a general global maldevelopment . . . and the corresponding increase in ecological and environmental [degradation]. . . . The end of the Cold War itself does not appear to have improved the prospects for successfully dealing with these issues." Zhang Yunling, in *Whose World Order? Uneven Globalization and the End of the Cold War*, ed. by Hans-Henrik Holm and Georg Sorensen (Boulder, Colo.: Westview Press, 1995), 94.

17. Eddie Koch, "Environment: New Vision Vital to Novel World Order," *Inter Press Service* (May 6, 1992).

2

Environmental Insecurity

Environmental degradation does not just threaten the animal and plant kingdoms; it poses an equal if not greater threat to human security. Environmental degradation has the potential to break down world order and international relations. This chapter traces the relationship between environmental issues and interstate and intrastate security issues. This examination of environmental insecurity illustrates the need for an environmental approach that recognizes the interconnectedness of environmental issues and development and security concerns.

Realization

As the harms associated with environmental degradation become more apparent, the causal link between environmental problems and economic decline, social strife, and war have become more evident. These threats have emerged with greater clarity in the post-Cold War era. Global environmental change has far-reaching implications. Environmental problems threaten both ecological and national stability. They menace human and ecological health while disrupting economic, political, and social well-being. They endanger national and international security.

Environmental security may be defined in a number of ways. It may be defined by some as having clean air to breath and water to drink. To others it can mean the security of ecological and economic sustainability. In discourse today, environmental security has come to concern how environmental degradation causes violent conflict and destroys the well-being of societies throughout the world. Each of these definitions has one aspect in common: it begins (and perhaps ends) with environmental degradation.

Perhaps the most alarming account of the potential for environmental deterioration was presented in the final report of the World Commission on Environment and Development, otherwise know as the Brundtland Report.[1] A 1988 conference on the Brundtland Report issued the following warning:

> Humanity is conducting an uncontrolled, globally pervasive experiment whose ultimate consequences could be second only to a global nuclear war. The best predictions available indicate potentially severe economic and social dislocation . . . which will worsen international tensions and increase the risk of conflicts among and within nations. These . . . changes may well become the major non-military threat to international security and the future of the global economy.[2]

Prior to the end of the Cold War, this gloomy scenario was not given the attention it deserved; only a sparse body of literature existed that explored the connections between acute conflict and environmental degradation. The end of the Cold War has increased the attention devoted to this relationship. The demise of the East-West conflict and the emergence of a "new" world order allow other threats to security such as environmental degradation to emerge with greater clarity and importance.[3] This greater clarity is described by John Last, who details how environmental degradation can lead to conflict:

> When people outrun their local or regional carrying capacity and cannot afford to import food they are caught in a demographic trap: they starve, become dependent on food aid, or must emigrate. Before this happens their frantic efforts to provide themselves with food, water, and fuel wood can degrade an already fragile ecosystem into a desert that may take centuries to recover. This has happened or is happening in parts of Africa south of the Sahara, in alpine foothills of the Himalayas and the Andes, in crowded small nations such as Haiti and Honduras, and elsewhere in Central and South America. Another outcome is conflict, seen in horrifying form in Rwanda in 1994 (although that genocide had other causes too). In future conflicts environmental stress will be an increasingly important factor, both as a cause and as a consequence of warfare.[4]

Environmental degradation undermines the economic base and social fabric of states, both strong and weak, rich and poor. Estimates place the economic costs of environmental degradation at 5 to 15 percent of national incomes.[5] That number will increase as economies that are tied to environmental conditions begin to feel the true costs of land and resource degradation. Environmental degradation also generates and exacerbates intra- and interstate tensions and conflicts, due in large part to the increased flow of environmental refugees. From a realist's perspective, environmental issues are a prime example of the conflict-ridden and anarchical structure of international relations. Environmental matters open up new sources of power and leverage that heighten the risk of international conflict and anarchy.

As environmental degradation intensifies, violent conflicts involving environmental components have increased.[6] Considerable research illustrates the ability of environmental issues to generate conflict. Social and military conflicts occur when environmental degradation undermines the social stability and economic viability of a society and leads to a breakdown in political order and an increased flow of refugees.[7] These complex interactions have come to be known as the environmental security thesis, which has generated a substantial amount of research and scholarship in recent years.[8] There is now wide support for the link between environmental decline and conflict.[9] Research shows that environmental scarcities are already contributing to violent conflict in regimes throughout the world.[10]

Environmental degradation, encroaching deserts, erosion, and over-farming are destroying vast tracks of arable land. These conditions force people to leave their homes and create tension between ethnic and political groups as competition increases for scarce resources. Chapter 3 will illustrate how such factors are playing a role in states such as Somalia, Ethiopia, and Haiti.[11]

In some developing countries, the multiple effects of environmental scarcity increase the demands on the state, stimulate predatory elite behavior, reduce social trust and useful intergroup interaction, and depress state tax revenues. These processes in turn weaken the administrative capacity and legitimacy of the state.[12] Richard Norton-Taylor explains that "[c]onflicts over resources—land, food and water—will threaten the existing order, and exacerbate simmering tensions between rich and poor, north and south. The rich, including Europe, are already raising their drawbridges and targeting immigrants and asylum seekers. They are attacking the symptoms rather than the cause."[13] For years, the academic community engaged in numerous debates on the relationship between environmental issues and the cause of conflict.[14] While some discount the entire thesis, others go as far as to describe environmental security as the "ultimate security" because all other types of security are dependent upon it.[15]

Scholars are not the only people taking notice. Those who monitor U.S. national security now recognize emerging environmental dangers as genuine threats to national security.[16] Failure to make this recognition earlier has been described as possibly "the gravest political and moral failure of our generation."[17] Environmental issues are becoming a driving force in U.S. foreign policy. The United States no longer confines its definition of national security threats to nuclear arsenals, arms balances, and hostile alliances. Environmental problems, with their ability to cause political and social disorder, are now receiving increased attention from U.S. foreign policymakers. Former senator Sam Nunn explains that there is "a new and different threat to our national security emerging—the destruction of our environment. The defense establishment has a clear stake in countering this growing threat [and] one of our key national security objectives must be to reverse the accelerating pace of environmental destruction around the globe."[18]

The United States government has begun to take serious interest in the environmental security thesis. There is now a Global Environmental Affairs Directorate at the National Security Council and an Office of Environmental Security, headed by a deputy undersecretary of defense, at the Pentagon. The Department of State has highlighted the need to consider famine, water shortages, greenhouse gasses, and other concerns when conducting foreign diplomacy. Department of State officials now pay closer attention to environmental issues and regional bureaus are required to identify how environment and resource issues affect key U.S. interests.[19] The deputy undersecretary of defense of environmental security described the mission of environmental security:

> to integrate environmental concerns into our national defense policies—from ensuring responsible performance in our operations at home—to deterring regional conflicts caused by scarcity or denial of resources—to mitigating threats such as ozone depletion or loss of biodiversity that can lead to international instability and global degradation.[20]

Environmental issues are also surfacing at the top of the agenda of intelligence agencies because environmental trends are among the underlying forces that affect a nation's economy, its social stability, its behavior in world markets, and its attitude towards neighbors.[21] The Central Intelligence Agency (CIA) has started to use its resources to monitor environmental degradation and the security issues that arise from such degradation. Former spy satellites are being used to monitor compliance with environmental treaties such as the Montreal Protocol on Substances that Deplete the Stratospheric Ozone Layer, and the London Convention regulating the dumping at sea of radioactive and other wastes. CIA director John Deutch delivered a keynote speech in the summer of 1996 entitled "The Environment on the Intelligence Agenda." Deutch explained that the environment has an important place on the U.S. intelligence agenda because environmental factors "influence the internal and external political, economic, and military actions of nations important to our national security."[22]

The CIA is not the only intelligence agency involved in environmental security matters.[23] Great Britain's MI5 and other European intelligence agencies are combating the symptoms of environmental degradation. The efforts of these agencies, however, are not always targeting the root causes. Some are concentrating on the effects of environmental degradation by placing obstacles in the way of migrant workers and asylum seekers.[24]

World leaders are also taking note of the environmental security thesis. The British foreign secretary, Malcolm Rifkind, suggests that "[e]nvironmental problems may not be a prima facie cause of conflict, but they undoubtedly contribute to disputes and war."[25] Germany's environment minister advanced the argument that the greenhouse effect, desertification, and water scarcity were likely to cause "violent conflicts and millions of environmental refugees."[26] The secretary-general of the 1996 U.N. Habitat II, Wally D'Now, dramatically exclaimed that the next major war would be fought over an environmental issue—water.[27]

Scholars and leaders alike now realize the link between environmental issues and security. Notions of environmental security are evolving to include not only environmental threats to physical security, but also to include environmental threats to economic, political, and social security. The question now becomes how to address these threats.

Prospects for the Future

Recently, two political scientists, Francis Fukuyama and Samuel Huntington, predicted the end of history and the clash of civilizations, respectively.[28] These predictions drew much debate and discussion within the academic and political communities.[29] Any prediction of the future, however, should include the threat of environmental insecurity. In fact, a strong argument can be made that the primary threat to human civilization will be environmental calamity.[30] New research shows that the next wave of wars, and perhaps the next major war, will be caused by a combination of population and environmental factors.

Egypt is a prime example of how population and environmental factors may spark conflict. Egypt's population has increased eightfold this century, while its arable land has decreased. The doubling time of population is thirty-one years, faster even than India, China, and Mexico. Cairo is one of the most stifling cities in the world. The Egyptian countryside is not much different. For example, Asyut, a provincial capital on the Upper Nile about 200 miles south of Cairo, has had its population quadruple in the recent decades as rural migrants in search of a better life arrive from the surrounding countryside. According to Egyptian social scientists, the influx of migrants combined with tens of thousands of students enrolled in its overcrowded university are combustive elements, making Asyut a center of radical fundamentalism.[31]

Land is required for many things—living, privacy, enjoyment—but its most important use is arguably food production. Ecologists explain that when land can no longer support a population, it will just give up. Egypt's Nile valley has nourished civilizations for 7,000 years. It is questionable whether it will be able to nourish much longer. One leading ecologist predicts that this point will be no later than 2030, when the population will have at least doubled from its current level. At this same point, Chinese imports of meat and grain will cause international prices to soar. Even if the market makes grain available, Egypt will be unable to afford it.[32]

Egypt also faces the threat of global warming. As sea levels rise,[33] one of the early candidates for inundation is the Nile Delta, where much of Egypt's food is grown. In the past, in the face of downturns in Egypt's food production or economy, Egyptians could migrate to other areas. Currently, Egyptians are not welcome even in the Gulf, which suffers its own environmental problems, namely water scarcity.

Although the topic of recent news reports, water scarcity in the Middle East is not a new threat. One of the first recorded wars took place between Mesopotamian cities in 4500 B.C., presumably over water.[34] A quick survey of the water sources in the area illustrates the potential for conflict.[35] The Jordan River is practically the only source of potable water for Israel, Syria, Lebanon, and the Palestines. A recent peace treaty between Israel and Jordan is an attempt to relieve problems of water shortage. While this illustrates the potential for cooperation, most experts believe there is just not enough water to go around for growing populations.[36]

Perhaps a more pressing issue is the crisis brewing over the Euphrates River. The river flows through Turkey, Syria, and then into Iraq. The Turks have begun the construction of a network of twenty-two dams on the

Euphrates and Tigris Rivers to provide hydroelectric power and irrigation. Due to their dependence on these rivers, Syria and Iraq are seriously threatened but too weak to confront Turkey. In an effort to increase their bargaining power, both Syria and Iraq have provided asylum to the Kurdish rebels fighting in eastern Turkey. Turkey has quietly threatened to turn off the water flowing downstream.[37] Even if water scarcity is overcome, the perception that water rights are inequitably distributed could be a greater incentive to conflict than the actual supply situation.[38]

Environmental problems are not unique to less-developed countries.[39] The potential for future energy wars and international disputes amongst economically developed countries increases as the resources needed to sustain them dwindle. Milton Viorst poses the following questions:

> Does a nation have a *casus belli* if another's pollution destroys forests, poisons water sources, promotes respiratory ailments? Surely a society has a right of self-preservation. Cannot the inhabitants of one country assert a natural law that bars the destruction of community property—that is, the Earth—by the inhabitants of another country? Americans need not anticipate war with Canada, but the world will undoubtedly see much more environmental disputes, of much greater seriousness, in the next century. . . . The Chernobyl cases pose another problem. If a country operates obsolete and dangerous nuclear reactors, could that be seen as a cause for war? Chernobyl spread cancerous radiation over much of Europe during its 1986 accident. The next accident could well be worse. Is this, in effect, a form of aggression? Will it—or should it—be in the domain of a new, expanded NATO?[40]

Answers to such questions are confusing at best, troubling and catastrophic at worst. The future could very well greet humanity with environmental conflicts of such magnitude never seen before.

Environmental Conflicts?

Thus far humanity has witnessed numerous conflicts at least partly attributed to natural resource scarcity.[41] One could argue that the struggle over natural resources played a role in every recorded war:[42] the two world wars, the Chaco War between Paraguay and Bolivia (1932-1935), the "Soccer War" between El Salvador and Honduras in 1969, the "Cod War" between Britain and Iceland (1972-1973), the Algerian War, the Falkland clashes between Britain and Argentina in 1982, and the Gulf War of 1991. Each of these conflicts resulted at least partly from the resort to military force to achieve a policy objective involving natural resources.[43]

The extent of environmental security depends upon the scope in which we wish to discuss the problem.[44] For example, wars over oil are not really environmentally induced conflicts. The extraction of oil is not by itself environmental degradation. Even if oil stocks were totally depleted, this would not cause any destabilization of the ecosystem (though the use of oil to produce power does cause serious environmental problems). However, the depletion of oil stocks would cause serious economic problems in today's global petroleum economy and inevitably lead to conflicts over the control of remaining stocks. Environmentally induced conflicts should be limited only to those in which actual environmental degradation causes the conflict.[45] Unfortunately, it is often difficult to separate conflicts caused by natural resource scarcity and those caused by environmental degradation.

It may be helpful to think of four different types of resource scarcity, each of which may contribute to conflict. First is physical scarcity. This occurs when a resource, such as coal, is only available in a finite amount. This is akin to the oil example discussed above. The second type of scarcity is geopolitical, which occurs when resources are distributed unequally on the surface of the earth so that some countries depend on the international flow and delivery of them. We currently see this type of scarcity with respect to oil where certain regions and states control or attempt to control the extraction and flow of oil. The third type of scarcity is called socio-economic scarcity, which concerns the unequal distribution of purchasing power and of property rights to provide natural resources between or within societies.[46] The last type is called environmental scarcity—scarcity caused by environmental degradation. An example of this type of scarcity occurs when oil burning causes global warming or acid rain that then spoils crops, inundates land, and alters climates. While each of these resource scarcities contributes to conflict, only the fourth type—environmental scarcity—is responsible for environmental conflict.

Defining Environmental Conflict

True environmental conflict is caused by the *environmental scarcity* of a resource. In other words, it is a conflict caused by a human-made disturbance of the normal resource regeneration rate. Thus, environmental scarcity can result from the exploitation of a renewable resource or from overstraining the ecosystem's sink capacity. Both can result in the deterioration of the environment.[47]

The Environment and Conflicts Project (ENCOP) adopted a similar definition. Environmental conflicts were defined as manifesting "themselves as political, social, economic, ethnic, religious, or territorial conflicts, or conflicts over resources or national interests, or any other type of conflict. They are traditional conflicts *induced by an environmental degradation.*"[48] While defining environmental conflict is important to understanding the problem, identifying its causes is considerably more critical (and more difficult) if we seek to create a solution.

Causes of Environmental Conflict

Environmental security literature points towards certain primary causes of environmental conflict: destruction of arable land, movement of refugees, population pressures, and water scarcity.[49] This latter source has been identified by many, and even many optimists, as perhaps the most likely and immediate cause of environmental conflict. A U.N. report explained that unless action is taken soon to improve water availability and access, worldwide "water shocks" are likely to arrest human development and place the world at risk of war over water scarcity.[50]

Thomas Homer-Dixon[51] is perhaps the preeminent scholar on the relationship between environmental scarcity and violent conflict.[52] His research on the relationship between environmental disaster and social violence suggests that environmental collapse caused by cropland depletion, rain forest destruction, and soil erosion could easily lead to food wars, roving gangs of water marauders, the devastation of marginal groups, national instability, and even open north-south conflict.[53]

Homer-Dixon lists seven problems that are likely to lead to environment conflict: (1) greenhouse warming, (2) stratospheric ozone depletion, (3) acid deposition, (4) deforestation, (5) degradation of agricultural land, (6) overuse and pollution of water supplies, and (7) depletion of fish stocks.[54] While the first two are global in nature, the last five involve more regional issues. These environmental problems are particularly problematic because they are more likely to cause certain social situations associated with environmental degradation: (a) decreases in agricultural production, (b) general economic decline, (c) population displacements, and (d) disruptions of institutions and social relations.[55]

It may be said that environmental issues are often the cause of conflict but rarely are they the object of contention. The Project on Environment, Population, and Security gathered, evaluated, and integrated data on linkages among population growth, renewable resource scarcities, migration, and violent conflict. The Project concluded that:

- Under certain circumstances, scarcities of renewable resources such as cropland, fresh water, and forests produce civil violence and instability. However, the role of this "environmental scarcity"

is often obscure. Environmental scarcity acts mainly by generating intermediate social effects, such as poverty and migrations, that analysts often interpret as conflict's immediate causes.
- Environmental scarcity is caused by the degradation and depletion of renewable resources, the increased demand for these resources, and/or their unequal distribution. These three sources of scarcity often interact and reinforce one another.
- Environmental scarcity often encourages powerful groups to capture valuable environmental resources and prompts marginal groups to migrate to ecologically sensitive areas. These two processes—called "resource capture" and "ecological marginalization"—in turn reinforce environmental scarcity and raise the potential for social instability.
- Societies can adapt to environmental scarcity either by using their indigenous environmental resources more efficiently or by decoupling from their dependence on these resources. In either case, the capacity to adapt depends upon the supply of social and technical "ingenuity" available in the society.
- If social and economic adaptation is unsuccessful, environmental scarcity constrains economic development and contributes to migrations.
- In the absence of adaptation, environmental scarcity sharpens existing distinctions among social groups.
- In the absence of adaptation, environmental scarcity weakens states.
- The intermediate social effects of environmental scarcity—including constrained economic productivity, population movements, social segmentation, and weakening of states—can in turn cause ethnic conflicts, insurgencies, and coups d'état.
- Environmental scarcity rarely contributes directly to interstate conflict.
- Conflicts generated in part by environmental scarcity can have significant indirect effects on the international community.[56]

These observations further our understanding of environmental scarcity and may be applied to specific instances of environmental conflict. One such scenario arises when national governments exploit the land where indigenous people live. This is exemplified by the situation on the island of Bougainville in Papua New Guinea. The national government of Papua New Guinea operated an enormous copper mine on the island that caused severe environmental damage. While proceeds from the mine filled the coffers of the national government, the environmental damage threatened the survival of the indigenous Bougainvilleans. As conditions for the indigenous people deteriorated, they started a sabotage campaign against the mine in 1988. This escalated into a guerrilla war.[57] At least one scholar predicts that "[w]hat is happening in Bougainville is also happening, or is likely to happen, in hundreds of Third World villages."[58] Such predictions are becoming reality as international and national forces alienate indigenous peoples from their traditional methods of sustainability.[59]

The destruction of traditional indigenous methods affects more than just indigenous and marginal groups. The economic costs of environmental degradation have begun to catch up with even the most powerful and prosperous governments. In China, experts estimate that environmental degradation such as water, soil, and air pollution, deforestation, and construction of dams will cost at least 15 percent of China's gross national product, a number expected to only increase in the coming years.[60] These economic costs strain national governments. As governments are unable to meet the needs of their citizens, political and legal institutions suffer a lack of legitimacy. This lack of legitimacy can lead to revolt and breakdown. China is not alone. For example, environmental degradation in Indonesia costs the country's agricultural economy half a billion dollars in discounted future income. In the Philippines, it will cost over one hundred dollars per hectare to compensate for the loss of nutrients due to the use of fertilizers in the Magat watershed on the northern Filipino island of Luzon.

Environmental Conflict Criticized

Not all scholars foresee such results. The environmental security thesis has been subject to some criticism. Some researchers advance the hypothesis that environmental degradation is irrelevant to political and social conflict. They discount the thesis that:

> environmental destruction and its disruptive effects not only create conflicts but also protract ongoing internal disorders. Because conflict is a "process," not a one-time event, environmental issues can add a new dimension to enduring social or ethnic disputes. That is, whereas environmental pressures trigger an intra- or interstate war, natural resource conflicts may evolve into long-term ethnic, political, and religious conflicts. Existing violent conflicts may also be protracted for environmental causes.[61]

They argue that resource scarcities, except perhaps water scarcity, do not promote very much direct conflict. For example, NATO's principal deputy undersecretary of defense for environmental security and co-chair of a NATO pilot study on environment and conflict, Gary Vest, argues that there is little evidence that environmental degradation leads directly to conflict.[62] Additionally, some warn against simplistic explanations of conflict in places such as Africa.[63] Researchers from the Department of Geography and Earth Sciences at Brunel University argue that flexibility is the key to understanding how people cope with distress. They show that migration can actually be part of a long-term strategy used by locals to reduce their exposure to risk. Research undertaken at Leeds University's Department of Politics shows that rather than war resulting from environmental scarcity it is environmental scarcity that results from warfare.[64]

In fact, some researchers have found the ecological and demographic stresses are declining factors in conflict. Even the critics, however, acknowledge that environmentally induced migration may spark ethnic conflict, and environmental harm can bring about institutional decay and economic deprivation, leading to civil strife.[65] Additionally, critics of the environmental security thesis concede that environmental degradation poses serious problems in much of the world.[66] These problems require action. Even if no worldwide conflict is on the horizon, the economic and social harms necessitate that we rethink are current approaches to environmental protection.

Conclusion

Environmental degradation manifests itself in many ways. While this chapter has concentrated on the security aspect of environmental degradation, the overall purpose of the book is to find ways to address environmental degradation, not just its many symptoms. This chapter introduces just one way in which environmental problems affect the stability and livability of this Earth. While this approach is admittedly anthropocentric by focusing on the human security concerns that environmental problems pose, the reader must recognize that this is but one ramification of environmental degradation. It may be the one that is best able to spur a reexamination of current approaches and force us as a society to develop new approaches. Despite the immense body of research illustrating the ecological effects of environmental degradation, policy-makers are less likely to take notice of solely "intangible" and "environmental" issues. War, violence, instability, revolution, and depression, on the other hand, have the ability to quickly attract attention to the problem, which we must remember is environmental degradation.

Awareness is only the first step. More is required. The recognition that environmental degradation poses a national security threat is drastically different from actually addressing the problem of environmental degradation. Awareness, however, is the first step. A quick glance around the world at specific case studies illustrates the pervasive instability and social strife that results from deterioration of environmental quality. These case studies show the positive linkage between environmental degradation and the breakdown of social and political order within states and the affinity for such instability to spill over borders.[67]

Notes

1. Jang B. Singh and Emily F. Carasco, "Business Ethics, Economic Development, and Protection of the Environment in the New World Order," *Journal of Business Ethics* 15, no. 3 (Mar. 1996): 297-307.

2. Jim MacNeill, "Towards 2000: Add Environmental Refugees to the List of Things to Worry about As We Proceed," *Policy Options* 10, no. 3 (Apr. 3, 1989).

3. Jose Gerardo A. Alampay, "Revisiting Environmental Security in the Philippines," *Journal of Environment and Development* 5, no. 3 (Sept. 1996): 329-337.

4. John Last, "Redefining the Unacceptable," *The Lancet* 346, no. 8991-92 (Dec. 23, 1995): 1642.

5. Hillary F. French, "Partnership for the Planet: An Environmental Agenda for the United Nations," *World Watch Paper* 126 (July 1995): 6.

6. Shin-wha Lee, "Not a One-Time Event: Environmental Change, Ethnic Rivalry, and Violent Conflict in the Third World," *Journal of Environment and Development* 6, no. 4 (Dec. 1997): 365.

7. See Andrew Hurrell and Benedict Kingsbury, *The International Politics of the Environment* (Oxford: Clarendon Press, 1992), 3, 5, 36.

8. Gerald B. Thomas, "U.S. Environmental Security Policy: Broad Concern or Narrow Interests," *Journal of Environment and Development* 6, no. 4 (Dec. 1997): 397. See Paul J. Runci, "Security and the Environment: An Annotated Bibliography," Dec. 5, 1996. Available from http://w3.pnl.gov:2080/ces/academic/runci.htm; Internet.

9. Lee, "Not a One-Time Event: Environmental Change, Ethnic Rivalry, and Violent Conflict in the Third World," 365.

10. Thomas F. Homer-Dixon, "Environmental Scarcities and Violent Conflict: Evidence from Cases," *International Security* 19, no. 1 (summer 1994): 5.

11. Richard Norton-Taylor, "Environment: CIA Turns Green," *Guardian* (London), 11 Sept. 1996, 4.

12. The Project on Environment, Population, and Security, "Project Description." Available from http://utl2.library.utoronto.ca/www/pcs/eps/descrip.htm; Internet.

13. Norton-Taylor, "Environment: CIA Turns Green," 4.

14. See Brian R. Shaw, "When Are Environmental Issues Security Issues?" *Report of the Environmental Change and Security Project, The Woodrow Wilson Center*, Issue 2 (spring 1996): 39. Available from http://w3.pnl.gov: 2080/ces/academic/ww_1shaw.htm; Internet. See also Editorial, "End of Cold War Requires New Thinking about National Security, Foreign Policy," *The Idaho Statesman*, 7 Nov. 1997, 12A.

15. Thomas, "U.S. Environmental Security Policy: Broad Concern or Narrow Interests," 397; Norma Myers, *Ultimate Security: The Environmental Basis of Political Stability* (New York: Norton, 1993).

16. This was not always the case. For years, "security" specialists ignored environmental dangers.

17. William C. French, "The New Environmental World Order," *Chicago Tribune*, 18 Apr. 1992, C17. However, Congress did pass the Strategic Environmental Research and Development Program (SERDP) in November 1990 (Pub. L. No. 101-510). See http://www.hgl.com/SERDP/; Internet.

18. Sam Nunn, Strategic Environmental Research and Development Program, Senate Floor Speech, June 28, 1990, 101st Congress, Second Session.

19. George Moffett, "'Green' Issues Become Force in Driving U.S. Foreign Policy," *Christian Science Monitor*, 8 April 1996, 1.

20. Sherri Goodman (deputy undersecretary of defense for environmental security), remarks to the Society of American Military Engineers, June 1, 1994, quoted in Gerald B. Thomas, "U.S. Environmental Security Policy: Broad Concern or Narrow Interests," *Journal of Environment and Development* 6, no. 4 (Dec. 1997): 397.

21. John Deutch, quoted in Richard Norton-Taylor, "Environment: CIA Turns Green," *Guardian* (London), 11 Sept. 1996, 4.

22. Norton-Taylor, "Environment: CIA Turns Green," 4.

23. One may ask: What does the involvement of the CIA in environmental issues symbolize? Intelligence and security agencies are organizations designed to counter perceived threats and seize new opportunities to protect the established order. Additionally, if only the United States possesses such intelligence, how is it to be shared and utilized by the world community or communities of the world in the pursuit of real environmental solutions?

24. Norton-Taylor, "Environment: CIA Turns Green," 4.

25. Nick Robins and Charlie Pye-Smith, "The Ecology of Violence," *New Scientist* (Mar. 8, 1997): 12 (quoting Rifkind).

26. Ibid. (quoting Merkel).

27. Ibid.

28. Samuel P. Huntington, *The Clash of Civilizations and the Remaking of World Order* (New York: Simon & Schuster, 1996); Francis Fukuyama, *The End of History and the Last Man* (New York: Free Press, 1992).

29. R. C. Longworth, "Others Won't Copy American-Style Democracy," *The Record*, 25 Feb. 1997, L11; Richard Grenier, "Choosing Sides over

History," *The Washington Times*, 6 Dec. 1996, A23; Michael Pakenham, "'The Clash of Civilizations': The Most Catalytic Work of Its Sort Since 'End of History,'" *The Sun* (Baltimore), 10 Nov. 1996, 4F; Richard Bernstein, "Books of The Times; A Scholar's Prophecy: Global Cultural Conflict," *The New York Times*, 6 Nov. 1996, C17.

30. Milton Viorst, "The Coming Instability," *The Washington Quarterly* 20, no. 4 (autumn 1997): 153.

31. Ibid.

32. Ibid.

33. Due to scientific uncertainty, the exact rise in sea level is difficult to predict. Part of this scientific uncertainty has its roots in recognizing linkages, since numerous feedbacks operate to both exacerbate and ameliorate sea level rise.

34. Viorst, "The Coming Instability," 153.

35. Egypt also faces problems on this front. Egypt depends on the downstream flow of water from the Nile for nearly all of its water needs. The Blue Nile rises in Ethiopia and then flows through Sudan, where it meets the White Nile. Both countries are contemplating irrigation projects that will substantially decrease water flow into Egypt. With Egypt already exceeding its allocation from a guarantee with Sudan, some experts feel that a showdown in the next ten years is quite likely.

36. Viorst, "The Coming Instability," 153.

37. Ibid.

38. Ronnie D. Lipschutz, "What Resources Will Matter? Environmental Degradation As a Security Issue." Proceedings from a AAA Annual Meeting Symposium, "Environmental Dimensions of Security," February 1992.

39. For example, the issue of environmentally induced migration is a problem facing France. Muslim immigrants are a source of rising tension in French society, which has now formally closed its borders to immigrants.

40. Viorst, "The Coming Instability," 153.

41. It should be worth noting that there is a distinction between environmental conflicts and those conflicts induced by natural resources.

42. Stephan Libiszewski, "What Is an Environmental Conflict?" *ENCOP Occasional Paper No. 1* (July 1992). Available from http://www.fsk.ethz.ch/encop/1/libisz92.htm.

43. Lee, "Not a One-Time Event: Environmental Change, Ethnic Rivalry, and Violent Conflict in the Third World," 365; Thomas F. Homer-Dixon, "On the Threshold: Environmental Changes As Causes of Acute Conflict," *International Security* 16, no. 2 (fall 1991): 76. Available from http://utl.library.utoronto.ca/www/pcs/thresh/thresh1.htm; Internet.

44. For example, the Project on Environmental Scarcities, State Capacity, and Civil Violence, developed a set of conceptual tools for deliberating about environmental scarcity. The project concluded that environmental scarcity had

three sources: (1) reduced resource supply (from degradation or depletion); (2) increased resource demand (from larger populations or higher per capita consumption); and (3) skewed resource distribution. The Project on Environmental Scarcities, State Capacity, and Civil Violence, "Key Findings." Available from http://utl1.library.utoronto.ca/www/pcs/state/-keyfind.htm. The conceptual tools helped the project reach conclusions about the interaction between environmental scarcity and civil violence. However, the project defined environmental security almost exclusively in resource terms.

45. Stephan Libiszewski, "What Is an Environmental Conflict?" *ENCOP Occasional Paper No. 1* (July 1992). Available from http://www.fsk.ethz.ch/encop/1/-libisz92.htm.

46. Ibid.

47. Ibid.

48. Ibid.

49. There are 214 major river basins that are shared by at least two countries—these could serve as the potential flash points for conflict.

50. Lee, "Not a One-Time Event: Environmental Change, Ethnic Rivalry, and Violent Conflict in the Third World," 365. Related to water wars are fish wars. A *Wall Street Journal* article explained that "[f]ishing conflicts are among the most visible of a new set of international security and diplomatic concerns caused by environmental degradation and resource depletion." See "Fisheries: Dwindling Resource Sparks Diplomatic Conflict," *Greenwire* (Nov. 25, 1997). Over 100 countries are involved in fishing disputes. These included confrontations between the Philippine navy and Chinese fishers to clashes between Danish and Icelandic coast guard fleets. "Fisheries: Dwindling Resource Sparks Diplomatic Conflict," *Greenwire* (Nov. 25, 1997). Fishing disputes can even cause conflict between the best of friends, as evidenced by those conflicts between the United States and Canada. See Paul Shwartz and Ray Suarez, "Water," National Public Radio, *Talk of the Nation* (Oct. 15, 1997, 2:00 pm ET), Transcript #97101502-211; Richard Harris and Robert Siegel, "Fish IV: Treaties," National Public Radio, *All Things Considered* (Aug. 28, 1997), Transcript #97082814-212; Editorial, "Strike a Salmon Deal with Canada," *The Bulletin* (Bend, OR), 30 July 1997, A6; Jane Clayson et al., "U.S. and Canada's Salmon War Heats Up," ABC News, *ABC World News This Morning* (July 21, 1997, 6:30 am ET), Transcript #97072108-j03; Jane Clayson and Carole Simpson, "Judge Orders Canadians to Stop Blockade," ABC News, *ABC World News Sunday* (July 20, 1997, 6:30 pm ET), Transcript #97072006-j06; Bill Redecker and Keven Newman, "U.S.-Canadian Salmon Tensions," ABC News, *ABC World News Saturday* (July 5, 1997, 6:30 pm ET), Transcript #97070505-j05; "High Seas Fishing; International Problems Created by the Law of the Sea," *U.N. Chronicle* 34, no. 2 (June 22, 1997): 30; Desmond Bill, "Fish War: The Same Old Stew Canada Has Fought over Fish for Centuries. The Latest Flare-Up

Is a Familiar Problem—On a Different Coast," *The Toronto Star*, 29 May 1997, A28(F).

51. Homer-Dixon is highly regarded by the political elite in the United States and elsewhere. President Clinton referred to his work in a speech to the National Academy of Sciences in Washington. Homer-Dixon has explored numerous case examples around the world, including El Salvador, Haiti, Peru, the Philippines, the West Bank, Rwanda, South Africa, and the Chiapas in Mexico. See Val Percival and Thomas Homer-Dixon, "Environmental Scarcity and Violent Conflict: The Case of Rwanda", *Journal of Environment and Development* 5, no. 3 (Sept. 1996): 270-291; Val Percival and Thomas Homer-Dixon, "Environmental Scarcity and Violent Conflict: The Case of South Africa," *Occasional Paper*, Toronto: Project on Environment, Population, and Security, October 1995; P. Howard and Thomas Homer-Dixon, "Environmental Scarcity and Violent Conflict: The Case of Chiapas, Mexico," *Occasional Paper*, Toronto: Project on Environment, Population, and Security, January 1996.

52. Thomas Homer-Dixon, "On the Threshold: Environmental Changes As Causes of Acute Conflict," *International Security* 16, no. 2 (fall 1991): 76-116. See also Thomas Homer-Dixon, "Environmental Scarcities and Violent Conflict: Evidence from Cases," *International Security* 19, no. 1 (summer 1994): 5-40.

53. Mark Kingwell, "Meet Tad the Doom-Meister; Professor Thomas Homer-Dixon," *Saturday Night* 110, no. 7 (Sept. 1995): 42.

54. Homer-Dixon, "On the Threshold: Environmental Changes As Causes of Acute Conflict," 76. Available from http://utl.library.utoronto.ca/www/pcs/thresh/-thresh1.htm; Internet. Others explain that environmental conflict is caused by: (1) resource inequity, (2) increased environmental decline, (3) heightened group identity, (4) economic decline, (5) forced migration, (6) social disintegration. See Lee, "Not a One-Time Event: Environmental Change, Ethnic Rivalry, and Violent Conflict in the Third World," 365.

55. See Libiszewski, "What Is an Environmental Conflict?"

56. The Project on Environment, Population, and Security, "Project Description." Available from http://utl2.library.utoronto.ca/www/pcs/eps/descrip.htm; Internet

57. B. Bogle, "Bougainville: A Classical Environmental Conflict?" *Occasional Paper No. 3, Environment and Conflicts Project* (1992).

58. Lee, "Not a One-Time Event: Environmental Change, Ethnic Rivalry, and Violent Conflict in the Third World," 365.

59. On the other hand, some argue that indigenous peoples are harmful to the environment. For example, woodstoves and open fires tend to consume more resources than energy-efficient petroleum-burning stoves and furnaces. While technology produces more resource-efficient devices, it also leads to more resource depletion as new technologies move societies toward higher resource-dependency.

60. Homer-Dixon, "Environmental Scarcities and Violent Conflict: Evidence from Cases," 5.

61. Lee, "Not a One-Time Event: Environmental Change, Ethnic Rivalry, and Violent Conflict in the Third World," 365.

62. See Nick Robins and Charlie Pye-Smith, "The Ecology of Violence," *New Scientist* (Mar. 8, 1997): 12.

63. See Dipankar De Sarkar, "Africa-Environment: Avoiding Simplistic Explanations of Conflict," *Inter Press Service* (July 4, 1997).

64. Ibid.

65. Marc A. Levy, "Time for a Third Wave of Environment and Security Scholarship," unpublished summary of article in *International Security* 20, no. 2 (fall 1995). Available from http://wwics.si.edu/PROGRAMS/DIS/ECS/report1/levy.htm; Internet.

66. However, some argue that "focusing on these environmental problems is a misguided method for attacking the problem of violent conflict." They acknowledge that the environment does play a role in political conflicts but maintain that "[m]ost sophisticated scholars of political conflict already knew that." Levy, "Time for a Third Wave of Environment and Security Scholarship."

67. In his study of conflict in Rwanda, Homer-Dixon notes that studies of civil strife in El Salvador, Haiti, Peru, the Philippines, and the West Bank indicate a strong link among renewable resource scarcities, escalating grievances, and the outbreak of violence. Val Percival and Thomas Homer-Dixon, "Environmental Scarcity and Violent Conflict: The Case of Rwanda," *Journal of Environment and Development* 5, no. 3 (Sept. 1996): 270. However, Homer-Dixon found that environmental factors do not provide an adequate explanation of the genocide in Rwanda. Though environmental scarcity produces four principal social effects that exacerbate conflict between groups, the motivational factors for the events that transpired in Rwanda were not intrinsically tied to environmental scarcity.

3

No Place, People, or Person Is Immune

Numerous states and peoples currently struggle with the all-too real effects of environmental degradation. In many areas environmental degradation contributes to the collapse of legal, social, and political stability. The world has witnessed more conflicts in the decade after the Cold War than at any other time this century. A large number of these conflicts have been attributed to ethnicity, but more and more, environmental factors are playing a role.

Environmental Degradation and Violent Conflict

Environmental degradation can lead to conflict in a number of ways. Environmental degradation shifts the balance of power between states either regionally or globally and produces instabilities. Environmental scarcities increase the disparity between the rich and poor, increasing the prospects for conflict between the two spheres. Consider the two most important global environmental problems: global warming and ozone depletion. Together they will (and presently do) have extreme impacts on agricultural production. At the same time they increase the rate of disease in humans and livestock. They also affect the weather. Changing weather patterns and sea level rise will affect countries such as Bangladesh and Egypt, which are extremely vulnerable to storm surges. Internationally, global warming may lead to contention over ice-free sea-lanes in the Arctic while overpopulation[1] and overuse of land will cause environmental refugees to spill across borders.

Environmental insecurity also arises from struggles over dwindling water supplies and the effects of upstream pollution. Environmental degradation raises the level of stress within national and regional societies, thereby increasing the likelihood of conflict and impeding the development of solutions.[2]

As the global population continues to grow exponentially and as environmental change threatens the quantity and quality of natural resources, the ability of nations to peacefully resolve conflicts over internationally distributed resources will increasingly be at the heart of stable and secure international relations.[3] Under circumstances of scarcity, resources such as water become a highly symbolic, and complicated, zero-sum, power and prestige-packed issue that is highly prone to conflict and extremely difficult to resolve.[4]

History is replete with examples of competition for shared resources, especially water. Maldistributions of fresh water together with current population and development trends suggest that it will be an increasingly salient part of international politics and conflict.[5] Many now predict that water security will soon rank with military security in the war rooms of Middle East defense ministries, since shortages and contamination of water supplies are bringing the region to the brink of crisis.[6] Unfortunately, water is not the only source of environmental insecurity. A look around the world highlights the many sources and subsequent effects of environmental security. These examples dot every region in the world, making no place, peoples, or person immune.

A Quick Trip around the World

Africa

Land degradation affects more than 3.6 billion hectares of land—about a quarter of the earth's total land surface—affecting over one billion people. The problem is particularly severe in Africa where desertification is causing a new wave of environmental refugees. Klaus Toepfer, the executive director of the United Nations Environment Program (UNEP), explains that "[t]he hardships suffered by the millions of those who decide to leave their impoverished surroundings to an even more miserable existence in an urban setting are the social manifestations of this malaise."[7] Unfortunately, land degradation is not the only environmental danger faced in Africa. Environmental insecurity is prevalent throughout much of the continent.

Sudan

Ecological stresses in central Sudan cause ethnic conflict within that state. Deteriorating environmental conditions in the drylands are a major obstacle to the region's development and stability. Desertification, crop failure, and famine plague the area as groups compete for scarce resources. Overgrazing and intensive, mechanized farming are destroying the Sahelian ecosystem in which 70 percent of the Sudanese people live. As land areas are degraded, people and livestock herds migrate from their previous ecological zone to an area already occupied by a different ethnic group.[8] From 1970 to 1985, Sudan suffered a rapid expansion of mechanized farming triggering more than twenty major regional tribal conferences to solve land disputes between various ethnic groups in the central rainlands.

In the past twenty-five years 4 to 5 million people have been displaced within the Sudan territory with another 2 to 3 million being forced to leave either as migrants or as refugees. The remaining forest lands in northern Sudan, an area the size of western Europe, has been denuded and half of the total usable land has lost topsoil and turned irreversibly to dust. Crop yields have fallen 30 percent of their previous levels in some areas as the rainfed agriculture population has grown 3 to 3.5 percent per year.[9]

The resulting migration has erupted in violent conflict. The civil war in the south exacerbated the situation. The interaction between conflict and environmental scarcity combine to form a spiral, whereas conflict leads to an excessive concentration of human and livestock populations in the ecological buffer zone in central Sudan, which is also a transitional area between northern and southern ethnic groups.[10] The resulting deterioration causes more conflict over the depleted resources.

These ecological conflicts have clearly protracted the Sudanese war. Environmental destruction, economic decline, social disintegration, population displacement, and protracted conflict are present in Sudan. The Sudanese civil war has gradually and consistently transformed from an ethnic and religious clash to a resource conflict triggered by environmental degradation.[11] Today the major cause of conflict is the struggle over resources.[12]

Kenya

Kenya has been described as "probably the most important state of East Africa in terms of political and economic power."[13] Like the rest of Africa, it faces serious environmental problems. Ten million of Kenya's 30 million people live in the arid and semi-arid belt expanse covering 80 percent of the country's surface. Its current population is increasing at an annual rate of 3.5 percent, making it one of the fastest growing populations on the planet. By the end of this century, population should reach 35 million and almost 80 million by the year 2025. Environmental degradation and increased competition for dwindling land have certainly added to the readiness to resort to violence as groups fight over existing ethnic rivalries and disputed land rights.[14]

The current political situation is one of apparent stability and democracy. Its economy, however, can not boast such an appearance. Environmental degradation plays a major role. Damage to the environment hampers agricultural production and adversely affects a very large part of the population.

While deforestation is not a prominent problem, erosion and water pollution are major problems.[15] Lake Victoria is the third largest fresh water lake in the world and is an important source of fresh water for Kenya, Tanzania, and Uganda. But the lake is threatened. As a food source, its fish stock is rapidly depleting due to overfishing and the introduction of foreign species. Additionally, rivers flowing into the lake carry with them human waste caused by activities of the dense population around the lake.[16] Just as environmental issues are interconnected, environmental issues are closely connected to the economy, which in turn is closely connected with political stability. Whenever we look to environmental problems such as the ones in Kenya, it must be with an eye towards the many ripples throughout society that environmental degradation can cause.

Tourism represents Kenya's biggest source of foreign currency, but tourists are also the country's biggest consumers (users) of resources such as water. People are attracted by Kenya's diverse biological reserves, but as more people visit game reserves, the flora and fauna in the parks need to be protected against them. Tourists are not the only outside threat to the state. Well-intentioned, but shortsighted, programs introduced by foreign "experts" have caused several ecological disasters. Officials from the Food and Agricultural Organization of the United Nations (FAO) were responsible for the introduction of the Nile perch in Lake Victoria, which pushed numerous native species past the brink of extinction. Foreign capital from international organizations and Western states made possible the drilling of wells. However, such well-intentioned efforts ultimately led to the destruction of vegetation because too many cattle gathered around these wells. These are just but a few examples of negative influences on the environment caused by "assistance" from abroad.[17]

Worsening environmental conditions, migration, and the poor economic situation have led to social divisions and a widespread decrease in social solidarity.[18] In 1991, fighting broke out among different groups. Kalenjin warriors and members of pastoralist tribes like the Masai repeatedly attacked Kikuyu in 1992 and 1993. Tribe members of the Luo, Luhya, Kamba, Meru, and Teso were killed and their houses and fields were looted and burned. These attacks led to counterattacks and retaliations, fueling additional conflict, resulting in 1500 persons being killed and 1 percent of the entire population being displaced. All of this occurred in just two years. Although environmental problems cannot be blamed for the entire conflict, the increasing pressure on limited resources affected both parties. The conflict also caused severe environmental degradation, increasing the likelihood of future environmentally induced conflict.

Traditionally, conflict includes struggles between competing groups. Environmentally induced violence may also manifest itself in conflict between state entities and state outlaws. In Kenya, this includes conflict between poachers and guards. Poachers are now equipped with modern weapons, communication facilities, and vehicles. Shoot-outs between poachers and park rangers are regular occurrences. Since 1990, however, these conflicts have subsided as rangers receive better equipment such as firearms, planes, and helicopters as well as the right to shoot poachers on sight.[19]

Environmentally induced conflict also extends beyond Kenya's borders. Potential international conflicts include clashes between Sudan and Kenya as well as the aforementioned conflict between countries dependent on the waters of the Nile. Kenya may be considered a linchpin—a country marred by environmental problems but one that is diligently working to reverse the trend and avoid violence. On the surface, Kenya is making great efforts to improve its environment, economy, and government. However, such changes must be made together in order to recognize linkages not only between environmental issues, but also those between the environment and economic and political stability.

South Africa

South Africa is another country affected by environmental insecurity. While one can claim that environmental scarcity is the sole cause of the country's recent turmoil, Percival and Homer-Dixon explain that if policymakers and social analysts ignore environmental problems they risk missing a factor that powerfully contributes to the violence in South Africa.[20] They explain that environmental scarcity contributed to reductions in agricultural productivity in the homelands, migrations to and within urban areas, and the deterioration of the local urban environment. These pressures inevitably undermined the ability of the government to provide for the needs of society. As the level of grievances within society rose, the transition from minority rule provided opportunities for the violent expression of these grievances.[21] Even though violence subsided in most areas of the country after the election of Nelson Mandela, civil strife continues in the KwaZulu-

Natal region, an indication that underlying stresses such as environmental scarcity remain.

Lesotho

An interesting political and military conflict caused by competition over environmental resources occurred in Lesotho. Lesotho has the luxury of being an "upstream" country. On the other hand, its neighbor, South Africa, is not. South Africa negotiated with Lesotho for thirty years to divert water from its mountains to the arid South African province of Transvaal. When Lesotho failed to cave in to its demand, South Africa gave support to a successful coup against Lesotho's tribal government. Within months the new Lesotho government reached an agreement with South Africa to construct the huge Highlands Water Project to meet South Africa's needs. According to Homer-Dixon, "[i]t seems likely . . . that the desire for water was an ulterior motive behind South African support for the coup."[22]

Somalia

Recent evidence from the Horn of Africa illustrates how environmental degradation creates insecurity. The civil strife in Somalia can be partly blamed on drought-related problems.[23] The strife illustrates the spiraling effect of societal breakdown and environmental degradation. Just as environmental degradation causes societal breakdown, so too does societal breakdown exacerbate environmental problems. In places such as Somalia, the fragmentation of the society into heavily armed clans prevents concerted efforts and reforms to address the underlying pressures of ecological degradation and overpopulation. It is difficult to determine the causal chain: whether environmental problems force people to go without food and water and then take up arms to survive or whether militarization cuts off food and water sources from the population.[24] Regardless, there is a close correlation between environmental degradation and violence. Such conflict has the potential to bring other countries and international organizations into the conflict.

Rwanda

The genocidal anarchy that exploded in April of 1994 in Rwanda can be at least partly attributed to environment and population pressures producing social stress that turns into violent conflict. Although Val Percival and Thomas Homer-Dixon explain that environmental factors do not provide an adequate explanation of the genocide in Rwanda, they concede that "environmental scarcity was correlated with conflict in Rwanda."[25] Environmental scarcities did cause social effects associated with environmentally induced conflict: agricultural production decreased, migration increased, and the state began to lose legitimacy. Environmental scarcities increased grievances within the Rwanda rural population and weakened the legitimacy of the regime.

Scarcity also limited the opportunities for wealth creation and for achieving economic and social status within Rwandan society. Additionally, civil war, structural adjustment, fall in coffee prices, and the lack of economic diversification boosted grievances and weakened regime legitimacy. Rising external and internal demands for democratization that compounded elite insecurity eroded its control of governmental institutions such as the army, policy, and bureaucracy. Although many other factors played a role, environmental scarcity contributed and stands to contribute even more heavily in the future.[26] Thus even though environmental scarcity alone is often insufficient to bring conflict to a region, such scarcity exacerbates almost every other flash point and thus facilitates the crossing of the threshold into violence.

Americas

Although not as severe as in Africa, environmental insecurity is emerging as a major problem in the Americas. Consider the cases of Mexico, Peru, and Haiti.

Mexico

In the early 1990s, factors combined in the Chiapas region of Mexico to produce a particularly explosive combination. A rapidly growing peasant population combined with structural imbalances in resource distribution and inadequate property rights protection to spark violent episodes. Local communities attempted to redistribute land and organize crop production for subsistence and export. These attempts were crushed by powerful interest groups. When the indigenas and campesinos of Chiapas were denied sustainable access to healthy environmental resources, conflict resulted.[27]

Peru

A similar course of events took place in Peru for many of the same reasons. Environmental degradation caused by soil loss and overpopulation led to ecological marginalization and the rise of the Sendero Luminoso (Shining Path) rebellion in Peru.[28] From 1980 to 1993, the Sendero Luminoso undermined the authority of Peru's central government on two-thirds of the national territory.[29] While land issues are a historic source of conflict, ecological marginalization is bringing a new wave of environmental insecurity to the country.

Haiti

Haiti provides another example of the destabilizing effects of environmental degradation. Many of the country's troubles can be traced to environmental degradation: widespread deforestation, soil erosion, and water shortages. Such environmental degradation has left tens of thousands of Haitians without a livelihood.[30] One source in the United States Department of State explained that "there's a direct link between this and why the government was overthrown and why 50,000 migrants left Haiti in 1994."[31] This is another instance of environmental scarcity spilling over borders to create conflict and chaos. Any solution to the situation in Haiti that does not involve environmental considerations will be a Band-Aid at best.

Asia

The diversity of environmental issues facing the continent of Asia is almost as great as the diversity of cultures and peoples. In some areas, the lack of water is a major problem, while in other areas too much water is the problem. Asia's environmental security will only be exacerbated if the continent continues its trend of rapid growth fueled by environmental resources.

Middle East

Water is a key source of contention in the Middle East.[32] The mix of scarce resources, rapid population growth, and intense agricultural activity combine with Israeli policies to produce a potentially volatile political environment in Gaza.[33] Water shortages are also a large problem in the occupied West Bank. Currently, Israel exceeds its average annual supply of renewable water by 10 percent. To cover the deficit, Israel overpumps the aquifers. As a result, water tables have dropped throughout Israel and the West Bank. The ecological effects are twofold: exhaustion of wells and the infiltration of sea water from the Mediterranean. In addition, most of Gaza's groundwater is polluted because of nitrate contamination due to wastewater mismanagement.[34] The fact that about 40 percent of Israel's water originates in occupied territories only compounds the pollution problem. Israel has imposed strict water limits on Jewish settlers and Arabs in the West Bank. However, the restrictions on Arab use are more severe. Israel restricts the number of Arab pumps and the amount of water pumped. Settlers use about four times the amount of water than their Arab counterparts. Such state policies only exacerbate current tensions in the region.

Arab agriculture in the region has suffered as a result of dry wells and saline from the nearby deeper Israeli wells. Although it is unclear what effects these water policies will have, "it seems reasonable to conclude that water scarcity and its consequent economic effects contributed to the grievances behind the intifada both on the West Bank and in Gaza."[35] Water scarcity in Gaza has "clearly aggravated socioeconomic conditions [and] in turn, have contributed to the grievances behind the ongoing violence against Israel and emerging tensions among Palestinians in Gaza."[36] The Middle East suffers from other environmental problems caused by war such as oil pollution and artillery waste. Water, however, will probably remain the most dangerous environmental issue.

Central Asia

Water-related problems are also creating environmental insecurity in Central Asia. As a result of short-sighted economic and environmental policies that attempted to transform the desert through intensive irrigation, the Aral Sea is quickly disappearing. Its drying is causing economic collapse and the potential for environmental refugees. The loss of the Aral Sea and associated environmental degradation will have immediate and direct consequences on the durability of Central Asian regional entities.[37]

The maldistribution of water resources is also a problem in the area. Kyrgyzstan and Tajikistan are water rich countries that hold the overwhelming share of the usable storage capacity of the two primary river basins in Central Asia. Uzbekistan controls 42 percent of the storage capacity of Amu Darya but only 16 percent of the water stored in reservoirs along the Amu Darya. Turkmenistan has no control over the storage capacity of the Amu Darya.

Uneven storage capacity among these four states results in different access and pollution control opportunities as well as different and often contradictory modes of water utilization.[38] Such environmental scarcities are more prone to contribute to violence in Central Asia because the states are facing a process of decolonization and nation building. They are "often violently searching for national, religious, and subnational identities."[39] In particular, ethnically mixed areas serve as potential hotbeds for conflict. There are currently twenty-six potential ethnoterritorial conflicts in Central Asia.

The formation of new states in Central Asia created upstream-downstream relationships between different independent countries. The new borders also created a whole series of politically separated irrigation networks that withdraw water from the same source. Under Soviet law, water resources were an exclusive state property and were provided as a free good. The costs of water utilization appeared only as charges for the development and maintenance of water supply schemes. Individuals were not charged for the amount of water consumed. This system contributed to the inefficient use of water supplies. After the republics declared sovereignty in 1990, the individual states assumed control over water management.[40]

This change created the potential for conflict within river basins. Conflict within international river basins usually occurs when upstream countries influence the river flow and diminish the possibilities of downstream countries to use river and water resources. When upstream countries use water for hydropower production or pollute the rivers, downstream countries are adversely affected. They may be unable to use the river for water-dependent activities such as agriculture, industry, and fresh water supply. In arid regions, the effects of upstream river degradation are felt even more. Drainage runoff degrades the quality, and river diversion reduces the quantity, of water. Downstream users experience a different set of constraints due to poor water quality.[41]

All countries in Central Asia share a portion of the Aral Sea basin. Uzbekistan and Kazakhstan share the Aral Sea itself while the two main basins of the Syr Darya and the Amu Darya are shared by several states. The Syr Darya leaves Kyrgyzstan, passes the Uzkekian part of the eastern Fergana Valley, crosses the Tajik stretch in the Western Fergana Valley and pours again into Uzbekistan. After crossing the Hunger Steppe the Syr Darya runs into Kazakhstan. The river not only creates interdependence between the states, but also significantly alters the relative power of upstream users versus downstream states. Conditions within those upstream states have spilled across borders.

Kyrgyzstan is facing serious economic problems, in part because of an energy shortage from Russian and neighboring countries. To overcome these problems, Kyrgyzstan attempts to maximize profits from its abundant water resources by lessening the water released for the downstream users of Uzbekistan, Tajikistan, and Kazakhstan. This has inevitably caused conflict between the countries. Water has been used as both a sword and a shield in negotiations between the countries on everything from energy to environmental protection.[42]

Disputes over shared irrigation systems have led to low-intensity conflicts between ethnic populations. There are twenty-three major irrigation systems for the Amu Darya and nine for the Syra Darya. The Fergana Valley, home to both Kyrgz and Uzbek populations, and the districts of Samarkand and Bukhara, home to both Uzbek and Tajik populations, have been identified as hotbeds of ethnoterritorial strife "with a high probability of water related disputes."[43]

According to one study sponsored by the Center for Security Policy and Conflict Research, "[a] low environmental consciousness and a widespread fatalism concerning the impoverishment of the living conditions, combined with a rather stable society and a modest food supply network, do not create the 'critical mass' of social upheaval taking the form of violent separatist movements."[44] While this prognosis may seem positive, it means that environmental degradation will worsen before it gets better and the underlying stresses will continue to build. Because the different countries of Central Asia have different interests and different values at stake, there is conflict over how to save the Aral Sea. The international ramifications of these disputes spill outside of the area. For example, serious water questions remain for Afghanistan. Unfortunately, social and economic crises place environmental protection and the development of ecological solutions on the back burner. Competition for scarce water resources will continue and intensify.[45]

Indian Subcontinent

The Indian subcontinent is one area of the world where environmentally induced conflict is particularly apparent. The current conflict between India, Pakistan, Bangladesh, and Nepal over the share of water from the Indus, the Ganges, and the Brahmaputra Rivers is but one example.[46] Water usage is not the only environmental problem causing conflict on the subcontinent.

The situation in Bangladesh provides an example of the spill-over effect. In the last few decades, large numbers of people have moved from Bangladesh to India. Population growth appears to be the primary cause. A bulging population combined with inadequate land and water supplies caused an estimated 10 million Bengalis to leave Bangladesh since the 1970s and migrate to the Indian states of Assam and Tripura. This influx of environmental refugees resulted in ethnic conflict, leading to thousands of deaths and serious strains in relations between India and Bangladesh.[47]

Bangladesh's cropland withstands serious degradation because of the annual flooding of the Ganges and Brahmaputra Rivers deposits nutrients. However, Bangladesh's population will double to 235 million by the year 2035. This will make currently scarce cropland even more scarce and exacerbate the migration of Bangladeshis across the border. The receiving regions, the Indian states of Assam, Tripura, and West Bengal, have suffered pervasive social fluctuations. Changes in land distribution, economic relations, and the balance of political power between religious and ethnic groups have triggered serious intergroup conflict.[48]

These interactions are typical of the cycle of environmental change and refugee flow. Refugees promote ethnic conflicts that spill across international lines. Population stresses cause further environmental decline and social tensions. Large numbers of Bangladeshi refugees are produced by population pressures and natural disasters. These refugees then play an active role in ethnopolitical conflicts at both the intra- and interstate levels.[49]

Interstate conflicts are manifesting themselves in India as Bangladeshis flee landlessness and poverty in their homeland; 10 million during the past fifty years. These environmental refugees, along with other Bengali-speaking people, now constitute the ethnic majority in the Indian state of Tripura. This situation exploded in February of 1997, when militants in the Indian state of Tripura slaughtered over sixty settlers, many of them of Bangladeshi origin. Those closest to the situation maintain that environmental problems had more to do with the massacres than religion or politics.[50]

A more general environmental threat is occurring throughout India. In rural areas throughout India, the combination of population growth, cropland scarcity and degradation, deforestation, and desertification results in resource scarcities. As competition for these resources increases, both amongst the people and between the people and the state, the potential for conflict increases. Additionally, scarcity and competition are driving people from rural areas into cites. These cities, such as Delhi, already suffer from overtaxed infrastructure, horrible air pollution, unavailable power and water, and inadequate sewage systems. These conditions combined to spark recent outbreaks of urban violence, mostly in the poorest slums. According to Homer-Dixon and Percival, "[t]hese pressures express themselves in a social environment already stressed by corruption and communal animosity."[51]

Evidence of environmental scarcity, resource capture, and ecological marginalization are also abundant in Pakistan. These problems constrain agriculture, exacerbate rural poverty, cause large waves of migration, and contribute to urban decay. The end result is a slowing of economic growth and disruption of legal institutions and social relations within society. Environmental degradation has resulted in declines in farm yields and the farming of marginal lands. Per capita agricultural growth has stagnated. Meanwhile, the population increases, thereby placing greater demands on the finite resource base. The final report of the Pakistan National Conservation Strategy concluded that in the absence of major change, food deficits are likely to threaten a number of regions while increasing disillusionment and the potential for conflict.[52]

Pakistani industrial areas experience severe air pollution. In Punjab, large segments of the population suffer from respiratory ailments and eye problems due to air pollution from chemical plants, cement factories, and other industrial sources. The pollution affects crops and livestock as well. Though Pakistan continues to grow economically, the development is uneven. The rich are growing richer while the poor grow poorer—increasing the potential for social conflict.[53] One study of the situation found that "[a]s resource scarcities mount grievances rise, especially across existing social cleavages within society; at the same time, the capacity of the state to address these grievances and to prevent violent challenges to its authority is diminished."[54] Clearly, environmental issues are not the sole driving force behind the potential for conflict within Pakistan. However, as this evidence indicates, environmental scarcity can contribute in many ways to the breakdown of society and the loss of political stability.

For example, the growing deprivation caused by environmental pressures among particular groups in rural areas has led to an increase in violence. For example, the rural Sind bandits illustrate this environmentally induced violence. The 1980s witnessed a sharp increase in the scope and frequency of banditry. Organized gangs were formed that had increased capabilities of eluding punishment by local authorities. Many of these bandits were former sharecroppers who lost their livelihoods because of multiple economic problems. As one researcher observed, "[t]he bandits place their criminal activities in a context of revolt against a landed elite whose control over resources has combined with severe resource scarcity to threaten the livelihood of rural laborers."[55] Forest areas also witnessed increased violence as the timber mafia, who have marginalized indigenous groups, create their own version of environmental insecurity in forest areas.

Urban migration caused by rural environmental scarcities has only worsened urban violence. As Pakistan's government attempts to deal with internal violence both in the countryside and in its cities, the ability of the government to provide basic social services diminishes. More critical yet is the loss of regime legitimacy. The government may undertake desperate measures, such as escalation of conflict with India. After a series of nuclear tests and border conflicts with India, the escalation appears well under way.

Southeast Asia

Turning from South Central Asia to Southeast Asia, the situation does not improve. For example, environmental pressures may cause the fragmentation of China. Only two poor populous countries have less arable land per capita than China: Egypt and Bangladesh. China is attempting to build its economy on coal. This is causing widespread and destructive air pollution. Meanwhile, uneven development, especially between coastal regions and inner areas, has resulted in destabilizing migration within China.

Perhaps China's biggest threat to environmental security centers on water. China suffers from extreme water scarcity. Chinese residents face a daily shortage of 28.8 million cubic meters of water. Shortages will be exacerbated by population growth, rising standards of living, and rapid industrialization.[56] Water scarcities increase demands on the state for new infrastructure—placing greater stress on the fiscal strength of the state. This will inevitably diminish state capacity.

Water scarcity and pollution have triggered violence in rural, as well as urban, areas. If scarcity continues to grow, especially in urban areas, a much more threatening form of urban civil violence may emerge. Such violence may involve migrant workers, unemployed state enterprise workers, grain-short urban dwellers, and disgruntled peasants.[57] Of course, environmental scarcity does not alone trigger such violence; rather, it is usually the government's response, or lack thereof, to such scarcity that ultimately results in conflict.

Local leaders have become increasingly vocal in their opposition to state environmental policies. For example, the governor of Sichuan is extremely vocal in his concern over Beijing's inadequate financial contribution for resettlement engendered by the Three Gorges Dam. Such opposition is a threat to legitimacy of the state. A loss of legitimacy and decline in the reach of the state contribute to social instability. Increased pollution levels result in growing interprovincial disputes over the responsibility and costs of treatment facilities and clean-up costs. The Chinese central government has yet to develop an effective mechanism for resolving such conflicts.[58]

Indonesia faces similar problems. To jump start its economy, the government used natural resources to fuel its economic growth. The second largest tract of tropical rain forests in the world is found in Indonesia. But now rain forests in Indonesia are declining at a rate of 1 million hectares per year. Battles over Indonesia's forests have turned violent in some instances by pitting the interests of local communities against those of the state. In addition, forest and land fires in 1997 and 1998 caused significant harm to both the economy and the environment.[59] They also displaced both endangered species and local communities. With three-fourths of the state claimed as "state forestland," pressure on those lands, forests, and resources is likely to intensify far beyond the current situation.

Oil reserves are quickly disappearing, leading some to predict that Indonesia will become an oil importer early in the next century. Powerful elites control most of the natural resource-based wealth—a situation that is becoming less tolerable to the general public. As its natural wealth dwindles, the New Order regime will be hard pressed to base its future growth on the exploitation of natural resources. Perhaps the current economic recession in most of the Pacific Rim is just a preview of larger events to come. The severe economic downturn during the closing years of the 1990s may be just the tip of the iceberg.

Environmental insecurity will intensify if current trends in natural resource control, exploitation, and distribution of benefits continue.[60] A further ramification of continued environmental degradation and resource scarcity will be the destruction of indigenous, sustainable practices. Deforestation will cause local forest-based communities to utilize secondary forest and scrub areas for tree crops, rattan, grazing fodder, and many other resources—resources that local communities do not have the hundreds of years of experience with preserving and living in equilibrium.[61]

The Philippines suffers from similar environmental degradation. Fueled in part by the overexploitation of renewable resources, population growth, and land degradation, the Philippines faces acute environmental degradation. The relative deprivation of the landless agricultural workers and poor farmers has forced them upland, where they cut down forests in an effort to survive.[62]

Recent data illustrates that environmental scarcities are beginning to have a serious effect on both economic and political stability. Logging and encroachment of farms since World War II have reduced the virgin second-growth forests from about 16 million hectares to about 7 million hectares. Logging and land clearing have accelerated erosion and changed regional hydrological cycles. This has decreased the land's ability to retain water and resulted in flash floods, which have seriously affected crop production. One study commissioned by the Philippine government and the European Economic Community found that only about half of the 36,000 hectares of irrigated farmland of the still unspoiled island of Palawan will actually be irrigable because of the hydrological effects of decreases in forest cover.[63]

Environmental degradation is beginning to hinder the Philippines' economic development. Heavy sedimentation in water bodies adversely affects irrigated crop production, which prevents rice production from keeping pace with population growth. Development has caused its own environmental problems. In 1994 alone, three oil spills nearly wiped out all the fish farms in Laguan de Bay. Landfills are popping up throughout the country, leaving some to worry whether the Philippines will choke on its own refuse.

Destruction of land and water resources uproots people. When combined with inequalities in access to rich agriculture lowlands, additional migration caused by population growth, and economic hardships brought about by environmental scarcity due to erosion and deforestation, the resulting volatile mix helps to spur insurgency and rebellion.[64] Internal conflict is not the only danger. For example, the Spratly Islands are claimed by the Philippines and five other states, including China. This situation is likely to be a flash point for conflict in the South China Sea.

Few places on the Earth are immune from environmental degradation and the destabilizing social, economic, and political problems it brings. Each of the brief case studies explored illustrates the link between environmental degradation and insecurity. Environmental insecurity, however, is but one ramification of environmental degradation. This chapter could have just as easily outlined the ecological harm or human suffering environmental degradation causes in each region of the world. Such harms are not isolated merely to less-developed nations. Even though the majority of case studies concentrated on developing states, industrialized states face many of the same problems, but because of sheer economic strength and political stability, do not face the same potential for internal collapse. Regardless, the most important task is now to move from identification of the problem to formulation of a solution.

From the Problem to a Solution

The Philippines offers more than just an exception to a "rule." The case of the Philippines and perhaps each case outlined above, however, is also an example of how an integrated and systemic approach to environmental issues can transform environmental insecurity to environmental security. It offers an example of how the environment can become a catalyst for cooperation with potential adversaries. It also illustrates how an integrated approach that involves international, national, and local components can solve environmental degradation and the insecurity it produces. At the international level, the Philippines and China can form closer bonds by cooperating over claims to the Spratlys. Furthermore, talks over protection of portions of the South China Sea can serve as a starting point for future interactions. At the national level, negotiations with Muslim secessionists can include talks about how both sides can work together to protect and substantially benefit from the island's vast resources.[65] At the local level, through empowerment of indigenous peoples and a return to sustainable local practices, the root problems of environmental degradation can be overcome. The events transpiring in the Philippines are but one example of how an integrated approach to environmental protection can achieve harmony and unity at the international level while producing stronger and more sustainable communities at the local level.

The purpose of this chapter is to highlight just one aspect of the pervasive nature of environmental degradation. It is not designed to provide in-depth analyses of all environmental problems (or even the many discussed in the chapter), nor does the chapter exhaustively describe the social and political ramifications of environmental degradation. There is just not enough room or time to take on such a task. Additionally, our current understanding and approaches to solve these problems are too elementary to accurately describe the situation. This chapter does, however, set the stage for a thoughtful and insightful look into the ability of the states and peoples of the world to overcome both environmental degradation and inter- and intrastate conflict by uniting in a multilevel web of interaction that is able to holistically approach environmental issues.

Notes

1. But see Thomas F. Homer-Dixon, "Population Growth and Conflict," *Environmental Dimensions of Security* (proceedings from a AAAS Annual Meeting Symposium, 9 February 1992): 9-15. The author's thesis is that there is no simple or clear causal relationship between population density, size, or rate of growth, and international or civil conflict. The relationship between population growth, size, or density and conflict is extremely complicated, involves many variables which are not linked in proximate or deterministic ways.

2. Thomas F. Homer-Dixon, "On the Threshold: Environmental Changes As Causes of Acute Conflict," *International Security* 16, no. 2 (fall 1991): 76. Available from http://utl.library.utoronto.ca/www/pcs/thresh/thresh1.htm; Internet.

3. Gail Bingham, Aaron Wolf, and Tim Wohlgenant, "Resolving Water Disputes: Conflict and Cooperation in the United States, the Near East, and Asia," an applied study prepared for the Bureau for Asia and the Near East of the U.S. Agency for International Development (Document No. ANE-0289-L-00-7044-00) by the Irrigation Support Project for Asia and the Near East, November 1994.

4. Thomas Naff, "Water Scarcity, Resource Management, and Conflict in the Middle East, Environmental Degradation As a Security Issue," *Environmental Dimensions of Security* (proceedings from a AAAS Annual Meeting Symposium, 9 February 1992): 25-30.

5. Peter H. Gleick, "Water and Conflict: Fresh Water Resources and International Security," *International Security* 18, no. 1 (summer 1993): 79-112.

6. Joyce R. Starr, "Water Wars," *Foreign Policy* 82 (spring 1991): 17-36.

7. Judith Achieng, "Environment-Africa: Desertification Still a Nagging Problem," *Inter Press Service* (June 18, 1998).

8. Mohamed Suliman, "Civil War in Sudan: The Impact of Ecological Degradation," *International Project on Violence and Conflicts Caused by Environmental Degradation and Peaceful Conflict Resolution* (Dec. 1992). Available from http://ifaa.org/encop1.html; Internet.

9. Ibid.

10. Shin-wha Lee, "Not a One-Time Event: Environmental Change, Ethnic Rivalry, and Violent Conflict in the Third World," *Journal of Environment and Development* 6, no. 4 (Dec. 1997): 365.

11. Ibid.

12. Mohamed Suliman, "Civil War in Sudan: The Impact of Ecological Degradation," *International Project on Violence and Conflicts Caused by Environmental Degradation and Peaceful Conflict Resolution* (Dec. 1992). Available from http://ifaa.org/encop1.html; Internet. For example, the first attacks by the Sudan People's Liberation Army (SPLA) were directed against the Jonglei Canal and oil-exploration companies.

13. Christoph I. Lang, "Environmental Degradation in Kenya As a Cause of Political Conflict, Social Stress, and Ethnic Tensions," *ENCOP Occasional*

Paper No. 12 (Center for Security Policy and Conflict Research: Zurich, 1995). Available from http://www.fsk.ethz.ch/fsk/encop/12/en12-con.htm; Internet.

14. Ibid.
15. Ibid.
16. Ibid.
17. Ibid.
18. Ibid. Unfortunately, women are the main victims of these social changes.
19. Ibid.
20. Valerie Percival and Thomas Homer-Dixon, "Environmental Scarcity and Violent Conflict: The Case of South Africa," *Occasional Paper* (Project on Environment, Population and Security: Washington, D.C., Oct. 1995). Available from http://utl1.library.utoronto.ca/www/pcs/eps/south/sa1.htm; Internet.
21. Ibid.
22. Thomas F. Homer-Dixon, "Environmental Scarcities and Violent Conflict: Evidence from Cases," *International Security* 19, no. 1 (summer 1994): 5.
23. Judith Achieng, "Environment-Africa: Desertification Still a Nagging Problem," *Inter Press Service* (June 18, 1998).
24. "Thomas Homer-Dixon; Director, Peace and Conflict Studies University of Toronto," *Defense News* (Mar. 27/Apr. 2, 1995): 46.
25. Val Percival and Thomas Homer-Dixon, "Environmental Scarcity and Violent Conflict: The Case of Rwanda," *Journal of Environment and Development* 5, no. 3 (Sept. 1996): 270.
26. Ibid.; Valerie Percival and Thomas Homer-Dixon, "Environmental Scarcity and Violent Conflict: The Case of Rwanda," *Occasional Paper* (Project on Environment, Population, and Security: Washington, D.C., June 1995). Available from http://utl1.library.utoronto.ca/www/pcs/eps/rwanda/rwanda1.htm; Internet.
27. Philip Howard and Thomas Homer-Dixon, "Environmental Scarcity and Violent Conflict: The Case of Chiapas, Mexico," *Occasional Paper* (Project on Environment, Population, and Security: Washington, D.C., Jan. 1996). Available from http://utl1.library.utoronto.ca/www/pcs/eps/chiapas1.htm; Internet.
28. Thomas F. Homer-Dixon, "Environmental Scarcities and Violent Conflict: Evidence from Cases," *International Security* 19, no. 1 (summer 1994): 5.
29. Abraham Lama, "Population-Peru: Migration Changes the Face of Lima," *Inter Press Service* (Jan. 18, 1999).
30. George Moffett, "'Green' Issues Become Force in Driving U.S. Foreign Policy," *Christian Science Monitor*, 8 April 1996, 1.
31. Ibid.
32. Priit J. Vesilind, "The Middle East's Water: Critical Resource," *National Geographic* 183, no. 5 (May 1993): 38-70. The author surveys the problems arising from the scarcity of water throughout the region: Turkey,

Israel, Jordan, and Syria. He argues that inefficiency of use exacerbates the inherent scarcity of water in the region, heightening environmental and health effects and political tensions. "If you want a reason to fight, water provides ample opportunity," Miriam R. Lowi, "Bridging the Divide: Transboundary Resource Disputes and the Case of West Bank Water," *International Security* 18, no. 1: 113-138. Lowi considers the linkage between "low" and "high" politics in conflict resolution, as it relates to resource scarcity, resource dependence, and particularly with the issue of shared water in the Jordan River basin. She focuses specifically on Israel's dependence on subterranean water supplies of the West Bank and its effects on the prospects for a political settlement in the region.

33. Kimberley Kelly and Thomas Homer-Dixon, "Environmental Scarcity and Violent Conflict: The Case of Gaza," *Ocassional Paper* (Project on Environment, Population, and Security: Washington, D.C., June 1995). Available from http://utl1.library.utoronto.ca/www/pcs/eps/gaza/gaza1.htm; Internet.

34. "Gaza Groundwater Crisis," *Environment News Service* (Apr. 11, 1997). Available from http://www.envirolink.org/archives/enews/0371.html; Internet.

35. Homer-Dixon, "Environmental Scarcities and Violent Conflict: Evidence from Cases," 5.

36. Kimberley Kelly and Thomas Homer-Dixon, "Environmental Scarcity and Violent Conflict: The Case of Gaza," *Ocassional Paper* (Project on Environment, Population, and Security: Washington, D.C., June 1995). Available from http://utl1.library.utoronto.ca/www/pcs/eps/gaza/gaza1.htm; Internet.

37. Brian R. Shaw, "When Are Environmental Issues Security Issues?" *Report of the Environmental Change and Security Project, The Woodrow Wilson Center*, Issue 2 (spring 1996): 39. Available from http://w3.pnl.gov:2080/ces/academic/ww_1shaw.htm; Internet.

38. Sefan Klötzli, "The Water and Soil Crisis in Central Asia—A Source for Future Conflicts?" *ENCOP Occasional Paper No. 11* (Center for Security Policy and Conflict Research: Berne, May 1994). Available from http://www.fsk.ethz.ch/fsk/encop/11/en11-con.htm; Internet.

39. Ibid.
40. Ibid.
41. Ibid.
42. Ibid.
43. Ibid.
44. Ibid.

45. On the other hand, these disputes are spurring some cooperative efforts. For instance, Turkmenistan and Iran are negotiating about building river dams in the border zone.

46. Gowher Rizvi, "South Asia and the New World Order," in *Whose World Order? Uneven Globalization and the End of the Cold War*, ed. by Hans-Henrik Holm and Georg Sorensen (Boulder, Colo.: Westview Press, 1995), 79.

47. Moffett, "'Green' Issues Become Force in Driving US Foreign Policy," 1.

48. Thomas F. Homer-Dixon, "Environmental Scarcities and Violent Conflict: Evidence from Cases," *International Security* 19, no. 1 (summer 1994): 5.

49. Shin-wha Lee, "Not a One-Time Event: Environmental Change, Ethnic Rivalry, and Violent Conflict in the Third World," *Journal of Environment and Development* 6, no. 4 (Dec. 1997): 365.

50. See Nick Robins and Charlie Pye-Smith, "The Ecology of Violence," *New Scientist* (Mar. 8, 1997): 12.

51. Thomas Homer-Dixon and Valerie Percival, "The Case Study of Bihar, India." Available from http://utl1.library.ca/www/pcs/state/india/indiasum.htm.

52. Peter Gizewski and Thomas Homer-Dixon, "Environmental Scarcity and Violent Conflict: The Case of Pakistan." Available from http://utl1.library. utoronto.ca/www/pcs/eps/pakistan/pak3.htm; Internet.

53. Ibid.
54. Ibid.
55. Ibid.

56. Elizabeth Economy, "The Case Study of China: Reforms and Resources: The Implications for State Capacity in the PRC," *Occasional Paper, Project on Environmental Scarcities, State Capacity, and Civil Violence* (Cambridge: American Academy of Arts and Sciences and the University of Toronto, 1997). Available from http://utl1.library.utoronto.ca/www/pcs/state /china/china1.htm; Internet.

57. Ibid.
58. Ibid.

59. Esther Tan, "Factors and Impacts of Forest Fires," *New Straits Times* (Malaysia) (Jan. 31, 1999): 13; "Habibie Seeks Review of Forestry Policies," *Jakarta Post* (Dec. 18, 1998); John Aglionby, "Orang-Utans in Danger of Extinction; Indonesia Forest Fires Have Left Men and Apes Competing for Scarce Resources, and the Apes Are Losing," *Guardian* (London) (Dec. 18, 1998): Foreign Page, p. 17.

60. Charles Victor Barber, "The Case Study of Indonesia." Available from http://utl1.library.utoronto.ca/www/pcs/state/indon/indonsum.htm; Internet.

61. Ibid.

62. However, current events in the Philippines illustrate that the linkages between political stability and the environment may not be as predictable as forecasted. Despite the Philippines' environmental woes, economic growth had remained stable (GNP growth at 6 percent) until the 1998 recession that hit the Pacific Rim. Jose Gerardo A. Alampay, "Revisiting Environmental Security in

the Philippines," *Journal of Environment and Development* 5, no. 3 (Sept. 1996): 329-337.

63. Thomas F. Homer-Dixon, "On the Threshold: Environmental Changes As Causes of Acute Conflict," *International Security* 16, no. 2 (fall 1991): 76. Available from http://utl.library.utoronto.ca/www/pcs/thresh/thresh1.htm; Internet.

64. Some research shows that the potential for conflict in the Philippines is diminishing. Jose Gerardo Alampay, "Revisiting Environmental Security in the Philippines," *Journal of Environment and Development* 5, no. 3 (Sept. 1996): 329.

65. Ibid.

4

A Natural Approach to Nature

How do we prevent environmental degradation and the social, political, economic, and even ecological fallout that it produces? The previous chapters outlined just one ramification of environmental degradation—environmental insecurity. Unfortunately, global disorder and conflict caused by environmental degradation is not even the most terrifying of the potential threats associated with environmental problems. The real security threats posed by environmental degradation include threats to the health and well-being of all living creatures.[1] Any world, even one filled with conflict, is better then no world at all—a situation that the combined power of global warming and ozone depletion can bring. A country may be able to fend off invasion or even social strife from within, but how does it prevent hurricanes, genetic mutation, or crop destruction? We must remember that the real problem is environmental degradation and thus any solution should address the root causes of environmental degradation.[2]

So what does our future hold? Answers to such questions have occupied the thoughts of some of our greatest thinkers. Unfortunately, the answers have been less than exceptional. One group of fifteen development professionals called the Global Scenario Group devised three possible scenarios for the future of the planet. The scenarios, and their variants, provide a glimpse into the future based on the threats of environmental degradation and how we respond to those threats. The first scenario is described as the "Conventional Worlds" scenario in which current trends continue without fundamental change in institutions or values. The first variant of this scenario incorporates mid-range population and development projects and explains how technology will gradually evolve to promote clean production, efficient resource use, and sustainable agriculture. A second variant includes comprehensive and coordinated government action to achieve greater environmental protection and social harmony.[3]

The second scenario describes a world in which the social, economic, and moral underpinnings of civilization deteriorate as emerging problems overwhelm the coping capacity of both markets and policy reforms. The first variant envisions global breakdown and unbridled conflict and economic collapse. The second variant involves an authoritarian response to the threat of breakdown.[4]

The third scenario sees visionary solutions to the sustainable challenge, including new socioeconomic arrangements and fundamental changes in value. One variant of this scenario incorporates localism, small technology, and economic autonomy. The second variant builds a more humane and equitable global civilization through international action.[5]

Which of these worlds does our future hold? Research on environmental degradation and human change can be found to support each of these scenarios. Perhaps the better question is which of these worlds is most desirable and how do we achieve it. This chapter attempts to answer this query.

Introduction to the Linkage Paradigm

The task at hand is to identify a framework that is best able to capture a visionary solution and avoid further environmental degradation and global breakdown caused by environmental insecurity. To solve environmental degradation it makes sense to mimic nature's own approach. In nature, everything is connected. Animals are dependent upon plants, which produce protein, carbohydrates, and fats through their photosynthesis. In turn, plant populations are controlled by animals, while both are influenced by bacteria. When biologists study nature they recognize that it is impossible to study organisms in isolation from the role and function they play within ecosystems. Additionally, an ecosystem's biological integrity is intact to the extent that it has the ability to maintain "a balanced, integrated, adaptive community of organisms having a species composition, diversity, and functional organization comparable to the natural habitat to the region."[6] Thus, an approach to environmental protection must recognize the interconnectedness of environmental issues while simultaneously building goodwill between states and building up local legal, political, and social institutions. To accomplish such a goal, this book proposes a synergistic linkage framework. A synergistic linkage model focuses on the appropriate actors and actions in environmental policymaking. It includes two levels, the policy level and the personal level.

At both the policy and personal levels, the paradigm is based on the doctrine of holism and the laws of ecology. Holism is a scientific principle that examines the relations between all living things.[7] The first law of ecology embodies the notion of interconnectedness. It explains that everything is connected to everything else. Each part of an ecosystem is connected to other parts, often in multiple ways. It follows then, that it is difficult, if not impossible, to affect only one part of an ecosystem. Any disruption in one area causes a rippling effect that affects many other areas in the overall ecosystem.[8] For example, the overextraction of one resource in an ecosystem can produce ramifying scarcities in the surrounding ecological system.[9] This is one way environmental degradation causes environmental insecurity. The synergistic linkage paradigm recognizes the interconnectedness of all environmental issues. It attempts to uncover the linkages not only between different environmental problems but also between environmental issues and development, population, economic growth, consumption, and politics, to name a few.

The linkage paradigm teaches us that what appear to be unrelated and diverse problems are actually part of an interrelated web of synergistic linkages. For example, "first-world overconsumption leads to secondworld industrial production problems, which leads to thirdworld resource depletion and underconsumption. Resultant poverty in the third world leads to increasing population, exacerbating ecological decline even more. Everything affects everything else."[10] Environmental connections are manifested through numerous linkages.[11] These linkages move from locality to locality, across horizons and borders, and even around the entire globe.[12] As the pace of globalization accelerates and the world becomes more interdependent and intertwined, the importance of linkages will become more, not less, important to policymakers at all levels of governance.

Consider just some of the linkages and variables that influence environmental problems and policies: population growth, demographic structure, patterns of population distribution, patterns of land distribution, family and community structure, economic and legal incentives to consume and produce goods, perceptions of the probability of long-run political and economic stability, historically rooted patterns of trade and interaction with other societies, form and effectiveness of governance, and values about the relationship between humans and nature.[13]

When linkages combine, the result yields not just compounded effects but usually multiplied effects. Problems are magnified through synergistic interactions. Synergistic interactions produce an effect greater than the sum of the whole based on the exponential effect of multidimensional interactions. The repercussions of these linked linkages usually transcend national borders and could soon become a pervasive aspect of international relations. Norma Myers has identified a number of these linkages: the hamburger connection and the songbird connection between the United States and Central America, the cassava connection between Europe and Southeast Asia, the cash-crop/desertification connection between Europe and the Sahel, and the debt/development connection between the rich world and the developing world.[14]

When one problem interacts with another, they do not produce a double-problem but rather a super-problem. Take for instance the manner in which plants react to stress. A plant's tolerance of one stress tends to decrease when other stresses are at work. Cold weather increases a plant's vulnerability to low sunlight. Conversely, low sunlight reduces a plant's photosynthetic activity and thus the plant becomes more susceptible to cold weather.[15] Perhaps a more apparent example is the combined effect of asbestos exposure and smoking in causing lung cancer.[16] By themselves, they pose a significant but not substantial risk. Together, they create a risk much greater than the sum of their individual probabilities.

Examples of Linkages

Linkages can be very complex and include numerous chains. Besides making them difficult to explain, this complexity has made research difficult. Consider the numerous parts of just one fairly well-known linkage. Acid deposition injures agricultural land, fisheries, and forests. At the same time, greenhouse warming is caused by and contributes to deforestation by moving northward the optimal temperature and precipitation zones for many tree species. It also increases the severity of windstorms and wildfires and expands the range of pests and diseases. In addition, the release of carbon from these dying forests subsequently reinforces the greenhouse effect. The increased incidence of ultraviolet radiation due to the depletion of the ozone layer also damages trees and crops, and harms phytoplankton at the bottom of the ocean food chain.[17]

Climate Change, Acid Rain, and Ozone Depletion

Climate change due to the warming of the Earth has been the topic of much environmental discourse. Many place the threat of global warming second only to worldwide nuclear war. From a linkage paradigm, this is extremely troubling. For if the associated linkages are taken into consideration, the interactions between global warming and other environmental problems may pose an even greater threat. Additionally, current policy initiatives advocated to abate greenhouse gases may actually exacerbate the problem (or lead to new ones).[18]

Global warming occurs when greenhouse gases build up in the atmosphere. These gases originate primarily from the combustion of fossil fuels. One of the primary fossil fuels is coal. It now powers many countries of the world, including some of the fastest growing ones such as China. When coal is burned, both carbon dioxide and sulfur dioxide are released. While the former contributes to global warming, the latter contributes to global cooling. Scientists contend that global warming has been held in check, at least in part, due to the cooling effect of sulfur dioxide. Unfortunately, sulfur dioxide is also the key element in acid rain. Acid rain has been found to deteriorate lakes and river ways as well as to destroy forests and wildlife habitats (not to mention the damage associated with the corrosion of buildings and other structures).

Given that coal burning contributes to both acid rain and global warming, it makes sense, at least on first glance, to do whatever possible to curb emissions from coal-burning power plants. While such an approach will significantly reduce sulfur dioxide, it may actually exacerbate global warming. If we were to stop all fossil fuel burning tomorrow, the Earth would undergo considerable warming. This ironic twist is explained by the fact that carbon dioxide stays in the atmosphere for about fifty years and sulfur dioxide falls out of the atmosphere in about three to five days (hence acid rain). Thus, the warming effect of carbon dioxide would no longer be held in check and massive warming would occur if we stopped burning pollution-causing coal.

To complicate the issue further, the problem of ozone depletion is also related to the two above environmental problems. Currently, tropospheric ozone is produced when hydrocarbons and greenhouse gases interact with sunlight to form smog. While there are health effects related to the formation of smog, it does help protect humans and the environment from an even greater threat: ultraviolet radiation that reaches the Earth due to a diminished stratospheric ozone layer. Thus, efforts to abate pollution in the name of stopping acid rain or global warming may increase the instances of skin cancer and other harmful spin-offs from ultraviolet radiation; this is not to mention the interaction between global warming and the formation of stratospheric ozone.

Finally, as stratospheric ozone decreases and more UV-B radiation reaches the Earth, another synergistic linkage occurs. The oceans serve as a significant sink of carbon dioxide, which means actions that hurt the health of the oceans increase the amount of carbon dioxide in the atmosphere and accelerate global warming. Marine phytoplankton absorb as much as 40 percent of annual emissions of atmospheric carbon dioxide.[19] However, phytoplankton are especially sensitive to enhanced UV-B radiation. If marine phytoplankton were to decline as a result of a hole in the ozone layer, the oceans' capacity to absorb carbon dioxide would be greatly reduced and the prospects for accelerated global warming would be much greater. The interconnectedness of ozone depletion, global warming, and acid rain are but one of many linked linkages that policymakers must understand.[20] The figure below illustrates but a few of these interactions and linkages.

The Oceans

The oceans serve as both a provider of food and natural resources as well as a pit for pollution and waste. As illustrated above, the oceans are intrinsically linked to global warming. But the synergistic linkages that connect the oceans to almost every aspect of life on this planet run much deeper. The oceans are affected by an array of human activities: fishing, transportation, recreation, resource extraction, energy production, dumping, disposal, research, and so forth. This is not to mention land-based activities

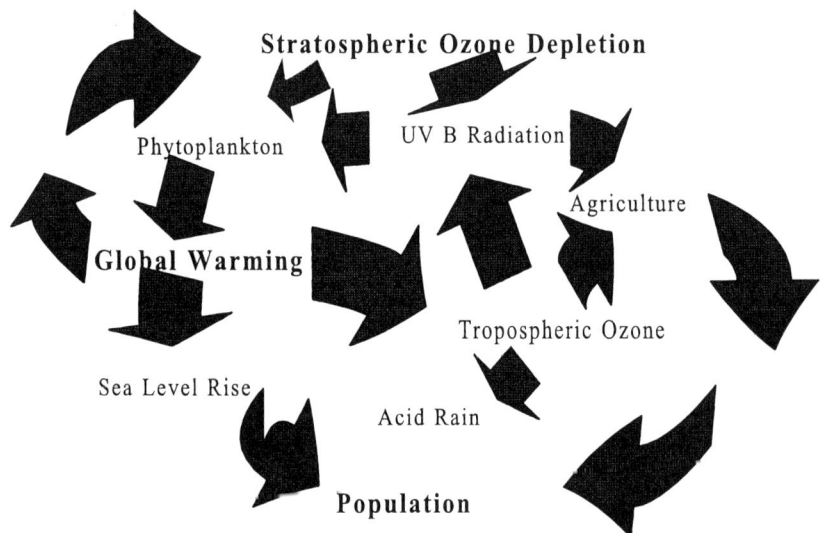

such as agriculture, industry, deforestation, land development, port facilities, and human settlements that can drastically affect the oceans. The broad spectrum of these activities has many calling for an integrated, holistic approach to addressing the problem of ocean health.

Unfortunately, present ocean policy is carried out in a fragmented and piecemeal manner. According to Myers:

> It is precisely because of this disregard for linkages that many oceans problems are increasing in size and number. When land use planners decide to site industries in coastal zones, they unwittingly foster use of the marine realm as a costless sewer whereupon pollution depletes ecosystem health in the oceans with adverse effects on fish stocks and biodiversity generally. When fisheries experts develop plans for sustained-yield harvests in developing-nations waters, they tend to limit their analyses to scientific and technical factors, overlooking the often impoverished status of fisheries communities that fosters overharvesting.[21]

Many people naively view the ocean as limitless or unalterable. They fail to heed the warnings of a rising sea level and instead build closer and more densely on the coast. For some, they have learned the hard way that human action in some distant place in the biosphere can have irrevocable effects on the health of the ocean ecosystem; for "there are few human industries or activities that do not ultimately affect the oceans in one way or another."[22] Policymakers need to realize that actions that may appear to be benign could have adverse effects on the most important bodies of water in the world. On the other hand, actions that may appear adverse could indeed be benign.

Other Linkages

One area where policymakers have attempted to act in a manner consistent with a linkage paradigm is that of arctic resources. To protect the polar bear, a whole ecosystem approach was devised to protect not only the bear, but also the entire ecosystem. Member nations recognized the link between ecosystem health, human activity, and the survival of the polar bear.[23] Unfortunately, there is a move away from a whole ecosystem approach to protect arctic seals. While such an approach was adopted in the 1970s, the recent decades have brought less concern for the seal and sustainability.[24] The arctic is influenced by a number of linkages, ranging from global warming to stratospheric ozone depletion. In fact, every region of the world is linked in some shape or form to every other region and every action influences not just one issue, but rather many throughout the ecosystem. Perhaps Newton was not quite correct: every action does not have only one equal and opposite reaction; rather, every action has many unpredictable and very unequal reactions.

Linkages affect all states and peoples of the world. Consider the situation in Indonesia. Logging concessions in Indonesia are depleting not only timber, but also water supplies, wildlife, reefs, and fisheries, along with other nontimber forest products. The Indonesian state apparatus is not equipped to provide the kind of innovative solutions needed to deal with such complex environmental interactions. The government's highly sectoralized forests bureaucracy is just one hurdle. The lack of resource accounting, which fails to internalize the costs of deforestation, encourages the exploitation of timber. Additionally, "the requirement for ingenuity to understand and manage complex systems such as tropical rainforests and coral reefs rises sharply when the current synergistic processes of degradation are underway."[25] For example, heavy siltations caused by deforestation destroy reefs, which subsequently diminish fisheries on which most poor coastal communities depend. Linkages thus manifest themselves in many ways. Understanding how and why they manifest themselves is still largely unknown.

Linkages and Scientific Research

The previous examples of linkages are just an illustration of the various linkages between environmental issues. Many of these linkages manifest themselves in the environmental insecurity discussed in chapters 2 and 3. Little scientific research has focused on synergistic linkages and that which has looked into the subject has been too limited and almost entirely uncoordinated.[26] Fortunately, some research is progressing. For example, recent research on UV-B radiation and organism growth discovered numerous linkages previously unknown.[27] However, Thomas Homer-Dixon warns that:

> [t]here is no a priori reason to expect that human scientific and technical ingenuity can always surmount all types of scarcity. Human beings may not have the mental capacity to understand adequately the complexities of environmental-social systems. Or it may simply be impossible, given the physical, biological, and social laws governing these systems, to reduce all scarcity or to repair all environmental damage.[28]

Everything we do know, however, points toward the need for a whole ecosystem approach. For example, scientists who monitor the health of forest ecosystems now advocate whole ecosystem approaches. Dr. Dennis LeMaster, head of the Purdue University Department of Forestry and Natural Resources, states, "'more and more we understand we have to look at the forest as a whole and the ecosystem approach is the best management strategy we have.'"[29] Scientists agree that the forest must be treated as a community of plants, animals, and microorganisms that combine to form an intricate web of life.

Scientific research continues to explore the various linkages between environmental issues. While the cases described previously are well documented, more research is needed to uncover other linkages. Additionally, scientists must constantly keep watch for the unequal and unanticipated reactions to environmental policies that may actually exacerbate other problems. Scientists agree that policymakers must change how they approach environmental protection. The question is how to effectuate that change.

Policy Implications

The vast array of linkages and linked linkages is enough to make many policymakers and students of environmental policy throw in the towel. But for those who want to address environmental degradation, they have no choice but to adopt a whole ecosystem, or synergistic linkage, approach. Policymakers must look to systems and examine linkages before administering policies. It is impossible to avoid linkages; they are all around us:

> Nature and human culture are intricately linked. Human overpopulation, for example, will likely increase greenhouse-effect gases and, therefore, climate changes. In turn, these can lead to the endangerment and extinction of animal and plant species. A solution to one ecological or social problem must not cause or exacerbate other social or ecological problems; when possible, it should help solve the others.[30]

In order to incorporate linkages into policymaking, policymakers need to alter their way of thinking. What is required is "a radical reorientation to shift policy makers' outlook from their erstwhile mode of linear thinking (i.e., nonlinkages thinking). Attitudes and perceptions are deeply entrenched in myriad ways. . . . The longer we delay in adopting corrective measure, the more deeply the present patterns of activity will become entrenched. Time is at a premium."[31] A move towards a linkage paradigm incorporates a number of policy changes.

First, policymakers must not focus on a single problem or issue unless that issue encompasses the whole. They must look to entire ecosystems. Sometimes the "ecosystem" will include a forest, other times it will include an entire continent. Such determinations should be scientific, not political. When policy agendas fragment issues, piecemeal solutions are frequently the end result. Problems should not be defined in a vacuum, for no issue is truly isolated. The manner in which an issue is framed significantly contributes to how the solution is derived. Additionally, solutions should not be focused solely on people.[32] Because people and the environment are connected through a myriad of linkages, when the environment is abused, people inevitably suffer.

When policymakers ignore linkages, they risk global catastrophe. The linkage between fossil fuels and global warming and acid rain was discovered a hundred years ago. Had policymakers acted then, it is doubtful the problem would be as dire as it is today. In 1972, the linkage between chlorofluorocarbons and ozone depletion was established. Yet world leaders waited ten years to take action.[33] Some observers warn that every year linkages are ignored, the impact of environmental degradation is increased geometrically. A linkage paradigm recognizes the interconnectedness of development and environmental protection. The ability of the linkage paradigm to incorporate human needs alongside ecological ones makes the paradigm a sustainable framework under which policymakers may operate.[34] It makes environmental policy politically possible while enabling long-term thinking.

One example of an environmental policy that incorporates a linkage paradigm is grand-scale tree planting in the humid tropics. Not only do the trees generate a sink for atmospheric carbon dioxide to counter global warming, but they also supply many spin-off benefits, such as relieving excessive logging pressures on remaining natural forests. Additionally, reduced deforestation preserves biological diversity that may yield great economic value. Finally, tree plantations and natural forests regulate water flow and reduce downstream flooding.[35] Thus, the environment and the human condition is improved through thoughtful policies that recognize the interconnectedness of environmental and human needs.

Ethical Implications

A change in how we approach environmental issues should be accompanied by a change in how we regard the environment. Any change at the systemic level should be accompanied by a change at the personal or moral level. A

A Natural Approach to Nature 57

change at the moral level could borrow from the land ethic of Aldo Leopold, which "changes the role of *Homo sapiens* from conqueror of the land-community to plain member and citizen of it. It implies respect for his fellow-members, and also respect for the community as such."[36] Such a change calls for humans to look at the environment in different ways.[37] In other words, it requires a manifestation of the synergistic linkage paradigm not only on the policy level, but also on the personal level.

A land ethic incorporates a holistic approach. It extends our ethical framework to include nature: "the land ethic simply enlarges the boundaries of the community to include soils, waters, plants, and animals, or collectively: the land."[38] A land ethic will make us question our relation to, and our relationship within, the natural world. An environmental ethic based on the land ethic is an integral part of a synergistic linkage paradigm.

Under such a framework, humans will no longer claim a special right to dominate or destroy the environment, including other life forms. Such an approach forces us to develop holistic understandings. Humans should not, and must not, place themselves too far above other species. This may be the only way to realize the full benefits of a linkage approach.[39]

An environmental ethic challenges us to think differently about the environment.[40] It asks us to understand the effect of our ecological crisis on the living and nonliving earth, and the peril that much of the environment faces.[41] The current state of environmental insecurity puts the future of the Earth in the hands of everyone. We must deal with threats such as deforestation and subsequent species loss. The only way to solve such problems is through a paradigm that incorporates a linkage approach both at the policy and the personal levels An environmental ethic that respects all living beings allows us to question our underlying assumptions. For example, instead of viewing the use of fossil fuels as an energy crisis, we must realize that it is really a consumption crisis.[42]

Many question the workability of such an environmental philosophy, but the Maori people illustrate how the environmental ethic can make for a better environment. The Maori people have no word for an environmental ethic. It is just the way they live and it preserves their environment. A change in ethics is the key to finding the roots of environmental problems.[43] In addition to being able to solve for the roots of environmental problems, an environmental ethic has many other benefits if instituted at the personal level worldwide. A change in ethics also has the ability to mobilize an entire people while allowing decentralization of environmental policy.[44]

An environmental ethic goes beyond anthropocentric means to solve environmental insecurity. First, it focuses on the causes and not the symptoms. It advocates an entirely new way of thinking. It attempts to find a way of putting people first *in order to protect the environment*.[45] Second, a change at the individual level will inevitably lead to policy changes at the local, national, and international levels. Each of the ecological changes humanity takes to preserve the environment will relieve stress on the social and governmental structures.[46] A type of global Maori people will not only be able to change the individuals relationship to nature, but also will be able to change the ethics of the entire international system.[47]

The past decade has witnessed a large increase in local environmental action and concern. One study found over 100 million members of grassroots movements and organizations in the rural areas of less-developed states.[48] The comprehensive study found that environmentalism is a global phenomenon, found in both rich and poor states.[49] The desire to protect the environment extends throughout the world. Unfortunately, current approaches to environmental protection fail to harness this energy.

One consequence of this failure is that environmental insecurity is becoming a pervasive problem throughout the world. It is time to devise approaches that celebrate rather than harness this energy.[50] As the Chinese philosopher Zhuangzi said, "only the selfless person can live up to the standards of nature because your body is just one temporary form in nature's constantly changing process. Selfishness is trying to hang on to what you have."[51] At the very core environmental degradation is the value of selfishness. It is selfishness at the entire species level.

Ethical judgments are inextricably embedded in policymaking and even in science.[52] A change in environmental outlook may be the only way to ensure a change in policy. Moreover, such a change is possible. Prior to the eighteenth century, most people had difficulty fathoming the idea of democracy. People were so used to monarchy, or rule by dictatorship, that mass democracy was seen as nothing more than a utopian concept with no grounding in reality. But democracy, in a relatively short period of time, has swept the entire globe. Major paradigm shifts are not only possible but, as in the case of an environmental ethic, they are also desirable. We cannot fully understand every result of each of our actions. It is time to reject the notion that humans can solve all problems by scientific, technological, and even governmental management.[53] Nature has a peculiar way of healing itself. If humans do not alter their ethical outlook in order to effectuate change at the policy level, nature may find a cure for its illness by itself; a cure that may not include humans at all. The issue is whether changes at the policy and personal levels are possible. A look at the status quo illustrates that while we still have a long way to go, change is very much possible.

Signs of Linkages in the Status Quo

There are some signs that the status quo is moving towards a linkage paradigm, both here and abroad.[54] At the national level, policymakers such as Bruce Babbitt are stressing a whole ecosystem approach to the Endangered Species Act.[55] The Environmental Protection Agency (EPA) has also endorsed a more holistic approach to its policymaking.[56] It seeks greater latitude to make policy and be able to invest in scientific research of linkages.[57] At the local level, states and local governments are moving towards a whole ecosystem approach. For example, in Florida, environmental policymaking was recently concentrated into one agency in hopes that it would be able to adopt a more holistic approach to environmental management.[58]

The linkage movement also influences the international level. Many international conferences now concentrate on the linkage between environment and development.[59] The Rio Earth Summit, despite all of the criticism it received, was a positive step towards a linkage paradigm. Its primary achievement was that it recognized the linkage between development and the environment.[60] Unlike the Stockholm Conference, the Rio Summit was able to garner greater consensus for both development and the environment.[61]

Despite these positive steps at both the national and international levels, experience has shown that a linkage paradigm remains the exception instead of the norm. At the international level, specialized agencies have been set up to tackle single, isolated issues. There is the FAO for food, WHO for health, and UNESCO for education, science, and culture. The United Nations (U.N.) established UNEP and UNDP for environmental protection and development, respectively. From a linkage perspective, one would expect that the two agencies would be in constant collaboration. Unfortunately, interaction is kept to a minimum. The U.N. "system hardly functions as a system."[62] Even the United Nations Population Fund and UNICEF do not always work together on issues concerning child welfare. Linkages are ignored and action goes uncoordinated. Despite the proclamations laid forth in the Brundtland report, there has been little attempt on the part of governments and international agencies to adapt their policy (or ethical) strategies accordingly. Many have resisted changing their current nonlinkage mind-set while others are perhaps daunted by the task that lies ahead of them. However, there are some policies that can help this transition towards a linkage paradigm.

Resource Accounting

One practical way to implement a linkage paradigm, at both the policy and personal levels, is through resource accounting.[63] Resource accounting entails a revision in the way in which governments assess the health of their economies. Currently, the environment is not viewed as productive capital even though we use it as such. National budgets and GNP should consider the depletion of natural resources. When we exploit forests, croplands, waterways, and the air, GNP goes up, not down. Likewise, when we engage in costly cleanup efforts and improve the condition of the "productive capital," GNP goes down. Yet if we were to treat any other type of productive capital, such as buildings or machinery in a similar manner, the very opposite would occur.

In response, some have called for a system that factors environmental health into GNP.[64] A country's gross national product may grow at 10 percent, but if it comes at the expense of resource depletion and environmental degradation, that number should be lowered accordingly. Thus there would exist an explicit economic incentive in maintaining a sustainable environment. It would also help to uncover other linkages between development and the environment.

Another way to arrive at similar results involves environmental cost pricing.[65] Environmental cost pricing takes into consideration the real price of a product, not the price the economic market assigns it. For example, markets currently decide the price of goods based on supply and demand, with little regard for environmental externalities. Under a system of environmental cost pricing, the environmental and social cost of products will be added to the current price to determine the *actual* price of a commodity. For example, the price of gasoline would reflect the cost of oil spills, air pollution, and military involvement. Additionally, the cost of fossil fuels would reflect the cost of acid rain, global warming, and other forms of pollution. The hope is that if products bear their true cost to society and the environment, a change in values may occur. Some feel this approach is desperately needed if we are to ever change the way in which we treat the environment (and one another).[66] Environmental cost pricing would internalize most of the environmental costs we currently externalize. It would remind the consumer on a daily basis of the true costs of products. It would also help to uncover linkages between development and the environment.

Implementing a Linkage Paradigm through an Integrated Approach to Environmental Protection

Many questions remain concerning the implementation of a linkage paradigm. For example, how do policymakers incorporate synergisms within their analytical and ethical frameworks? When should research stop and action begin? This book is concerned with questions concerning how best to implement a linkage paradigm throughout the world and the appropriate actors for such action. Some commentators observe that the whole ecosystem approach bolsters the push toward national control. They explain that "[i]f the environment is one giant web of interconnections, then local action is too narrow and must be inferior to centralized coordination. Indeed, environmental activists have shifted focus again, seeking international, not just national, regulations to deal with global issues such as endangered species, climate change, or ozone depletion."[67]

It is important to recognize that just as linkages exist between environmental issues, so too do linkages exist between various environmental actors. To achieve environmental protection, an integrated approach that incorporates all levels of governance is required. An integrated approach is also derived from nature: each species and organism depends upon a web of relationships within its ecosystem; "conversely, the stability and integrity of an ecosystem is dependent upon the function, role, and operation of various species interacting in mutually beneficial ways."[68] To achieve this result, unification and communication across international lines are required. We must identify those who have a stake in environmental policy and involve them.[69] Only a concentrated effort can achieve an integrated approach. A concentrated approach, however, does not mean a centralized one. An international framework that is able to bring peoples together is just a first step. While certain issues require international cooperation, all environmental protection requires community involvement. The rest of this book explains this interaction and illustrates how local action within global frameworks best implements a synergistic linkage paradigm at both the policy and personal levels.

Notes

1. See Report of the 24th U.N. of the Next Decade Conference, *Environmental Problems: A Global Security Threat* (Muscatine, Iowa: The Stanley Foundation, 1989), 1-3.

2. Our anthropocentric framework and our skepticism (or disbelief) of global environmental catastrophe make the problems associated with worldwide breakdown more credible and influential in spurring action than predictions of

environmental disaster. For example, it is the human suffering associated with environmental degradation that led Kofi Annan, the secretary general of the United Nations, to observe that "[f]ailure to act now could endanger our planet irreversibly, unleashing a spiral of increased hunger, deprivation, disease, and squalor. Ultimately, we could face the destabilizing effects of conflict over vital natural resources." Interview of Kofi Annan, "Gore Visits Earth Summit Plus Five," *All Things Considered;* NPR (June 23, 1997), Transcript No. 97062314-212.

3. Gliberto C. Gallopin and Paul Raskin, "Windows on the Future: Global Scenarios and Sustainability," *Environment* 40, no. 3 (Apr. 1998): 6.

4. Ibid.

5. Ibid.

6. J. R. Karr and D. R. Dudley, "Ecological Perspectives on Water Quality Goals," *Environmental Management* 5 (1981): 55.

7. Don E. Marietta Jr., *For People and the Planet: Holism and Humanism in Environmental Ethics* (Philadelphia: Temple University Press, 1994): 55.

8. Zachary A. Smith, *The Environmental Policy Paradox* (Englewood Cliffs: Prentice Hall, 1995): 2.

9. Thomas F. Homer-Dixon, "The Ingenuity Gap: Can Poor Countries Adapt to Resource Scarcity?" *Population and Development Review* 21, no. 3 (Sept. 1995): 595.

10. William E. Kilbourne and Joshua Lyle Wiener, review of *Radical Ecology: The Search for a Livable World, Journal of Public Policy and Marketing* 13, no. 2 (fall 1994): 323.

11. Norma Myers produced perhaps the best account of linkages in the environment and development field.

12. Norma Myers, "The Question of Linkages in Environment and Development," *BioScience* 43, no. 5 (May 1993): 302.

13. Thomas F. Homer-Dixon, "On the Threshold: Environmental Changes as Causes of Acute Conflict," *International Security* 16, no. 2 (fall 1991): 76. Available from http://utl.library.utoronto.ca/www/pcs/thresh/thresh1.htm; Internet.

14. Norma Myers, "The Question of Linkages in Environment and Development," 302.

15. Ibid.

16. Miguel A. Santos, *Managing Planet Earth: Perspectives on Population, Ecology, and the Law* (New York: Bergrin & Garvey Publishers, 1990): 64-65 (describing how pollutants combine to produce greater influence than the sum of the individual effect).

17. Thomas F. Homer-Dixon, "On the Threshold: Environmental Changes As Causes of Acute Conflict," *International Security* 16, no. 2 (fall 1991): 76. Available from http://utl.library.utoronto.ca/www/pcs/thresh/thresh1.htm; Internet.

18. Scientific uncertainty may also be responsible for preventing action. Although there is near consensus that the earth is warming, considerable debate exists as to how to abate the warming. One might ask if our limited scientific knowledge will prevent us from doing anything. A constant theme throughout this book is information dissemination. However, that information must first be gathered. Only a concerted scientific effort coupled with political support will be able to find linkages and devise plans of action to address those linkages.

19. Norma Myers, "The Question of Linkages in Environment and Development," 302.

20. This discussion is not even complete. Studies have shown that global warming has had both negative and positive effects on the formation of stratospheric ozone; just one more layer in the intricate web of environmental interconnectedness. Additionally, Norma Myers notes that global warming is linked synergistically with genetic depletion. Greenhouse warming produces higher temperatures and reduced soil moisture that will hurt agricultural crops. To overcome increased drought resistance, the genetic adaptability of crops needs to be expanded. This can be done through germ plasm variability. Unfortunately, the gene reservoirs of many crop plants have been depleted due to broad-scale elimination of biodiversity. Finally, global warming is intrinsically linked to population. As population increases so too does global warming due to increased human activity. But as the Earth warms, the seas rise and inundate land causing increased overcrowding due to less territory and more people. These are but a few of the linkages surrounding global warming!

21. Myers, "The Question of Linkages in Environment and Development," 302.

22. Peter Weber, "Abandoned Seas: Reversing the Decline of the Oceans," *World Watch Paper* 116 (November 1993): 55.

23. Oran R. Young, *International Governance: Protecting the Environment in a Stateless Society* (Ithaca: Cornell University Press, 1994), 71-72.

24. Ibid., 76.

25. Charles Victor Barber, "The Case Study of Indonesia." Available from http://utl1.library.utoronto.ca/www/pcs/state/indon/indonsum.htm; Internet.

26. Myers, "The Question of Linkages in Environment and Development," 302.

27. Max L. Bothwell et al., "Ecosystem Response to Solar Ultraviolet-B Radiation: Influence of Trophic-Level Interactions," *Science* 265, no. 5168 (July 1, 1994): 97.

28. Thomas F. Homer-Dixon, "On the Threshold: Environmental Changes As Causes of Acute Conflict," *International Security* 16, no. 2 (fall 1991): 76. Available from http://utl.library.utoronto.ca/www/pcs/thresh/thresh1.htm; Internet.

29. "Foresters Emphasize Ecosystem Management," *United Press International* (Dec. 12, 1991).

30. James A. Nash, *The Christian Century* (August 26-September 2, 1992): 774.

31. Myers, "The Question of Linkages in Environment and Development," 302.

32. Sherry Salway Black, review of *Paradigm in Progress: Life beyond Economics*, *Christianity and Crisis* 53, no. 2 (February 15, 1993): 46.

33. Myers, "The Question of Linkages in Environment and Development," 302.

34. Raymond E. Grizzle, "Environmentalism Should Include Human Ecological Needs," *BioScience* 44, no. 4 (April 1994): 263.

35. Myers, "The Question of Linkages in Environment and Development," 302.

36. Aldo Leopold, *A Sand County Almanac* (1949; reprint, New York: Ballantine Books, 1966), 240.

37. Rodney Aitchtey, "The Ways of Deep Ecology," *Contemporary Review* 260, no. 1513 (Feb. 1992): 193.

38. Leopold, *A Sand County Almanac*, 239.

39. Others argue that this will allow us to move "beyond a limited piecemeal shallow approach to environmental problems and attitudes to articulate a comprehensive religious and philosophical worldview." George Sessions and Bill Devall, "Deep Ecology," in Roderick Nash's *American Environmentalism: Readings in Conversation History* (New York: McGraw-Hill, Inc., 1990), 314.

40. Currently, institutions at both the local and international levels operate within an anthropocentric framework. For example, current calls from international and local institutions for species preservation are based on what species can provide humans. They discuss how species are critical to the invention of new medicines. This perspective views species as a resource. An ethical solution, on the other hand, would change this perspective. They would be preserved because they have an inherent worth separate from whatever value humans assign to them. We can already see signs of such an approach in the way some endangered species are giving inherent as opposed to extrinsic worth. Merrit P. Drucker, "The Military Commander's Responsibility for the Environment," *Environmental Ethics* 11, no. 2 (summer 1989): 138. By thinking about nature as not something separate from and outside the human individual but as a totality, which includes human relations, change may be possible. It also allows us to start to realize the many linkages around us. Mark Hoffman, "Normative International Theory: Approaches and Issues," in Groom and Light's *Contemporary International Relations: A Guide to Theory* (New York: Pinter Publishers, 1994), 37.

41. Kirkpatrick Sale, "Deep Ecology and Its Critics," *The Nation* 246, no. 19 (May 14, 1988): 673.

42. Aitchtey, "The Ways of Deep Ecology," 96.

43. David Rothenberg, *Ecology, Community, and Lifestyles: Outlines for an Ecosophy* (Cambridge: Cambridge University Press, 1989), 12.

44. The transnational global environmental movement is part of the move towards globalization. "Now, globalization holds the hope of a constantly shared consciousness for humanity, regardless of differing political, social, and cultural realities. In this sense, the Earth *is* a new world." George A. Lopez et al., "The Global Tide," *Bulletin of the Atomic Scientist* 51, no. 4 (July/August 1995): 39. An environmental ethic may also be able to stop social dominance. No longer will the world be witness to rich over poor, men over women, north over south, or humans over nature. Though the main goal of an environmental ethic is to reestablish the human relationship with the environment, ethics are able to unite the people of the world to stop social as well as ecological dominance.

45. Ibid., 9.

46. Daniel H. Henning and William R. Mangum, *Managing the Environmental Crisis* (Durham: Duke University Press, 1989), 25.

47. Some, however, caution against use of the idea of the "noble savage" in which indigenous people value and preserve the earth's natural resources. See Kathleen A. Galvin, "Traditional Peoples and Biodiversity Conservation in Large Tropical Landscapes; Book Reviews," *Bioscience* 2, no. 48 (Feb. 1998): 131.

48. Steven R. Brechin and Willett Kempton, "Global Environmentalism: A Challenge to the Postmaterialism Thesis?" *Social Science Quarterly* 72, no. 2 (June 1994): 247.

49. "Arguing from two types of new evidence—widespread grass roots environmental activism and two cross-national opinion surveys—[the study] conclude[s] that public environmental concern exists globally; it is not restricted only to advanced industrialized countries." Ibid., 265.

50. Christopher Manes, *Green Rage: Radical Environmentalism and the Unmaking of Civilization* (Boston: Little, Brown and Company, 1990), 248.

51. Zhuangzi, as adapted and illustrated by Tsai Chih Chung, *Zhuangzi Speaks: The Music of Nature* (Princeton: Princeton University Press, 1992), 54.

52. Henry Shue, "Ethics: The Environmental and the Changing International Order," *International Affairs* 71, no. 3 (July 1995): 456.

53. Henning and Mangum, *Managing the Environmental Crisis*, 7.

54. See Erik A. Devereux, "Editorial: It'll Never Work," *Pittsburgh Post-Gazette*, 12 September 1993, C4. Devereux explains that "[t]oday we recognize the important linkages between the environment, economic growth and the quality of human life; no longer can we consider 'the environment' by itself. Addressing the environment requires a focused, holistic approach that exploits linkages with the economy to serve the public good." He advocates the consolidation of federal agencies into one Department of the Environment in order to overcome the current fragmented and hostile pattern of relationships between federal agencies.

55. "ESA: Babbitt Stresses Whole Ecosystem Approach," *Greenwire* (February 17, 1993).

56. William Reilly, "Testimony of William Reilly, EPA Administrator to the 27th International Geographic Congress, Sponsored by the National Academy of Sciences," *Federal News Service* (August 10, 1992).

57. Brandon Loomis, "Regulations 'Fight Is On'—Environmental Issues Are up for Debate, Says Crapo Aide," *Idaho Falls Post Register*, 4 April 1996, C2.

58. Jon East, "One Voice for Florida's Environment," *St. Petersberg Times*, 14 February 1993, 4D.

59. Horace Awori, "Africa-Environment: Task Force to Crack Smuggling Rings," *Inter Press Service* (Sept. 3, 1994).

60. Mohamed T. El-Ashry, "The World Bank's Post-Rio Strategy," *EPA Journal* (April, May, June 1993): 22; Nathan Keyfitz, "The Preservation of the Planet—Only One World: Our Own to Make and to Keep by Gerard Piel," *Scientific American* 268, no. 2 (Feb. 1993): 114.

61. Tommy T. B. Koh, "The Road to and from Rio," *The Straits Times* (July 31, 1992): 32.

62. Myers, "The Question of Linkages in Environment and Development," 302.

63. Current measurements of national incomes do not incorporate measures of resource depletion. For example, a country can deplete and pollute its aquifers, cut down its forests, erode its soil, exhaust its mineral reserves, and destroy its biological reserves without affecting its measured income. This encourages societies to generate present income at the expense of their potential for future income. Thomas F. Homer-Dixon, "On the Threshold: Environmental Changes As Causes of Acute Conflict," *International Security* 16, no. 2 (fall 1991): 76. Available from http://utl.library.utoronto.ca/www/pcs/thresh/thresh1.htm; Internet.

64. See also Charles E. Di Leva, "International Environmental Law and Development," *Georgetown International Environmental Law Review* 10 (winter 1998): 501 (describing how green accounting is still inexact and efforts need to be intensified to improve the use of environmental indicators).

65. Ibid.

66. Alan Durning, "After the Deluge: The Changing Worldview," *World Watch* (Jan./Feb. 1997): 27-31.

67. Terry L. Anderson and Peter J. Hill, "Environmental Federalism: Thinking Smaller" in *Environmental Federalism*, Terry L. Anderson and Peter J. Hill, ed. (New York: Rowman & Littlefield Publishers, Inc., 1997), xiii. See also David Schoenbrod, "Why States, Not EPA, Should Set Pollution Standards," in *Environmental Federalism*, Terry L. Anderson and Peter J. Hill, ed. (New York: Rowman & Littlefield Publishers, Inc., 1997), 260.

68. Ronald E. Purser et al., "Limits to Anthropocentrism: Toward an Ecocentric Organization Paradigm?" *Academy of Management Review* 20, no. 4 (Oct. 1995): 1053.

69. Samual G. Pooley and Ralph E. Townsend, "A Community Corporation Approach to Management of Marine Fisheries: With Some Potential Application to Hawaii," in *Managing the Commons* (2d ed.), ed. John A. Boden and Douglas S. Noonan (Bloomington: Indiana University Press, 1998), 154-158.

5

Getting There Together

Catastrophic events can either lead to resentment, complacency, and delusion or they can serve as rallying points whereby individuals, groups, and states come together to address the consequences and work to avoid repeats of the catastrophic event. Environmental disasters, such as the *Torrey Canyon, Amoco Cadiz, Exxon Valdez,* and Chernobyl accidents, resulted in new international rules and principles.[1] Cooperation has already occurred in the international arena on marine pollution, Antarctica, the stratospheric ozone layer, and to a lesser extent acid rain and the transboundary movement of hazardous wastes.[2] International cooperation, however, is not enough. Local communities must be a part of any international plan of action. Frameworks, like international conventions, protocols, and laws, can provide opportunities for local communities to make a big difference.[3]

International action frequently occurs when states acknowledge that they cannot solve particular environmental problems alone and that solving such problems is in the best interest of the state after considering issues such as sovereignty and dependency. Frequently, calls for action only occur when issues are framed as resource ones and not ones of environmental protection.[4] From a linkage perspective, this is unfortunate because it indicates current policies are unable to achieve the personal level of the synergistic linkage paradigm. Fortunately, there are signs that states are becoming more concerned about the environment for purely environmental reasons. Extending the principle of "good neighbourliness," detailed in Article 74 of the U.N. Charter to environmental matters, will be an important starting point for international cooperation.[5] Already, international efforts have spawned numerous environmental initiatives.

International Agreements

The treaty/convention method is one way in which international cooperation may be achieved. Although some characterize it as time consuming, restrictive, and expensive, it allows for the expression of differences among states and the creation of new and innovative responses to these differences. The 1987 Montreal Protocol on Substances that Deplete the Ozone Layer[6] and the 1989 Basel Convention on the Control of Transboundary Movements of Hazardous Wastes and Their Disposal[7] are examples of the growing success of the treaty/convention method.[8] They "have led to new hope for international cooperation in the creation of international environmental law."[9] The world, in fact, has been witness to a long history of environmental cooperation through the treaty/convention method.[10] Each agreement had the benefit of building on their predecessors.

Before this century, few bilateral or multilateral agreements on international environmental issues existed. One of the first treaties to actually address *environmental* concerns was the 1909 United States-United Kingdom Boundary Waters Treaty, which provided in Article IV that water "shall not be polluted on either side to the injury of health or property of the other."[11] The 1916 Convention for the Protection of Migratory Birds in the United States and Canada[12] and the Treaty for the Preservation and Protection of Fur Seals[13] are early examples of international cooperation concerning wildlife, even if the parties were not always motivated by environmental considerations.[14]

Subsequent to these agreements but prior to 1972, only a handful of international agreements were reached.[15] In 1972 the world met at the United Nations Stockholm Conference on the Human Environment. The Conference established the United Nations Environment Programme (UNEP).[16] The Stockholm Declaration called for "[i]nternational co-operation . . . in order to raise resources to support the developing countries in carrying out their [environmental] responsibilities."[17] It also appealed for international cooperation in Principle 24:

> International matter concerning the protection and improvement of the environment should be handled in a co-operative spirit by all countries,

big or small, on an equal footing. Co-operation through multilateral or bilateral arrangements or other appropriate means is essential to effectively control, prevent, reduce and eliminate adverse environmental effects resulting from activities conducted in all spheres, in such a way that due account is taken of the sovereignty and interests of all States.[18]

Since 1972, states have concluded literally hundreds of multilateral and bilateral environmental agreements. Today, there are over nine hundred international legal "instruments that are either primarily directed to international environmental issues or contain important provisions on them."[19] The International Court of Justice, in one advisory opinion, proclaimed that "[t]aken together, these provisions embody a general obligation to protect the natural environment against widespread, long-term and severe environmental damage."[20]

International environment law is setting the pace for both international environmental cooperation and the development of international law in other areas. The scope of international agreements has experienced great growth as well. More aspects of the environment are covered than ever before, ranging from river basins within national borders to the movement of global transboundary pollution. The duties and responsibilities of the parties to these agreements have also become more comprehensive. Agreements now call on states to undertake research and monitoring roles as well as to prevent and reduce certain pollutants. It is notable that there is not a single example in which provisions of an earlier convention were weakened or diluted; rather, they have been strengthened, enlarged, or expanded.[21]

The experience gained by the international community helps the various parties to become very skilled at negotiating international agreements.[22] Whereas it took more than nine years to conclude negotiations on the Law of the Sea Convention, countries today are negotiating agreements just as complex in only a few years. The Climate Framework Convention took fifteen months (from February 1991 to May 1992) and the Environmental Protocol to the Antarctic Treaty and the Biological Diversity Convention required less than two years.[23] Additionally, nongovernmental organizations such as Greenpeace and the Sierra Club heighten international awareness of the need for protection of the global commons.

The implications for environmental security from this increase in international cooperation are twofold. First, the increasing number of international agreements signifies greater cooperation and interdependence between states. Second, the increasing scope of agreements indicates a willingness of states to begin to cede greater amounts of sovereignty and commit higher quantities of resources to international efforts on environmental protection. Just the coming together of states should help them learn from one another and recognize both differences and similarities that may help in negotiating other aspects of international law, thereby spurring cooperation on other issues.

From the perspective of the United States, the harmonizing and unifying effects of environmental protection play a special role in reversing the trend of environmental insecurity. The United States can lead international efforts and transfer the positive developments of its environmental policies to other states.[24] This process may occur in a number of ways. For example, the U.S. could use its influence to build consensus to establish new environmental protection agreements and to strengthen existing ones. In the Middle East, U.S. officials have added environmental problems like water shortages to its policy agenda in order to encourage regional cooperation.[25] Businesses in the United States can also apply lessons learned in countries where environmental legislation and awareness are "advanced" to their operations in less-developed countries.[26] This is not, however, without risks. The United States must be careful about imposing environmental policies on less-developed states. At the same time it must be sensitive to the needs of developing countries as well as to accusations of hypocrisy.

Cooperative efforts are traditionally only possible when North/South issues are properly handled and then only workable with the help of non-governmental organizations. The relations between the North and South as related to the environment and environmental security deserve attention. Although the North/South divide poses a serious obstacle for environmental security, cooperation on environmental issues presents a tremendous opportunity for better North/South relations and hence improved environmental security. Environmental concerns directly affect the security in the South.[27] Most of the empirical examples provided in the previous chapters of environmentally induced violence and social disorder occurred in less-developed countries. Developing countries are intrinsically tied to their environment, for it is where most derive their fuel for economic development. The push for economic development often means that developing states do not have the resources to devote to the protection of the environment. In many cases, the administrative organ of the state stands as an obstacle to environmental protection and conservation.[28]

The gap between the rich and the poor has doubled over the past twenty years.[29] As the gap increases, so too do the complexities of environmental cooperation. North/South issues have been at the forefront of international environmental conferences for many years. At the Stockholm Conference, the head of the Brazilian delegation stated: "A country that has not yet reached minimum satisfactory levels in the supply of essentials is not in a position to divert considerable resources to environmental protection."[30] An equally important point was made by the Ugandan delegate who stated, "[W]e are not confronted with an environment that has degenerated into pollution as a result of development. On the contrary, we are faced with an environment many of whose inherent aspects are prohibitive to development and injurious to human comfort."[31] Differing needs and abilities to respond to environmental degradation between countries in the North and the South require them to first understand each other. Perhaps the greatest contribution of the Earth Summit was not so much the specific agreements or proposals, but rather the heightened awareness it brought to the highest levels of government of all countries. The Earth Summit helped more-developed countries realize the importance of development issues while it helped less-developed countries realize the importance of environmental protection. Such awareness, however, has not always filtered through to the implementation and enforcement level. Many developed countries continue to impose their ecological views while many less-developed countries[32] maintain full speed ahead on economic growth despite being under ecological siege.[33]

It is likely that the North/South divide will remain a contentious issue in environmental cooperation, if for no other reason than that developed countries see environmental protection differently than developing ones. Developed countries view the environment as an inherent good requiring protection. Their priorities include protecting rain forests, saving the ozone layer, preserving biological diversity, and maintaining their comfortable lifestyles. Developing countries tend not to view the environment in isolation from economic considerations. Many see poverty as the root cause of environmental degradation in their countries. Thus, countries must first alleviate poverty in order to even begin to protect the environment. Whereas developed states view tropical rain forests as bastions of species diversity, developing countries see them as plentiful sources of firewood and grazing land to fuel their economic development.[34] They look to how developed countries achieved their economic power and see the inherent hypocrisy in "do what we say, not as how we do." The difficulty thus becomes how, and to what extent, developing countries should be assisted by their more developed brethren. Industrialized states favor cooperation, but frequently emphasize that the exchanges should occur on a commercial basis.

Two basic issues will probably decide the fate of North/South relations with respect to environmental protection. The first involves the harmonization of national legislation. Developing and developed states need to agree on a baseline of environmental protection. This ensures an even playing field in the economic realm while providing for environmental considerations. Second, developed states need to be willing to engage in the transfer of appropriate technologies with developing countries.[35]

Cooperation that cuts across the North/South divide will have great effects on environmental security. As the East/West divide dissolves, the primary threat to world order will come from a gap between the "haves" and the "have-nots." The North must be careful not to ignore the concerns of the South while at the same time ensuring that the environment be protected. Some developing countries argue that developed countries' concerns for the environment are, in part, a conspiracy to stop their economic growth—a form of eco-imperialism. Such perceptions will only hinder cooperation. The environment can serve as a harmonizing mechanism for world order only as far as it can harmonize relations between the North and the South. Should environmental cooperation between the North and the South become a reality, there is no doubt that cooperation will spread to other issues such as nuclear proliferation, economic development, and international terrorism.

Currently, attempts to overcome the North/South divide are being both helped and hindered by the explosion of nongovernmental organizations (NGOs). Thus far, the primary focus of this book has concentrated on the relations between states, mentioning the role of NGOs only in passing. But NGOs deserve attention for the critical role they play in the realm of environmental protection and environmental security. Whereas less-developed states may be weary of Northern states, they may have less reservations about working with NGOs (though suspicion may run high towards them as well). In addition, NGOs play an important role in the formation of international law.[36] They identify issues requiring international response, participate as observers in international organizations, and ensure states uphold treaty obligations. According to one international relations observer, "although states remain far and away the most important actors, international organizations and non-governmental groups have played a central role in creating the international environmental legal order."[37]

Nongovernmental organizations serve as a link between the public and the national government. They allow individuals to influence the international environmental agreement process. Many nongovernmental organizations have become permanent fixtures at the official negotiations of international environmental agreements. A wide array of NGOs monitored the negotiations of the Climate Convention. NGOs are even representing microstates at international conferences and have joined the official delegations of some rather large states, such as in the negotiations for the Environmental Protocol to the Antarctic Treaty.[38]

NGOs work with states to reform domestic policy, which helps make international cooperation and agreement easier. They increase awareness and change individual attitudes and lifestyles.[39] Environmental NGOs have set up camps throughout the world, both in the North and the South. Though some NGOs are viewed with distrust, especially in less-developed states, they have been generally accepted as a positive force in environmental protection and environmental security. Many NGOs stress education and environmental awareness as the cure for environmental protection:

> Ultimately, our environmental crisis will be solved . . . by ecologically literate citizens of all countries acting in an environmentally responsible way. . . . Ecological illiteracy is a prime cause of pollution. . . . Any normal human being who has the knowledge necessary to understand that all of nature is interrelated will not only desist from actions harmful to the environment but will be alert to the actions of the environmentally irresponsible . . . environmental education is still a subject on the fringe . . . few teachers in the West, and less in the developing countries, have an understanding of and are committed to environmental education.[40]

NGOs are able to spread environmental education and awareness. Through education and awareness the prospects for world harmony and environmental security through environmental cooperation are high. The new world order that environmentalists envision may only be possible through education.[41] Thus whether it is educating individuals, supervising states, or formulating policy, NGOs play a critical role in environmental protection and world order.

Community Considerations

International cooperation must involve communities in the formation and implementation of solutions to environmental degradation. However, community action is not without its drawbacks. Communities tend to be isolated from one another and do not always consider the ramifications of their actions on other, distant locales. Local political institutions are only accountable to the local electorate; thus, if local leaders can prevent a landfill or nuclear waste dump from coming into their community, they are viewed as heroes. The global result, however, is that another community, usually poorer or less powerful, must bear that cost. Local governments tend to view pollution problems as nuisances rather than resource consumption problems.

Without international frameworks, communities do not have the luxury of global environmental research. For each new environmental problem, local leaders and scientists must craft new solutions from scratch without the benefit of learning from others. On one hand, this produces truly local solutions that are best designed to protect local environments. On the other hand, this creates inefficiency and prevents the dissemination of information that might be helpful to thousands of communities. In addition, it may lead to NIMBY ("Not In My Back Yard") sentiments since communities are unaware of the pervasive nature of the problem and end up fighting against one another to absorb each other's pollution.

Another problem associated with community action is interest politics. Some feel that local governing institutions are more vulnerable to special interests because of their smaller size. Thus in some communities, a small but powerful elite may be able to control environmental policy to the detriment of both the population and the environment. Even in those communities not controlled by a handful of elites, the mere identification of environmental problems may be impossible because they either have downstream or downwind effects or they are so localized as to not gain much attention. Each of these relative weaknesses associated with community action, however, may be either completely overcome or significantly assuaged by global frameworks that are able to bring communities together.

The State

Although nongovernmental organizations and other nonstate actors are playing an increasingly prominent role in international environmental protection, states remain the predominant players. From a synergistic linkage paradigm, this is problematic. State leaders closely guard the concept of state sovereignty for hundreds of years. For example, Principle 21 of the Stockholm Declaration on the Human Environment explains that "states have, in accordance with the Charter of the United Nations and the principles of international law, the sovereign right to exploit their own resources pursuant to their own environmental policies."[42] Though in recent years, many have challenged the notion of total state sovereignty. The threat posed by environmental insecurity presents the most dynamic challenge that state sovereignty has ever faced.

The problem of the global commons is raised in any discussion of an international topic that affects every state but is no one state's problem. Environmental problems at the global level seem to be regarded as everyone's problem and therefore as no one's problem.[43] Despite this belief, "one common ideological basis exists for all environmental programs—the involvement of government with social goals and problems relating to the environment and natural resources."[44] Because nation-states are sovereign, they are seen as the critical actors.[45] Though many nongovernmental organizations have increased their activities and have become actors on the international scene (as well as some inroads made by independent intergovernmental organizations), states are still the decisive actors.

One criticism of state action is that they do not ensure continuity. This is more of a problem in democracies where administrations can change frequently. National governments often operate on a crisis basis, oriented toward immediate and crucial problem solving. The modern political climate, which is fraught with changing conditions, does not appear to allow for much stability in policy.[46] Significant environmental problems, such as climate change and ozone depletion, are not readily ascertainable over a brief period of time. The linkages discussed previously reinforce this observation. The effects of such environmental problems should be measured from year to year or even generation to generation instead of day to day or month to month. The effects of environmental degradation are rarely perceived to have an impact on traditional concerns of the political establishment.[47]

For example, a resolution to population and environmental problems requires a sustained effort that will yield more immediate pain than visible results. A solution will demand patience, a commodity that modern societies, including democracies, do not have in abundance. It often demands lifestyle changes, which endears the effort neither to the rich nor the poor.[48] This does not endorse fascism, but rather recognizes that a long-term approach is needed to address the root causes of the problem. Frequently, administrations in the Western world are more concerned about producing short-term results to help reelection bids than about signing international agreements or participating in international institutions that will not benefit the state for twenty to thirty years (and long after the next election).

Additionally, thinking of environmental security as a traditional "national security" issue is problematic. Identifying environmental degradation as a threat to national security can be useful if the two phenomena—security from violence and from environmental threats—are similar. Unfortunately, they have little in common. Among other differences, the sources and scope of threats to environmental well-being and national security are very different, as are the types of threat each poses.[49]

Besides only adopting short-term policies or those that equate environmental security with national security, states often do not act in the best interest of the global environment. This is important because "the state is the only one that is accorded 'sovereign' power domestically and is franchised to act independently and 'legitimately' in the international and global systems."[50] If the state is the only sovereign and legitimate international actor, then the world has two choices. One is to put all trust into the state to make the right decisions. The second is to take all trust away from the state and create an international system that respects all actors, from individuals through international bodies. Since the beginning of the state system, a single paradigm has dominated global politics: "'power politics' . . . and the 'state-centric' model, this paradigm assumes global politics to be a contest for power among sovereign nation-states in an anarchic environment."[51] Can a state-centric model really address environmental insecurity?

The state-centric model has had very limited success in dealing with environmental problems. Thus an increasing number of international agreements have been created that regulate state behavior.[52] But is this enough? After all,

> [t]he emergence of a new and unprecedented set of environmental challenges has highlighted the disjuncture between a single integrated, enormously complex and deeply interdependent ecosystem and the still dominant form of global political organization: a fragmented system of sovereign states, normatively built around the mutual recognition of sovereignty, and politically forming an anarchical system in which cooperation has historically been limited and in which war and conflict are deeply rooted, and for many an inherent feature.[53]

All states contribute to the problem but no one state can solve the problem.[54] As early as 1916, with the migratory birds treaty, states realized that they could not do it alone.[55] But states still jealously guard the notion of sovereignty. States often assert "sovereignty" in international negotiations. On one hand, sovereignty can prevent one state from trying to force its own cultural, political, and economic preferences upon others, which may have perfectly valid reasons for differing values, priorities, and policies. But state sovereignty has its ugly side. At times during the United Nations Conference on Environment and Development (UNCED), sovereignty seemed "to become almost a totem with which many developing countries sought to ward off discussion on various uncomfortable issues. . . . As such it became a symbolic word, treated as an absolute, and used as a way of trying to block a number of areas of discussion, most notably on forests."[56] Additionally, emphasis on the state divides the world into territorially distinct and single-minded entities. This de-emphasizes the transboundary nature of environmental problems.[57]

Many have called for greater flexibility with respect to the very notion of sovereignty.[58] This is a necessity if the political discussion on global sustainability is to advance. Currently, there is the potential for conflict "between international demands for environmental conservation and a state's claim to the right to control the resources within its borders touches directly upon state sovereignty."[59] Brazil is one state that is currently facing such a dilemma. There are strong international calls for preservation of the rain forests, with some governmental and nongovernmental actors going as far as to offer to buy Brazilian land to protect it. All of these actions are perceived by Brazil to be threats to its sovereignty. The other central tension is between perceived sovereign national interests and international responsibilities.[60] What is needed is a formation of national interests that mirror the interests of the international system.

At one point in time, sovereignty was a "dreamed-up" idea. Today, the notion of absolute sovereignty has come full circle. A synergistic linkage paradigm recognizes the usefulness of state action, but notes that it must be supplemented, or even supplanted in certain instances, by both international and local action. In other words, it advocates hyper-pluralism.[61] This reconceptualization of the state-centric model and of state sovereignty is the first step in implementing a synergistic linkage paradigm committed to the preservation of the environment.

Reconsidering International Institutions

Many critics of state sovereignty favor stronger international institutions to address the causes and solutions of the environmental crisis. What remains to be answered is whether such international institutions are desirable. More importantly, however, is how best can international institutions be utilized in a hyper-pluralism world.

Though it remains a critical question whether the states will be able to cope with the environmental crisis, one thing is certain: the environmental movement will continue to grow. It will continue to make a considerable impact at the national and international levels.[62] The world gathered in Rio de Janeiro in 1992 to discuss ways to work together to address the environmental crisis. Though over 500 nongovernmental organizations and over one hundred sovereign states attended, the conference produced more hot air than real action. Despite the calls for "radical change in the whole structure of development and international cooperation, even those close to the process hoped for much more than actually emerged."[63]

Advocates of international cooperation must realize that the environmental movement is in its infancy and there "is much that we do not understand about the systemic interactions in question."[64] International relations theory tends to conclude that the international system is anarchy with "no governing authority."[65] However, the world has entered a new period, one of profound change in our thinking about governance and governing in international society.[66] Considerable research has been undertaken to illustrate and assess environmental diplomacy and negotiation.[67] Unfortunately, little attention has been paid to a linkage paradigm.

Environmental problems are forcing states to cooperate.[68] A sense of urgency is bringing states together for the first time to cooperate at the international level.[69] Many now advocate new international institutions to address the harms of environmental degradation. States are engaged in a grand enterprise to build an international regime that can safeguard the environment of the entire planet. This enterprise is fraught with uncertainty, with possibly great and controversial costs, and with potentially divisive political implications.[70] International regimes can also be a mere guise for state sovereignty. In creating international regimes, we must be careful that the regimes are not merely tools of states used to pursue their national interests.[71] Additionally, we must recognize that the United Nations alone cannot handle the environmental crisis. It may, however, be able to start to bridge cultural differences that currently preclude cooperation.

Despite the political and economic barriers inherent in international cooperation, a number of environmental agreements have been implemented.[72] These environmental agreements may signify a new understanding of the problems. The growth of the environmental movement to international and global proportions is a historical development. Hopefully, subsequent generations will view this as a major change in the state of human affairs—an awakening to a new awareness of the threat of environmental insecurity.[73]

The very nature of the environmental threat increases international interdependencies. These pressures, despite the anarchical nature of the international system, will allow for the emergence of international institutions.[74] One necessary ingredient of international agreements is the practice of bargaining, which is a means for achieving coordination in decentralized social choice.[75] State regime bargaining has its limitations, for no international environmental regulation will ever be successful unless states confer some of their sovereignty to the international system. Such limitations are inherent in any treaty or public international lawmaking process.

Optimists maintain that most states comply with international law most of the time.[76] Perhaps this willingness to comply with international law is due to the inherent weakness and diluted manner of international agreements and statutory regulations. The bargaining process panders to all sides of an issue. Frequently, calls for tough environmental action are weeded out by those states interested in maintaining the status quo. One empirical example is the 1992 UNCED in Rio. President Bush advised his negotiating delegation not to sign any agreement. Such arrogance and tunnel vision is perhaps the Achilles' heal of the bargaining process. Fortunately, there are signs the United States is changing its policy.

It is probably true that the world needs international governmental organizations to secure peace, order, and justice.[77] States are capable of solving many problems, but they need the proper international institutions to coordinate and even enforce policy. A number of international treaties already exist. Without explicit international cooperation, however, member nations will only do what is in their interests instead of doing what is best for the greater good.

Even the proponents of international institutions and regimes recognize that certain environmental issues are able to capture the attention of the international community, while other just as important and linked issues fall by the wayside.[78] Additionally, questions remain about the ability of states not only to cooperate to reach an agreement, but also to maintain the cooperation to carry out the agreement. Agreements may be highly unstable because of the continuing temptation to defect by taking a free ride on the cooperative behavior of other actors.[79]

One final question that cast doubts over the legitimacy of international agreements is that of accountability. International treaties and institutions are agreements or compacts between sovereign states, not individuals.

Individuals must go through their own governments to have an effect, albeit indirect, on international agreements and actions. However, "this theory is increasingly breaking down in practice. In fact, a range of nonstate actors— including environmental groups, scientists, and the business community— now exert a direct and powerful influence in international environmental negotiations and institutions,"[80] but still not to the degree of the sovereign state.

International agreements can compensate for the current inept state-centric model. Oran Young explains:

> Critical threats to the earth's habitability demand that humankind rise to the challenge of creating new and more effective systems of international environmental governance. These threats are largely anthropogenic in origin and manifest themselves in such forms as desertification, deforestation, ozone depletion, climate change, the loss of biological diversity, disruptions of the global hydrological cycle, and ultimately, perturbations in coupled atmosphere/ocean/land systems capable of triggering worldwide ecological crises.[81]

Rather than replacing the state centric system, international regimes should develop frameworks within which state and local governments can best utilize their resources in order to achieve an integrated approach.

Developing Effective International Frameworks

The first step in developing a synergistic linkage paradigm is acknowledgment of the complexity of both the environmental problem[82] and what I describe as the action problem, or the problem associated with approaches to solve environmental degradation. We have come a long way towards acknowledging the complexity of environmental issues. Peoples throughout the world have taken notice of the problem. This is evidenced by the increase in the number of world conferences on environmental protection. The Earth Summit held in 1992 brought peoples from around the world to discuss and act upon environmental issues.[83] According to President Bush, the Earth Summit "signaled the next era in world history— one characterized by the recognition that environmental protection, economic development, and public participation in decision making are interrelated and crucial to our future quality of life."[84] A slew of smaller conferences, workshops, and agreements has also taken place in the last ten years in an attempt to address environmental issues. Unfortunately, much more needs to be done. While we have come a long way in recognizing the problem, we have struggled to develop a coherent and effective approach to solve these problems. What follows is a look at cooperative efforts aimed at solving regional and global environmental degradation. Based on the lessons learned from these efforts, it is possible to create global frameworks under which an integrated approach may blossom.[85]

Notes

1. Philippe Sands, in *Greening International Law*, ed. Philippe Sands (New York: The New Press, 1994), xxiii.

2. Andrew Hurrell and Benedict Kingsbury, *The International Politics of the Environment* (Oxford: Clarendon Press, 1992), 46. See, for example, the Vienna Convention on the Protection of the Ozone Layer, the Montreal Protocol on Substances that Deplete the Ozone Layer with the London Adjustments and Amendments, the Protocol on Environmental Protection (with annexes) to the Antartic Treaty, the Basel Convention on the Transboundary Movements of Hazardous Wastes and Their Disposal, the two International Atomic Energy Agency Conventions on Early Notification of a Nuclear Accident and on Assistance in the Case of a Nuclear Accident or Radiological Emergency, the International Convention on Oil Pollution Preparedness, Response, and Cooperation, the Framework Convention on Climate Change, the Convention on Biological Diversity, the Principles on Forests, the Nonbinding Legal Instrument of the Arctic Environmental Protection Strategy, and the London Guidelines for the Exchange of Information on Chemicals in International Trade.

3. Unfortunately, the regimes designated to carry out and enforce such international frameworks are formed by the states and are not always given the proper amount of power to maintain environmental goals.

4. Martin List and Volker Rittberger, *The International Politics of the Environment*, ed. Hurrell and Kingsbury (Oxford: Clarendon Press, 1992), 86, 93.

5. Sands, *Greening International Law*, xxxiii.

6. Montreal Protocol on Substances that Deplete the Ozone Layer, Sept. 1987, S. TREATY DOC. No. 10, 100th Cong., 1st Sess. 2 (1987), 26 I.L.M. 1550 (entered into force Jan. 1, 1989).

7. Convention on the Control of Transboundary Movements of Hazardous Wastes and Their Disposal, Mar. 22, 1989, S. TREATY DOC. No. 5, 102d Cong., 1st Sess. (1991), 28 I.L.M. 657.

8. Other treaties include: The Antarctic-Environmental Protocol (1959); The Convention on the Prohibition of Military or Any Other Hostile Use of Environmental Modification Techniques (1976); The Convention on Long-Range Transboundary Air Pollution (1979); Basel Convention on the Control of

Transboundary Movements of Hazardous Wastes and Their Disposal (1989); The Convention on Biological Diversity (1992); and, The United Nations Framework Convention on Climate Change (1992).

9. Jang B Singh and Emily F. Carasco, "Business Ethics, Economic Development, and Protection of the Environment in the New World Order," *Journal of Business Ethics* 15, no. 3 (March 1996): 297-307.

10. For a history of environmental cooperation see Hillary F. French, "Partnership for the Planet: An Environmental Agenda for the United Nations," *World Watch Paper* 126 (July 1995): 7.

11. Treaty Relating to Boundary Waters between the United States and Canada, Jan. 11, 1909, U.S.-Gr. Brit.., 36 Stat. 2448.

12. Convention for the Protection of Migratory Birds, Aug. 16, 1916, U.S.-Gr. Brit., 37 Stat. 1538.

13. Treaty for the Preservation and Protection of Fur Seals, Feb. 7, 1911, U.S.-Gr. Brit., 37 Stat. 1538.

14. See also Convention for the Protection of Birds Useful to Agriculture, Mar. 19, 1902, 102 B.F.S.P. 969 (entered into force May 11, 1907).

15. Convention on the Preservation of Fauna and Flora in Their Natural State, Nov. 8, 1993, 172 L.N.T.S. 241; Convention on Nature Protection and Wild Life Preservation in the Western Hemisphere, Oct. 12, 1940, 56 Stat. 1354, 161 U.N.T.S. 193; Convention for the Regulation of Whaling, Sept. 24, 1931, 49 Stat. 3079, 155 L.N.T.S. 349; Convention for the Northwest Atlantic Fisheries, Feb. 8, 1949, 1 U.S.T. 477, 157 U.N.T.S. 157; Convention for the Protection of Migratory Birds and Game Mammals, Feb. 7, 1936, U.S.-Mex., 50 Stat. 1311. See also Edith Brown Weiss, "International Environmental Law: Contemporary Issues and the Emergence of a New World Order," *Georgetown Law Journal* 81 (March 1993): 675.

16. *Report of the United Nations Conference on the Human Environment at Stockholm*, 11 I.L.M. 1416 (1972).

17. Ibid., prmbl. 7.

18. Ibid., princ. 24.

19. Edith Brown Weiss, "International Environmental Law: Contemporary Issues and the Emergence of a New World Order," *Georgetown Law Journal* 81 (March 1993): 675.

20. "Legality of the Threat or Use of Nuclear Weapons," Advisory Opinion. 1996 ICJ 222 (¶ 31).

21. Weiss, "International Environmental Law: Contemporary Issues and the Emergence of a New World Order," 675.

22. Ibid.

23. Ibid.

24. See George Bush, "Letter to Congressional Leaders on the National Strategy on the Environment", *Public Papers of the Presidents*, January 13,

1993, 29 Weekly Comp. Pres. Doc. 39. Bush wrote of United States international leadership efforts, "We insisted that a new world order include a cleaner world environment and reached 27 new international environmental agreements. We made America the world leader in phasing out ozone-depleting chlorofluorocarbons (CFCs) and led the way to a global ban on driftnet fishing. We launched a Forests for the Future initiative that proposed doubling international aid for forest conservation as a step toward halting global deforestation and dieback. We reduced Poland's debt to help that nation fund a new environmental foundation, and we launched the East-West Environmental Center in Budapest, Hungary, to help countries in Central and Eastern Europe. We addressed environmental protection in trade negotiations with Mexico, expanded debt-for-nature swaps to protect rainforests in Latin America, and created a network for environmental cooperation with Asia."

25. George Moffett, "'Green' Issues Become Force in Driving U.S. Foreign Policy," *The Christian Science Monitor*, 8 April 1996, 1. Additionally, while briefly working at the Department of State, I assisted in organizing regional conferences in the Middle East on water issues. Though many feel that the next war in the Middle East will be over water, not oil, there are promising signs that water will create an environment of cooperation instead of conflict.

26. Singh and Carasco, "Business Ethics, Economic Development and Protection of the Environment in the New World Order," 297-307.

27. Shahram Chubin, "The South and the New World Order," in Brad Robert's *Order and Disorder after the Cold War* (Cambridge: The MIT Press, 1995), 434.

28. Ronnie D. Lipschutz and Judith Mayer, *Global Civil Society and Global Environmental Governance* (Albany: State University of New York Press, 1996), 28.

29. John R. Beaumont, "A New World Order and Managing the Environment," *Futures* (March 1993): 197.

30. Singh and Carasco, "Business Ethics, Economic Development, and Protection of the Environment in the New World Order," 297-307.

31. Ibid.

32. See Michael Vatikiotis, "Malaysian Forests: Clearcut Mandate," *Far Eastern Economic Review* (Oct. 28, 1993): 54; Adam Schwarz, "Biological Resources: Banking on Diversity," *Far Eastern Economic Review* (Oct. 28, 1993): 55; Mark Clifford, "Hongkong Electric Power: Watts Less Is More," *Far Eastern Economic Review* (Oct. 28, 1993): 60; Darryl D'Monte, "India: A Dam Too Far," *Far Eastern Economic Review* (Oct. 28, 1993): 62.

33. Adam Schwarz, "Looking Back at Rio: 'Give Us Trade, Not Aid': Environmental Values vs. Economic Growth," *Far Eastern Economic Review* (Oct. 28, 1993): 48-50.

34. Ibid, 50-52.

35. John R. Beaumont, "A New World Order and Managing the Environment," *Futures* (March 1993): 197.

36. Edith Brown Weiss, "International Environmental Law: Contemporary Issues and the Emergence of a New World Order," *Georgetown Law Journal* 81 (March 1993): 675.

37. Philippe Sands, in *Greening International Law*, ed. Philippe Sands (New York: The New Press, 1994), xviii, xx.

38. Weiss, "International Environmental Law: Contemporary Issues and the Emergence of a New World Order," 675.

39. Andrew Hurrell and Benedict Kingsbury, *The International Politics of the Environment* (Oxford: Clarendon Press, 1992), 9.

40. Singh and Carasco, "Business Ethics, Economic Development, and Protection of the Environment in the New World Order," 297-307.

41. Some environmentalists, however, have a different vision of environmental security, one that no longer places the state at the center. While they feel that educating and supervising states are a necessary stopgap measure for NGOs to undertake, they want more drastic change. Called "The Mandate," some grassroots efforts are attempting to establish a supercourt to safeguard the world from the actions of individual states. According to founder Dr. Paul Clark, "We are in a box that we can't get out of when it comes to tackling the environmental problems that face us. We have to reconsider the notion of national sovereignty. It's still might versus right on the international level. We are still chattel property of our governments." Tony Caplan, "Environmentalists Seek Support for New World Order," *U.P.I.* (Mar. 31, 1991). A supercourt would indeed change the dimensions of world order and environmental protection; but unless it was sensitive to local needs and initiates, it may hinder rather than help the cause of environmental security.

42. Declaration of the United Nations Conference on the Human Environment, June 16, 1972, 11 I.L.M. 1416, 1420.

43. Rod Hague et al., *Political Science: A Comparative Introduction* (New York: St. Martin's Press, 1992), 111.

44. Daniel H. Henning and William R. Mangum, *Managing the Environmental Crisis* (Durham: Duke University Press, 1989), 19.

45. Richard W. Mansbach and John A. Vasquez, *In Search of Theory: A New Paradigm for Global Politics* (New York: Columbia University Press, 1981), 5.

46. Henning and Mangum, *Managing the Environmental Crisis*, 19.

47. Brian R. Shaw, "When Are Environmental Issues Security Issues?" *Report of the Environmental Change and Security Project, The Woodrow Wilson Center*, Issue 2 (spring 1996): 39. Available from http://w3.pnl.gov:2080/ces/academic/ww_1shaw.htm; Internet.

48. Milton Viorst, "The Coming Instability," *The Washington Quarterly* 20, no. 4 (autumn 1997): 153.

49. Daniel Deudney, "Environment and Security: Muddled Thinking," *Bulletin of the Atomic Scientists* (Apr. 1991): 22-28. On the other hand, environmental security devalues the state. It recognizes that many modern environmental threats, such as ocean pollution, global warming, climate change, ozone depletion, and deforestation are problems too big to be solved by one state. Gerald B. Thomas, "U.S. Environmental Security Policy: Broad Concern or Narrow Interests," *Journal of Environment and Development* 6, no. 4 (Dec. 1997): 397.

50. Nazli Choucri, "Introduction: Theoretical, Empirical, and Policy Perspectives," in Nazli Choucri's *Global Accord: Environmental Challenges and International Responses* (Cambridge: The MIT Press, 1993), 11.

51. Mansbach and Vasquez, *In Search of Theory: A New Paradigm for Global Politics*, 5.

52. Andrew Hurrell, "The Global Environment," in Booth and Smith's *International Relations Today* (University Park: The Pennsylvania State University Press, 1995), 135-40.

53. Ibid., 132.

54. Hague et al., *Political Science: A Comparative Introduction*, 112.

55. Henning and Mangum, *Managing the Environmental Crisis*, 275.

56. Michael Grub et al., *The "Earth Summit" Agreements: A Guide and Assessment* (London: Earthscan Publications Ltd, 1993), 34.

57. Thomas F. Homer-Dixon, "On the Threshold: Environmental Changes As Causes of Acute Conflict," *International Security* 16, no. 2 (fall 1991): 76. Available from http://utl.library.utoronto.ca/www/pcs/thresh/thresh1.htm; Internet.

58. Ibid.

59. Ann Marie Clark, "Non-Governmental Organizations and Their Influence on International Society," *Journal of International Affairs* 48, no. 2 (winter 1995): 511.

60. Grub et al., *The "Earth Summit" Agreements: A Guide and Assessment*, 56.

61. Clark, "Non-Governmental Organizations and Their Influence on International Society," 512.

62. Sheldon Kamieniecki, "Political Mobilization, Agenda Building, and International Environmental Policy," *Journal of International Affairs* 44, no. 2 (winter 1991): 339.

63. Grub et al., *The "Earth Summit" Agreements: A Guide and Assessment*, 55.

64. Oran R. Young, *International Governance: Protecting the Environment in a Stateless Society* (Ithaca: Cornell University Press, 1994), 40.

65. John S. Dryzek, *Rational Ecology: Environment and Political Economy* (New York: Basil Blackwood, Inc., 1987), 162.

66. Young, *International Governance: Protecting the Environment in a Stateless Society*, 12.

67. A. J. R. Groom and Dominic Powell, "From a World Politics to Global Governance—A Theme in Need of a Focus," in Groom and Light's *Contemporary International Relations: A Guide to Theory* (New York: Pinter Publishers, 1994), 86.

68. Hurrell, "The Global Environment," 133.

69. Sheldon Kamieniecki, "Political Mobilization, Agenda Building, and International Environmental Policy," *Journal of International Affairs* 44, no. 2 (winter 1991): 339.

70. David G. Victor et al., "Pragmatic Approaches to Regime Building for Complex International Problems," in Nazli Choucri's *Global Accord: Environmental Challenges and International Responses* (Cambridge: The MIT Press, 1993), 453.

71. Clark, "Non-Governmental Organizations and Their Influence on International Society," 510.

72. Kamieniecki, "Political Mobilization, Agenda Building and International Environmental Policy," 339.

73. Ibid. (quoting Caldwell).

74. Young, *International Governance: Protecting the Environment in a Stateless Society*, 181-82.

75. John S. Dryzek, *Rational Ecology: Environment and Political Economy* (New York: Basil Blackwood, Inc., 1987), 169; Victor et al., "Pragmatic Approaches to Regime Building for Complex International Problems," 455.

76. Dryzek, *Rational Ecology: Environment and Political Economy*, 177.

77. Young, *International Governance: Protecting the Environment in a Stateless Society*, 13.

78. Ibid., 81.

79. Dryzek, *Rational Ecology: Environment and Political Economy*, 173.

80. Hillary F. French, "Partnership for the Planet: An Environmental Agenda for the United Nations," *World Watch Paper* 126 (July 1995): 45.

81. Young, *International Governance: Protecting the Environment in a Stateless Society*, 140.

82. Similar to our ability to understand linkages between environmental issues, our ability to conclude treaties and conventions has been hampered by limits in scientific knowledge. Weiss, "International Environmental Law: Contemporary Issues and the Emergence of a New World Order," 675.

83. For a summary and analysis of the Earth Summit, including a compilation of the key documents, see Stanley P. Johnson, *The Earth Summit:*

The U.N. Conference on Environment and Development (UNCED) (Boston: Graham & Trotman, 1993).

84. George Bush, "Letter to Congressional Leaders on the National Strategy on the Environment," *Public Papers of the Presidents*, January 13, 1993, 29 Weekly Comp. Pres. Doc. 39.

85. Some positive signs already exist. For example, the UNCED adopted framework conventions and plans of action that led to follow-up steps to real solutions and implementation.

6

Creating Global Foundations

Any approach to environmental protection requires cooperation. More and more, environmental issues are sparking international cooperation and coordination. States are increasingly willing to come together to solve common environmental problems. Coming together, however, is just a beginning, for keeping together is progress and working together is success. Too often states cannot get past just coming together. Quite often the devil is in the details. And once details are ironed out, implementation and enforcement present their own issues.

Some international efforts have been effective. The most successful of these have utilized local actors. They have overcome the desire to micromanage environmental policy and instead sought to foster community empowerment. To achieve a truly integrated approach, international cooperation needs to be replaced by global cooperation at the community, state, and international levels. This chapter examines some of the most prominent international efforts, some successful, some not so successful. Each of these efforts, however, provides important clues on how to build and sustain meaningful global foundations for environmental protection.

Global Warming

Global climate change, particularly global warming, is an environmental problem that presents particular difficulties for global cooperation within a synergistic linkage paradigm. As with most transboundary atmospheric pollution, global warming affects not only the global commons,[1] but also areas within state borders. Because global warming affects both individual states and the world, an integrated approach that involves both local and international action is the best alternative. The current mindset, however, views global warming as solely an international phenomenon requiring a uniform answer. The difficulty arises when one considers that the environmental devastation caused by global warming is not uniform. Developed countries may be able to fend off a rising sea level, but low lying areas incapable of expending vast resources to build up shorelines, such as Bangladesh, may become completely inundated. The destruction of agriculture may also affect only certain parts of the world. In some areas, food and land shortages will cause massive numbers of environmental refugees (which in the example of Bangladesh has empirically led to environmental insecurity), while in others the effects will be minimized because states will be able to afford to adapt and to develop stopgap technological measures.

Many snares hamper global cooperation on global warming. First, the increased atmospheric concentration of greenhouse gases is a worldwide issue because the gases are widely dispersed in the upper atmosphere. Second, the rewards on restraints on greenhouse gas emissions come in the politically distant future while the costs are incurred in the political present. Finally, "the pervasive sources of greenhouse gas emissions—notably burning fossils fuels, cultivating wetlands, and raising cattle—imply that restraint will involve changes in behavior by hundreds of millions if not billions of people, not merely the fiat of 180 or so governments."[2]

Some feel that the dire scenarios and distant impacts will not be enough to unify the world community. They cite the frequent breakdown in discussions and fierce contention over details. Senator John Kerry explained, "It's one of those big, sweeping issues that's hard to bring down to a 'today decision,' it tends to overwhelm."[3] Others explain that the challenges facing climate negotiations are just too daunting: resistance from developing countries because they do not want to hamper economic growth, resistance from oil export countries over their soul source of capital, resistance from developed countries over the rate of emission reductions, and the list goes on.

Overcoming these challenges is difficult, but the international community is responding, due in large part to the threat of environmental insecurity. Both developed and developing countries are coming together to address climate change. The best example of such efforts is the Framework Convention on Climate Change,[4] which was hailed by many as a "landmark achievement in the history of international environmental management."[5]

Cooperation became possible because all countries realized that "a change of climate[,] which is attributable directly or indirectly to human activity . . . and its adverse effects[,] are a common concern of humankind."[6] The Convention acknowledges the disproportionate effects developed countries have had on greenhouse gas emissions and the special difficulties developing countries have in curbing emissions since their economies are particularly dependent on fossil fuels.[7] The Convention calls for a "stabilization of greenhouse gas concentrations in the atmosphere at a level that would prevent dangerous anthropogenic interference with the climate system."[8] It recommends that "[s]uch a level should be achieved within a time frame sufficient to allow ecosystems to adapt naturally to climate change, to ensure that food production is not threatened and to enable economic development to proceed in a sustainable manner."[9]

The Convention directs states to "take precautionary measures to anticipate, prevent or minimize the causes of climate change and mitigate its adverse effects."[10] It goes as far as to state that "[w]here there are threats of serious or irreversible damage, lack of full scientific certainty should not be used as a reason for postponing such measures."[11] Signatories to the Convention agreed to develop national inventories of emissions;[12] implement national programs to mitigate climate change;[13] cooperate in the process of technology transfer;[14] develop plans for conservation of sinks and reservoirs of greenhouse gases;[15] participate in educational programs to increase local awareness about climate change;[16] and develop international scientific and research programs.[17]

The Kyoto Protocol followed the Climate Convention. At Kyoto, 160 countries met to negotiate limits to greenhouse gas emissions from industrialized countries. The Protocol set varying emission targets for each country, representing a 5 percent reduction in greenhouse gas emissions below 1990 levels. The Protocol disallowed the banking of credits from reductions that had already occurred. In addition, all major greenhouse gases were included in the legal agreement. Unfortunately, the Protocol left open the issue of forest "sinks."[18] The Protocol was subject to criticism for not targeting developing countries and for providing too many loopholes to developed countries.[19] The Protocol was followed by the Buenos Aires talks, which took place in late 1998. The talks resulted in a firm schedule for settling issues left unresolved at Kyoto. In addition, the meeting served as a backdrop for several substantial steps forward in curbing global warming. the United States officially signed the protocol and two developing countries, Argentina and Kazakhstan, announced national greenhouse gas emission limits.[20]

The Climate Convention and the Kyoto Protocol are the first steps toward a new vision of global, not just international, cooperation on environmental problems.[21] The negotiations that occurred at the Rio Earth Summit pertaining to climate change were an important starting point that will serve as a mold for future treaties and conventions to come.[22] Important lessons can be learned from the climate negotiations at the Rio Earth Summit and at Kyoto. For example, success in climate negotiations only became possible when the participants "were able to forgo the need to assign blame for the current situation, and focus on finding a path through these difficult challenges."[23] Success was also possible because the participants recognized the role that individual states and localities must play if any effort is to be successful.

Success in climate negotiations is a relatively new phenomenon. In 1990, the EEC's Council of Ministers could not even agree on a reduction of CO_2 emissions and the European Community is supposed to be the most homogenous regional body in the world.[24] Perhaps it was this homogeneity and perceived need for a uniform solution that prevented cooperation in the first place. Though considerable progress has been made within the European Community since that time, disagreement continues to lag and stall international cooperative efforts. Germany recently criticized Russia for risking environmental disaster by stalling on an international convention to reduce global warming.[25]

Environmental insecurity, such as that caused by global warming, occurs at two levels. First, there is the level of the environmental degradation itself, with the ability for environmental scarcity to cause political and economic instability. Second, conflict can occur after and during the unifying effect of environmental problems, that is, during and after negotiations and treaties. Either one party (or parties) cannot come to agreement or a party feels it has sacrificed too much in return for a disproportionately low return.

To overcome the potential for conflict and disunity, cooperation must forge ahead in response to climate change. There are some positive signs. The G-7 recently pledged to increase cooperation on global levels. The G-7 chairman's statement issued after the 1996 political communiqué urged the global community to act on major issues such as environmental degradation and global warming.[26] Industrial countries also revived efforts to combat global warming. Countries pledged to seek a binding pact on cutting pollution blamed for the greenhouse effect.[27] Developed countries are not the only ones cooperating on climate change. The seven states of Central America have joined forces in the Central American Council on Climate Change to address the effects and causes of global warming. The countries are working together to conduct a study to examine regional vulnerability and adaptation options with respect to climate change and global warming. These countries have also joined international cooperative efforts by ratifying the Framework Convention on Climate Change.[28] The Organization for Economic Cooperation and Development (OECD) is now discussing a "harmonisation agenda" that would identify the most urgent areas for action (such as global warming). It seeks greater compatibility of trade policies in order to protect the environment. As these examples illustrate, throughout the world both regional and international efforts are rising to the task of combating global warming.

The United States has long been criticized for its approach toward cooperative efforts at addressing global climate change. Its rhetoric has consistently outpaced its action. Many attack the U.S. for not taking the risk of global warming seriously and delaying efforts for worldwide emissions reductions.[29] During Bush's administration, the president was accused of hypocrisy; on one hand he championed international cooperation in a "New World Order," but on the other he dismissed the risk of global warming.[30] During the Gulf War, *The Washington Post* carried an article entitled "Nuclear Winter, Petroleum Summer," which described the Gulf War as an effort to make the world not safe for democracy, but rather safe for global warming. It concluded by remarking that U.S. policy in the new world order must be towards cooperation on environmental security.[31]

Based on recent events, it appears as if U.S. policy is moving towards acknowledging the threat of global warming and the need for international cooperation. During a trip to Australia, President Clinton issued a sweeping statement that called for tougher international agreements to fight global warming. He said, "I call upon the community of nations to agree to legally binding commitments to fight climate change. . . . We must stand together against the threat of global warming. A greenhouse may be a good place to raise plants; it is no place to nurture our children."[32] A new White House proposal would reduce U.S. emissions to 1990 levels by the year 2000 and call upon other states to make binding targets and timetables for reducing emissions.[33]

Unfortunately, this rhetoric and public display is not translating into action. As of July 1998, 124 countries have become parties to the Kyoto Protocol to the Framework Convention on Climate Change.[34] Although the United States signed the Protocol in November of 1998, the Senate has yet to ratify the agreement. Many consider "[t]he Kyoto story [a]s part of a larger pattern of U.S. foot-dragging in international environmental affairs."[35] Additionally, many in the field oppose the Kyoto Protocol because they doubt its effectiveness. They are troubled that the agreement is premised on setting national emissions targets.[36] Signature states are allowed to pursue the agreed-upon national objectives whatever way they see fit. If the Kyoto Protocol on global warming is to be successful, it will require a manifestation of the linkage paradigm on a personal level. The international community has devised a framework under which peoples may come together and discuss environmental protection, but the treaty leaves the ultimate protection up to the states and communities of the world. It is clear that but for a global framework such as the Climate Convention, communities will not act, either because they do not want to or because they do not know how to. Communities, however, are the ones who must act. Thus, international regimes and states need to provide greater incentives and serve as educators so that these communities will both want to take action and know how to take action.[37] Global warming will continue to receive international attention and may be the key environmental issue that decides the future of environmental cooperation in the twenty-first century.[38] The question for all of us is how do we want that future to look.

Stratospheric Ozone Layer

While the Climate Convention and Kyoto Protocol illustrate the importance of global frameworks to facilitate local action, the Montreal Protocol and London Amendments on stratospheric ozone illustrate the important role global frameworks play in disseminating information. Twenty years have passed since the surfacing of the first report linking chloroflourocarbons (CFCs) with stratospheric ozone depletion. Initially, the theory was greeted with skepticism, but as a result of information dissemination, scientists around the world now acknowledge the ozone depleting abilities of chemicals such as CFCs and methyl bromide. Such broad international scientific agreement facilitated the creation of international treaties and protocols for the gradual (and in some instances, immediate) phase out of ozone-depleting substances. These efforts culminated with the Montreal Protocol on Substances that Deplete the Ozone Layer in 1987.[39] The Montreal Protocol is a recent and visible result of what happens when people are educated about the threat of environmental degradation. The extent of this undertaking, with 148 parties to the agreement (which was the largest number of states to an environmental treaty at the time), indicates how important education can be to addressing the environmental protection of the global commons. It also illustrates the power of concerted action.[40]

Although the Protocol and subsequent London Amendments are benchmarks for human progress and cooperation on international environmental issues, the road to agreement was fraught with difficulties and conflict. Even though the problem was agreed upon, the road to a successful agreement took considerable time and energy.[41] There was division within the Western camp over how to approach the issue. First, there was disagreement between the European Community (E.C.) and the United States. Just as these problems were being resolved, conflict emerged within the E.C. over how to best pursue an international protocol. Then, debate arose to the extent of chemical coverage. Just as this debate came to a resolution, questions arose concerning production versus consumption, standards for a base year, and the stringency and timing of reductions. An even more divisive issue surfaced with the divide between the North and the South. Countries such as India and China presented special considerations and problems. After sitting on the fence, many states from the South spoke out about their concerns over what they viewed as a disproportional burden they were being asked to carry. Resolving such issues took informed and sensitive negotiators as well as a common desire to protect the environment.[42]

The Montreal Protocol was successful because of four factors. First, there existed a core group of countries. These countries motivated others and brought their desires for a Protocol to fruition. The second factor involved the role of science and technology. The consensus among scientists from around the world provided a critical ingredient for action. Third, strong personalities helped to move along the talks and negotiations. Certain individuals were able to pull all the parts together and provide the required leadership. Finally, a willingness to compromise was required.[43]

According to U.S. negotiator Richard Benedick, a successful international agreement came only after everyone could agree on the harms and then build personal relationships with one another. The latter is an example of how environmental issues can harmonize world order by harmonizing the relationship between states at the individual level. But the Montreal Protocol itself is an example of a larger phenomenon: environmental threats serving as the impetus for multilateral diplomacy and cooperation. This development, however, has its drawbacks. While the Protocol will serve as a model for other agreements and illustrates how states of the world can cooperate and act together, future agreements will need to incorporate and empower communities into their overall scheme of environmental protection.[44] After all, international agreements can only go so far; abatement of ozone depleting chemicals requires changes in behavior of most citizens of the world.

Acid Rain

While ozone depletion is an environmental problem that affects the entire world in a somewhat uniform manner, acid rain is primarily regional and disproportional in its effects. It is also one that both international and regional as well as national and local institutions are playing a part in solving. Although acid rain was an environmental challenge before scientists even began to theorize about the depletion of the ozone layer, it is an issue that has proven more tenuous and difficult on which to reach a consensus at the international level. First, there were difficulties in locating the sources and transport of acid rain. Although much of acid rain comes from the high stacks of power plants, questions remain concerning causation and movement of acid rain. Additionally, unlike other pollutants, sulfur dioxide can move hundreds if not thousands of miles in the atmosphere, thereby removing those who create the pollution from those who suffer its effects. Recently, however, there have been signs of regional and local cooperation on the issue of acid rain.

On the North American front, the United States and Canada have signed a number of accords designed to curb acid rain and to reduce other air pollutants.[45] Though the problem of transboundary air pollution has been a contentious issue between the two states for some time, it is only in the last decade that the United States treated seriously the need for cooperation with Canada on the issue of acid rain.[46] From the Canadian perspective, cooperation with the United States is an important, if not essential, requirement to protect itself from acid deposition.[47] Although relations between the two states are relatively cordial, the problem of acid rain has traditionally served as a dividing stake that sometimes seeps over into other areas of bilateral relations. The recent accords and cooperative efforts should help to fortify overall relations.

Europe is another area of the world that faces problems from acid rain. Rather than just requiring the cooperation of two states, a plethora of states are involved in negotiations and efforts to protect streams, lakes, and forests from the effects of acid rain. Sulfur dioxide from almost any state in Europe can lead to acid rain in practically any other state in Europe. At the 1993 Lucerne Conferences, the states of Europe came together to discuss the issue.[48] Just as in the early stages of negotiations on ozone depletion, cooperation in the rather homogenous European Community was particularly difficult when environmental issues were raised. Nevertheless, the acknowledgment of a common problem and the recognition of the need for cooperation made acid rain a potentially harmonizing mechanism for regional environmental security.

While in North America and Europe, the parties involved in cooperation were primarily developed states; the situation is quite different in East Asia. Japan and South Korea have become increasingly worried about the threat of air pollution caused by coal consumption in China. Whereas Japan and South Korea (to a lesser extent) are economically developed states, China is still on the road (or superhighway if one prefers) to development. As a result, there is a conflict of value hierarchies among the states in this region of the world. Although Japan is fearful of offending its rather ominous neighbor, it recognizes that action is needed.[49] To curb regional pollution, Japan created a "Green Aid Plan," with most of its efforts directed at mainland China's coal plants. Japan invited officials from China, South

Korea, Mongolia, and Russia to discuss environmental cooperation on such issues as acid deposition. It also constructed a China-Japan Friendship Environmental Protection Center in Peking to transfer Japanese technology to help curb the pollutants that cause acid rain.[50] Both Japan and China have since formed bilateral agreements on environmental cooperation with a focus on the problem of acid rain.

Efforts to curb air pollution have spread to include many other states in Asia. An international symposium was held in 1995 in Japan, which brought together 500 experts, environmentalists, and government officials from ten Asian countries. The overarching theme of the symposium was the importance of cooperation among not only the states, but also between governments, citizen organizations, and private enterprises. With some viewing Asia as the region to watch over the next decade, cooperative relationships between the states are in everyone's interest. If environmental efforts can then lead to agreements in other areas, such as nuclear proliferation, arms sales, and population, the prospects for prosperity and peace in Asia are great.

Besides leading to regional cooperation, acid rain can also serve as a catalyst for worldwide cooperation as exemplified by the bilateral cooperation efforts between Japan and the European Community.[51] Acid rain is an environmental problem that requires a global framework to facilitate information and idea exchange. As states, communities, and individuals become more concerned with the health of lakes, streams, and forests, the push for global cooperation will be even greater. Steps to combat acid rain will lead to more regional cooperation and as the regions of the world recognize the common problem they share, regional cooperation will lead to world cooperation. Regional experimentation combined with international guidelines and local implementation can definitely serve as a harmonizing mechanism for world order. After all, what better way to address the problem of acid rain in North America than to learn from efforts undertaken in Europe or Asia?

Shared Bodies of Water

Whereas acid rain originates from primarily one source (atmospheric sulfur dioxide and nitrous oxides), the pollution of lakes and seas stems from a variety of sources. Nevertheless, the effects of common water body pollution reach many communities, states, and regions of the world.[52] The world is witnessing many regional efforts to preserve the ecological integrity and sustainability of shared water resources. The following examples are but a handful of current and past efforts.[53]

The states of Russia, Kazakhstan, Turkmenistan, Iran, and Azerbaijan border the Caspian Sea. Cooperation between these countries and others has been sparked by what some term as a sea "at risk" and even "near death."[54] The first international conference on the environmental degradation of the Caspian Sea convened in 1991 in the city of Baku. Countries represented included Russia, the former Soviet republics, Iran, Turkey, the United States, Canada, Britain, and Scandinavia.[55] These states met to discuss such ecological issues as the depletion and threatened extinction of many fish species of high commercial value. Proposals were made to set up joint ecological foundations as well as a unified monitoring system of interstate and interregional commissions and expeditions. The delegates also expressed a desire to form an international scientific research center to study the problems of the Caspian Sea.[56]

The conference was an example of regional cooperation that called upon the expertise of individuals and states outside of the immediate problem area. Just as some have claimed that green issues were the driving forces in ending the Cold War in Eastern Europe, environmental issues may also help to unite the former Soviet republics. These working bonds may translate into cooperation on other issues as well as begin the long process of reconciliation. Finally, common environmental problems may test Russia's ability to serve as a regional hegemony through the resolution of issues in its own sphere of influence.

Cooperative efforts to combat water pollution have also found success in parts of Africa. The Zambezi River flows either between or through Angola, Zambia, Namibia, Botswana, and Zimbabwe before being fed by tributaries from Tanzania and Malawi and then flowing through Mozambique en route to the Indian Ocean. In all, eight countries directly affect the ecological health of the river. Efforts to protect the Zambezi River were blocked by numerous obstacles.[57] Once support was garnered from the presidents of Botswana, Zambia, and Zimbabwe, the United Nations Environmental Programme helped to connect these countries with foreign assistance. After money was raised to conduct research and develop solutions, the affected states negotiated the Agreement on the Action Plan for the Environmentally Sound Management of the Common Zambezi River System.[58] The parties reached the agreement only once they realized that given the interconnectedness of the river and river basin, a cooperative effort was required to preserve the ecological health of the river.[59]

One area that faces both severe environmental degradation and extreme environmental insecurity is the Indian subcontinent. Environmental issues, however, may be able to spur cooperation. Bangladesh and India signed a thirty-year agreement in late 1996 that shared water from the Ganges River. The agreement settled a two-decade-long dispute between the two countries. Moreover, the prospects for further cooperation on such water-related issues as hydroelectric power, irrigation, and augmentation of the Ganges flow now seem possible. Some predict that "[f]uture accords may also address problems created by migration, environmental degradation, and separatist movements in the adjoining regions of both countries."[60]

Additionally, the bilateral agreement between Bangladesh and India may lead to multilateral agreements on the integrated development and protection of the larger Ganges-Brahmaputra-Barak river basin, which is shared by Bangladesh, Bhutan, China, India, and Nepal. The prospects for peace and prosperity in South Asia are closely tied to the cooperative development and use of shared rivers in an efficient, equitable, and sustainable manner:[61]

> Parts of the basin suffer from sporadic violence among different ethnic and religious groups—demands for autonomy and separatist rebellions that are often fueled by conflicts over natural resources such as land, water, forests, and minerals. Thus the recent Bangladesh-India agreement needs to be extended to include all the countries sharing the basin.[62]

Water may serve as either a pacifier or a spark for renewed violence between India and Pakistan. The Indus Water Treaty in 1960 ended a twelve-year dispute between Pakistan and India. The most interesting aspect of this treaty is that both countries honored the provisions of the treaty despite two subsequent wars and intermittent skirmishes over Kashmir.[63] Thus, while the Indus Water Treaty may have not led to broad-based cooperation, it did prevent conflict over water. With the area on the brink of nuclear war, it is appropriate to wonder if the threshold would have already been passed but for the treaty.

One of the most politically significant and economically important waterways in the world is the Baltic Sea. It serves as a prime port for ships in Europe as well as a prime deposit of economically important resources. The history of exploitation dates back to the fifteenth century. The Baltic Sea has been plagued by problems of mercury, chlorinated pesticides, oil spills, seal extinction, petroleum hydrocarbons, heavy metals, war pollution, and nuclear power plants and fallout. Some of these pollutants have caused irreversible damage to the ecosystem of this European artery. In the past fifteen years, there have been ten tanker accidents and the rise in tourism (10-15 million a year) has further exacerbated environmental degradation. The states bordering the Baltic Sea are now calling for cooperative efforts to preserve the ecological balance of the sea. These calls are not new. As early as 1919 states were concerned with the Baltic Sea. The Treaty of Versailles stipulated complete freedom of access to the Baltic Sea for ships of all countries.

102 Rethinking Environmental Protection

Today, there is a myriad of cooperate efforts ranging from international agreements to local entities working on the problem of pollution of the Baltic Sea. The 1974 Convention on the Protection of the Marine Environment of the Baltic Sea Area was a significant step in providing for the environmental protection of the Sea.[64] A more recent convention, the Baltic Sea Environmental Declaration, was signed in 1993. It covered the entire catchment area of the Baltic. Such regional cooperative efforts can help spur global cooperation. The Joint Comprehensive Environmental Action Program was carried out in collaboration with four international banks: the World Bank, the European Bank for Reconstruction and Development, the European Investment Bank, and the Nordic Investment Bank. Many international organizations such as the United Nations Environmental Programme (UNEP) and the World Meteorological Organization (WMO) have assisted in the environmental protection of the Baltic Sea. Additionally, numerous NGOs involved themselves in the process and even NGIs (nongovernment individuals) played a crucial role.[65] The Baltic Sea Convention succeeded by recognizing that the only way to protect oceans and seas is to ban all dumping of wastes.[66] The cooperative efforts have been another bridge between East and West and very well may include spin-offs into other areas of environmental and planetary protection.

While protection of the Baltic involved states of similar stature, the cooperative efforts to protect the Mediterranean Sea exemplify how environmental concerns can bring together different civilizations. In 1975, the sea-bordering states of the Mediterranean Sea met in Barcelona to launch a concerted effort to end pollution.[67] It is widely believed that had the states not acted when they did, the sea would have suffered irreversible damage. The Convention called upon each of the signatories to act both independently and collaboratively to protect and improve the sea environment. It is one of the first examples of an integrated approach that utilized both global frameworks and local ingenuity.

The countries have subsequently adopted two protocols, the Prevention of Pollution of the Mediterranean Sea by Dumping from Ships and Aircraft, and Cooperation in Combating Pollution of the Mediterranean Sea by Oil and Other Harmful Substances in Cases of Emergency, both of which provide a framework for ecological protection.[68] More recently, nearly all of the sea-bordering states signed a Protocol for protection against land-based pollution. Thirty countries were represented at the signing and agreed to the gradual elimination of persistent organic pollutants into rivers and the sea. These pollutants include derivatives of chlorine, such as DDT and dioxin. It is remarkable that any agreement was reached given the diversity of the region. States bordering the Mediterranean include both very industrialized and very poor ones as well as ones just beginning to recover from civil war.[69] Despite this diversity, the common desire to protect a common resource transcended such differences and unified the region, if only for this specific purpose.

Whereas the Baltic Sea Convention occurred amongst a highly diverse group of participants, efforts to protect the Great Lakes have centered on two countries that share a high degree of commonality: the United States and Canada. The history of cooperation on the Great Lakes dates back to 1912. Concern over environmental degradation of the Great Lakes has led to extensive and growing bilateral cooperation. The 1978 Great Lakes Water Quality Agreement was the result of years of negotiations.[70] The 1987 protocol addressed groundwater contamination affecting the Great Lakes and the airborne transport of chemicals into the Great Lakes. One of the cooperative efforts stemming from the protocol prohibited all direct discharges of persistent toxic chemicals into Lake Superior. The program was the end result of a recommendation made by the U.S.-Canadian International Joint Commission.[71] Such cooperation has "led to a growing sense of a shared major bioregion, to a depth of understanding of some biophysical phenomena of aquatic ecosystems that is acknowledged worldwide, and to the emergence of ecosystemic thinking that casts new light upon how humans must begin to adapt to and understand the ecosystem of which they are a part."[72]

While considerable progress has been achieved with respect to environmental protection of the Great Lakes, at times the action was slow and lacking. Ironically, cynicism about the institutional problems led to a transformation that resulted in improved institutions. Additionally, non-governmental organizations joined the cooperative efforts to save the Great Lakes. For the past twenty years, academics in both countries have organized a series of meetings entitled "Canada-United States Inter-University Seminars" for the Great Lakes. The series brings together about fifty participants from universities, government agencies, and NGOs. Other examples of NGO activity abound. The NGO, Great Lakes Tomorrow, sponsors educational classes and runs two Centers for the Great Lakes in Chicago and Toronto. The environmental degradation of the Great Lakes thus not only spurred environmental cooperation between the United States and Canada, but has also increased cooperation between the peoples of these two countries.

Unfortunately, cooperation is sometimes the exception rather than the rule. Take for instance the problem of cooperation among states in the Jordan and Euphrates River basins. The region has no binding international arrangements for water sharing, even though they desperately need such arrangements. Efforts at technical cooperation have failed in the absence of political cooperation among riparian states.[73] Fortunately, the plethora of agreements on shared water resources provides a number of models for success.

Other Case Studies

The aforementioned case studies illustrate the ability of environmental degradation to spur cooperation at the individual, state, regional, and international levels.[74] These instances of environmental cooperation are not alone. Concern over the Arctic elevated calls for international cooperative efforts.[75] States and nongovernmental organizations have frequently met to discuss how to best preserve the environment of the Arctic region.[76] Apprehension over hazardous waste led to the Basel Convention on the Transboundary Movements of Hazardous Wastes and Their Disposal.[77] The Convention, which was signed by 116 countries, overcame substantial North/South problems through a common desire to protect the environment.[78] The Antarctic Treaty,[79] which now has forty-three signatories and has safeguarded the natural environment for forty years, is another example of international concern that led to cooperation.

One case study omitted thus far is that of oceanic pollution. The oceans are the largest area of global commons and are used by practically every state. It would be difficult to find one person in the world who is not affected by actions that occur in, on, and over the oceans. Oceanic pollution has tremendous potential to cause environmental insecurity and conflict. One need only remember the Canadian coast guard firing upon a Spanish trawler for "invading" its coastal waters and numerous other oceanic skirmishes whether it be over whaling, fishing, or drilling.

Such conflict, however, has spurred international efforts to protect and govern the oceans. The Law of the Sea was the most ambitious attempt ever for international regimes. It represented a major step towards an integrated management regime for the oceans and "'a monumental achievement' for world order."[80] Though the Convention took nine years to negotiate, it serves as a benchmark for treaties and conventions that follow. In all senses of the word, the Law of the Sea Convention was a global agreement designed at procuring global cooperation. It was even able to overcome decisive North/South issues that continue to plague international cooperative efforts.[81]

Conclusion

These cases illustrate the ability of the states of the world to come together to solve environmental degradation. It also illustrates the ability of environmental degradation to spark cooperation and coordination. The most successful efforts were those that utilized local actors. The importance of global, and just international, cooperation is made stronger when we attempt to act holistically. The international cooperative efforts exemplified in this chapter primarily dealt with single environmental issues. The international community's limited success in addressing multiple environmental issues can be explained by its failure to use an integrated approach.

Fortunately, international efforts that take a holistic approach to environmental protection are emerging. For example, the Single European Act has brought together the entire continent to address environmental issues in a more holistic manner.[82] Other treaties are also beginning to take a related approach by focusing on systems rather than individual issues. For example, the ASEAN Convention on the Conservation of Resources addresses the conservation of endangered species through the conservation of the whole ecosystem.[83] The Biological Diversity Convention takes a similar approach by focusing on the conservation of ecosystems as a central means for preventing the extinction of species about which we know little or nothing.[84] Unfortunately, such efforts are few and far between.

Completion of a framework requires the inclusion of community and local efforts to solve environmental issues. Only by recognizing the linkages between various environmental actors can a linkage approach begin to solve environmental problems and the environmental insecurity they cause.

Notes

1. See David Adamson, *Defending the World: The Politics and Diplomacy of the Environment* (New York: I. B. Tauris & Co., 1990), 50-51.
2. Richard N. Cooper, "Toward a Real Global Warming Treaty," *Foreign Affairs* (Mar./Apr. 1998): 66.
3. Anthony Flint, "Culture Clashes to Mark Population Control Talks," *The Boston Globe*, 28 August 1994, 1.
4. Framework Convention on Climate Change, May 9, 1992, 31 I.L.M. 849.
5. Irving M. Mintzer and J. Amber Leonard, ed. *Negotiating Climate Change: The Inside Story of the Rio Convention* (Cambridge: Cambridge University Press, 1994), 21.
6. Framework Convention on Climate Change, May 9, 1992, 31 I.L.M. 849, Art. 1.2.
7. Ibid.
8. Ibid., Art. 2.
9. Ibid.
10. Ibid., Art. 3.3.
11. Ibid.
12. Ibid., Art. 4.1(a).
13. Ibid., Art. 4.1(b).
14. Ibid., Art. 4.1 (c).
15. Ibid., Art. 4.1 (d).

16. Ibid., Art. 4.1 (i).

17. Ibid., Art. 5(a). See Ranee K. Panjabi, *The Earth Summit at Rio: Politics, Economics, and the Environment* (Boston: Northeastern University Press, 1997), 169.

18. NRDC, "The Kyoto Protocol: A Few Wrinkles Still Need to Be Ironed Out of the Landmark Global Warming Agreement" (Feb. 5, 1998). Available from http://www.nrdc.org/bkgrd/gwkpanal.htm; Internet.

19. David M. Driesen, "Free Lunch or Cheap Fix?: The Emissions Trading Idea and the Climate Change Convention," 26 *Boston College Environmental Affairs Law Review* 1 (1998); Prasad Sharma, Comment, "Restoring Participatory Democracy: Why the United States Should Listen to Citizen Voices While Engaging in International Environmental Lawmaking," 12 *Emory International Law Review* 1215 (1998).

20. NRDC, "Details of the Kyoto Global Warming Treaty Remain to Be Resolved, but the U.S. Should Cut Pollution Now" (February 17, 1999). Available from http://www.nrdc.org/brief/global.htm; Internet.

21. Elizabeth Dowdeswell and Richard J. Kinley, in *Negotiating Climate Change: The Inside Story of the Rio Convention*, ed. Irving M. Mintzer and J. Amber Leonard (Cambridge: Cambridge University Press, 1994), 127.

22. Michael J. Chadwick, in *Negotiating Climate Change: The Inside Story of the Rio Convention*, ed. Irving M. Mintzer and J. Amber Leonard (Cambridge: Cambridge University Press, 1994), xiii.

23. Irving M. Mintzer and J. Amber Leonard, ed., *Negotiating Climate Change: The Inside Story of the Rio Convention* (Cambridge: Cambridge University Press, 1994), 333.

24. "Energy and Environment: Discussions on Joint General Warming," European Report, no. 1620 (Oct. 10, 1990), 13; Ranee K. Panjabi, *The Earth Summit at Rio: Politics, Economics, and the Environment* (Boston: Northeastern University Press, 1997), 99, 165.

25. "Action on Treaty Urged," *The Moscow Times*, 1 October 1996.

26. Rex Nutting, "G-7 to Cooperate More on Global Issues," *United Press International* (June 29, 1996).

27. Marcus Kabel, "Big Powers Seen Boosting Global Warming Fight," *Reuters Financial Service* (July 19, 1996).

28. "Central America Cooperates on Climate Change," *Global Warming Network Online Today* (August 14, 1996).

29. For example, the following statement by the outgoing President Bush made it appear that the United States was the world leader in tackling global warming. Bush stated, "Our comprehensive action-oriented approach to global climate change was adopted by the world community at the United Nations Conference on Environment and Development in Brazil and ratified unanimously by the United States Senate. The United States was the first industrialized nation to ratify the treaty and the first nation to set forth its action plan to reduce greenhouse gas emissions." George Bush, "Letter to Congres-

sional Leaders on the National Strategy on the Environment," 29 Weekly Comp. Pres. Doc. 39 (January 13, 1993).

30. Eric A. Davidson, "Leadership for a New Environmental Order," *Christian Science Monitor*, 27 February 1992, 19.

31. Joseph Romm, "Nuclear Winter, Petroleum Summer," *Washington Post*, 30 December 1990, X7.

32. John F. Harris, "Clinton Dives in Down Under; President Tours Great Barrier Reef, Calls for Environmental Pacts," *Washington Post*, 23 November 1996, A16; Ranee K. Panjabi, *The Earth Summit at Rio: Politics, Economics, and the Environment* (Boston: Northeastern University Press, 1997), 171.

33. "EIA Reports Utility CO2 Emissions Fell 0.2% with More Use of Nuclear, Hydro," *Utility Environment Report* (October 25, 1996): 3.

34. Kyoto Protocol to the United Nations Framework Convention on Climate Change, Dec. 10, 1997. Available from http://unfcc.de/homep.htm; Internet. The protocol sets an overall target of a 5.2 percent reduction in emissions of six greenhouse gases by the period 2008-2012, using 1990 as a base year. It must be ratified by all of the developed nations before it can enter into force. The agreement does allow some developed countries to increase emissions over 1990 levels. See Mostafa K. Tolba and Iwona Rummel-Bulska, *Global Environmental Diplomacy: Negotiating Environmental Agreements for the World, 1973-1992* (Cambridge: MIT Press, 1998), 96.

35. Hilary F. French, "U.S. on the Sidelines," *Worldwatch Report* (June 25, 1998). Available from http://www.enn.com:80/features/1998/06/062598/0625fea.asp.

36. Richard N. Cooper, "Toward a Real Global Warming Treaty," *Foreign Affairs* (Mar./Apr. 1998): 66.

37. Ibid.

38. For a synopsis of the Kyoto Protocol on Climate Change, see http://www.envirotrust.com/protocol.html. It provides a summary and discusses targets, timetables, covered gases, sinks, compliance, and ratification.

39. Montreal Protocol on Substances that Deplete the Ozone Layer, Sept. 1987, S. Treaty Doc. No. 10, 100th Cong., 1st Sess. 2 (1987), 26 I.L.M. 1550 (entered into force Jan. 1, 1989).

40. Brian R. Shaw, "When Are Environmental Issues Security Issues?" *Report of the Environmental Change and Security Project, The Woodrow Wilson Center*, Issue 2 (spring 1996): 39. Available from http://w3.pnl.gov:2080/ces/academic/ww_1shaw.htm; Internet.

41. David Adamson, *Defending the World: The Politics and Diplomacy of the Environment* (New York: I. B. Tauris & Co., 1990), 105.

42. Richard Elliot Benedick, *Ozone Diplomacy: New Dimensions in Safeguarding the Planet* (Cambridge: Harvard University Press, 1991).

43. Mostafa K. Tolba and Iwona Rummel-Bulska, *Global Environmental Diplomacy: Negotiating Environmental Agreements for the World, 1973-1992* (Cambridge: MIT Press, 1998), 83-84.

44. Benedick, *Ozone Diplomacy: New Dimensions in Safeguarding the Planet*, xiii, 2, 3, 22, 23, 36, 45, 47, 49, 68-69, 75-76, 101, 123-24, 148-52, 199, 200, 205, 210.
45. See, e.g., George Bush and Brian Mulroney, "Remarks by the President and Prime Minister Brian Mulroney of Canada at the Air Quality Agreement Signing Ceremony in Ottawa," *Weekly Comp. Pres. Doc.* 7 (March 12, 1991): 298; "Joint Statement Announcing Canada-United States Air Quality Negotiations," *Weekly Comp. Pres. Doc.* 26 (July 8, 1990): 1058. See also, Jessica Lee, "Bush Touches Base with Allied Leaders," *USA Today*, 14 March 1991, 1A (IE).
46. Robert Cooke, "Progress, Pressure on the Planet," *Newsday*, 22 April 1990, 2.
47. Max Kampelman, "Democracy and Human Dignity: Political and Religious Values," *Vital Speeches* 62, no. 16 (June 1, 1996): 482.
48. "Clean or Hot Air from Swiss Eco-Talks?" *Power Europe* (April 23, 1993).
49. "Air Pollutants From Mainland China Worry Neighbors," *Central News Agency*, (Nov. 7, 1992).
50. Clayton Jones, "Japanese Link Increased Acid Rain to Distant Coal Plants in China," *Christian Science Monitor*, 6 November 1992, 1.
51. "EEC/Japan: Closer Environmental Cooperation," *Europe Environment* (February 4, 1992).
52. Notable successes in establishing institutions that have helped resolve water disputes include the Rhine Commission in Europe and the Mekong Delta River Commission, in Southeast Asia, which is supported with Australian aid. But at the international level questions remain if U.N. institutions are equipped to deal with environmental security issues. See Nick Robins and Charlie Pye-Smith, "The Ecology of Violence," *New Scientist* (Mar. 8, 1997): 12.
53. See, for example, Kuwait Regional Convention for Cooperation on the Protection of the Marine Environment from Pollution (Kuwait, 1978); Protocol Concerning Regional Cooperation in Combating Pollution by Oil and Other Harmful Substances in Case of Emergency (Kuwait, 1978); Convention for Cooperation in the Protection and Development of the Marine and Coastal Environment of the West and Central African Region (Abidjan, 1981); Protocol Concerning Cooperating in Combating Pollution in Case of Emergency (Abidjan, 1981); Convention for the Protection of the Marine Environment and Coastal Area of the South-East Pacific (Lima, 1981); Agreement on Regional Cooperation in Combating Pollution of the South-East Pacific by Hydrocarbons or Other Harmful Substances in Cases of Emergency (Lima, 1981); Protocol for the Protection of South-East Pacific against Pollution from Land-Based Sources (Quito, 1983); Protocol for the Conservation and Management of Protected Marine and Coastal Areas of the South-East Pacific (Paipa, 1989); Protocol for the Protection of the South-East Pacific against Radioactive Contamination (Paipa, 1989); Regional Convention for the Conservation of the Red Sea and

Gulf of Aden Environment; Protocol Concerning Regional Cooperation in Combating Pollution by Oil and Other Harmful Substances in Case of Emergency (Jaddah, 1982); Convention for the Protection and Development of the Marine Environment of the Wider Caribbean Region (Cartagena, 1983); Protocol Concerning Cooperation in Combating Oil Spills in the Wider Caribbean Region (Cartagena, 1983); Protocol Concerning Specially Protected Areas of Wildlife to the Convention for the Protection and Development of the Marine Environment of the Wider Caribbean Region (Kingston, 1990); Convention for the Protection, Management, and Development of the Marine and Coastal Environment of the Eastern African Region (Nairobi, 1985); Protocol Concerning Protected Areas and Wild Fauna and Flora in the Eastern African Region (Nairobi, 1985); Protocol Concerning Cooperation in Combating Marine Pollution in Cases of Emergency in the Eastern African Region (Nairobi, 1985); Convention for the Protection of the Natural Resources and Environment of the South Pacific Region (Noumea, 1986); Protocol Concerning Cooperation in Combating Pollution Emergencies in the South Pacific Region (Noumea, 1986).

54. Kevin Stairs and Peter Taylor, in *The International Politics of the Environment*, ed. Andrew Hurrell and Benedict Kingsbury (Oxford: Clarendon Press, 1992).

55. Though the United States and other Western countries have strained relations with Iran, their leaders are willing to sit down with Iranian representatives and discuss joint efforts on environmental concerns.

56. "International Conference on Caspian Sea Pollution," *BBC Summary of World Broadcasts* (June 21, 1991): Part 1, The USSR; Weekly Economic Report (citing Telegraph Agency of the Soviet Union in Russian for abroad 1313 gmt 14 Jun 91).

57. Tolba and Rummel-Bulska, *Global Environmental Diplomacy: Negotiating Environmental Agreements for the World, 1973-1992*, 49-52.

58. Agreement on the Action Plan for the Environmentally Sound Management of the Common Zambezi River System, May 28, 1987, 27 I.L.M. 1109.

59. Tolba and Rummel-Bulska, *Global Environmental Diplomacy: Negotiating Environmental Agreements for the World, 1973-1992*, 50-51.

60. Arun P. Elhance, "From War to Water Pacts in Turbulent South Asia," *Christian Science Monitor*, 15 Jan. 1997, Opinion/Essay, 19.

61. Ibid.

62. Ibid.

63. Ibid.

64. One need not be reminded that this Convention was formed during the Cold War. It illustrates the far-reaching effect of environmental issues to unite even hostile states to cooperate on an issue.

65. Bengt-Owe Jansson and Harald Velner, in *Barriers and Bridges to the Renewal of Ecosystems and Institutions*, ed. Lance H. Gunderson et al. (New York: Columbia University Press, 1995), 292, 303-307, 331-33, 335, 344, 362.

66. Kevin Stairs and Peter Taylor, in *The International Politics of the Environment*, ed. Andrew Hurrell and Benedict Kingsbury (Oxford: Clarendon Press, 1992), 120.

67. The treaty was formerly called the Barcelona Convention for the Protection of the Mediterranean Sea against Pollution and included two protocols, one to prevent pollution of the Mediterranean by dumping from ships and aircraft and the other to achieve cooperation in fighting pollution.

68. Tolba and Rummel-Bulska, *Global Environmental Diplomacy: Negotiating Environmental Agreements for the World, 1973-1992*, 41; Lawrence Susskind and Connie Ozawa, *The International Politics of the Environment*, ed. Andrew Hurrell and Benedict Kingsbury (Oxford: Clarendon Press, 1992), 143, 145.

69. "Mediterranean Sea: International Protocol to Reduce Pollution," *Europe Environment* (March 19, 1996).

70. Agreement on Great Lakes Water Quality, Nov. 22, 1978, Can.-U.S., 30 U.S.T. 1383.

71. "International Lake Superior Pollution Program Announced," *United Press International* (Oct. 1, 1991).

72. George R. Francis and Henry A. Regier, in *Barriers and Bridges to the Renewal of Ecosystems and Institutions*, ed. Lance H. Gunderson et al. (New York: Columbia University Press, 1995), 241.

73. See chapter 2. See also Miriam R. Lowi, "Rivers of Conflict, Rivers of Peace," *Journal of International Affairs* 49, no. 1 (summer 1995): 123-144. Lowi concludes that effective political cooperation must precede effective resource administration and management, rather than the reverse as functionalist scholars have argued.

74. For an example of comprehensive regional cooperation, one can look to the European Council. The European Commission approved a communication to the European Council on the integration of environmental requirements into other European Union policies. Commission on the European Communities, "Partnership for Integration: Commission Presents Strategy on Integration of Environment into Other Policy Areas," *RAPID* (May 27, 1998). The goal is to integrate the environment into policies at all levels in all countries.

75. Though concern for the Arctic has spurred cooperation, this has not always been the case. Some scholars cite the example of the Falkland Islands as a war over subarctic resources. See David Adamson, *Defending the World: The Politics and Diplomacy of the Environment* (New York: I. B. Tauris & Co., 1990), 76.

76. See Shi-lin Chan, "Arctic Pollution Spurs Calls for International Cooperation," *Reuters North American Wire* (April 11, 1991). See also

"International Cooperation: Eight Countries To Discuss Pollution Control in the Arctic," *Europe Environment* (Sept. 14, 1993).

77. Convention on the Control of Transboundary Movements of Hazardous Wastes and Their Disposal, Mar. 22, 1989, S. Treaty Doc. No. 5, 102d Cong., 1st Sess. (1991), 28 I.L.M. 657. For a summary and analysis of the negotiations and issues of the Basel Convention see Mostafa K. Tolba and Iwona Rummel-Bulska, *Global Environmental Diplomacy: Negotiating Environmental Agreements for the World, 1973-1992* (Cambridge: MIT Press, 1998), 97-124.

78. Jang B. Singh and Emily F. Carasco, "Business Ethics, Economic Development, and Protection of the Environment in the New World Order," *Journal of Business Ethics* 15, no. 3 (March 1996): 297-307.

79. Treaty Respecting the Antarctic, Dec. 1, 1959, 12 U.S.T. 794, 402 U.N.T.S. 71; Protocol on Environmental Protection to the Treaty Regarding the Antarctic, June 21, 1991, S. Treaty Doc. No. 22, 102d Cong., 2d Sess. (1992), 30 I.L.M. 1455. See also Arctic Environmental Protection Strategy, June 24, 1991, 30 I.L.M. 1624.

80. Miriam Levering, *A New World Order: Can It Bring Security to the World's People*, ed. Walter Hoffman (Washington: World Federalist Association, 1991), 91.

81. Jack N. Barkenbus, *Deep Seabed Resources: Politics and Technology* (New York: The Free Press, 1979), 103, 108.

82. Single European Act, Feb. 17, 1986, 25 I.L.M. 503 (entered into force July 1, 1987).

83. Agreement on the Conservation of Nature and Natural Resources, July 9, 1985. See Edith Brown Weiss, "International Environmental Law: Contemporary Issues and the Emergence of a New World Order," *Georgetown Law Journal* 81 (March 1993): 675.

84. Convention on Biological Diversity, June 5, 1992, 31 I.L.M. 818.

7

All Pollution Is Local

Tip O'Neill made famous the phrase that all politics is local. Similarly, it may be said that all pollution is local. The previous chapters show that any approach to solving environmental degradation must involve international cooperation. Cooperation, however, is not the only answer. For, "[w]hen you find a man who knows his job and is willing to take responsibility, keep out of his way and don't bother him with unnecessary supervision. What you may think is co-operation is nothing but interference." What rang true for novelist and philosopher Thomas Dreier rings true for environmental protection. This chapter emphasizes the need for local action to both complement, and in some areas supplant, international cooperation.

The world is witnessing environmental degradation unlike anything it has ever seen. The effects of environmental degradation range from economic and development stagnation to social and political upheaval. During the Cold War, the primary perceived threat to the future of humanity was nuclear Armageddon. Today, that threat has been replaced by an even more perilous harm: global environmental catastrophe. Whereas global nuclear annihilation required action by people, it is inaction that has the potential to lead to an irreversible environmental calamity.[1] Many now believe that "[t]he conditions of global environmental interdependence require sustained levels of international cooperation not only to address threats to environmental security but also to promote proactive and forward-looking policies directed at the attainment of positive environmental security."[2]

David Adamson provides a somewhat pessimistic outlook on the prospects of international cooperation and environmental protection. He states:

> Governments have not been as irrational and totally careless of life as the experience of the Second World War led many to believe. These are factors which provide the basis on which the new environmental security regime can be built, although, sadly, it will probably take more than one catastrophe to shake the world into acceptance of the sacrifices of sovereignty and treasure which will be needed to make it effective. . . . Acknowledgment of humanity's common predicament should shape the moral stance, since the goal will be mutual survival.[3]

One can only hope that the unifying catastrophe will not be the one that ends humanity.

While Adamson feels the world will require a global catastrophe before it acts, the threat of environmental insecurity may be enough. As evidenced by the recent explosion of environmental cooperation and agreements, the world is coming together. The survey of case studies in the preceding chapters illustrates the multitude of international efforts to protect the environment.[4] These efforts embody bilateral, regional, and global agreements on a slew of issues. Many attempt to form international and regional management regimes to protect the environment.[5] Numerous heads of state and world leaders now feel there needs to be a "serious global commitment to environmental management and sustainable uses of our planet's resources."[6] International agreements have not only grown in number, but also in scope and importance.

Environmentalism encourages and influences states to establish regimes capable of protecting the global environment. It very well may be the most powerful expression of transnational civil society that uniquely has the ability to create a new "law of humanity."[7] This is perhaps one of the most unique aspects of environmentalism: "the idea of a world recreated free from . . . pollution . . . that is tremendously inspiring; it appeals to a drive, rooted in our culture at least as far back as the Renaissance, to seek perfection in this world."[8] Environmental problems are an obvious example of the necessity of pursuing democratic governance at the local, national, and international levels.[9] Such cooperative efforts equate to greater openness and decreased hostilities. Even Thomas Homer-Dixon, who has written extensively about the ability of environmental scarcity to spur violence, concludes that environmental cooperation through effective international institutions is crucial to the preservation of not only the environment, but also to the continuance of humanity.[10] Environmental issues already serve, and will serve to a much greater degree, as a harmonizing mechanism for environmental security. Through international cooperation, dialogue, and awareness, environmental issues will spur greater peace, prosperity, and productivity throughout the world.

Internationalism, an Incomplete Solution?

It would appear that global solutions implemented through international governmental bodies would best be able to effectuate a whole ecosystem approach. After all, are not environmental linkages global in nature? Are not local governments concerned only with local problems? Do they not view ecosystems as being self-contained units when they are really global in nature? Are not international governmental bodies the only way to address common environmental pollutants and organize the efforts of peoples around the world? Despite the evident tension between localism and linkages, the following chapters will illustrate how localism is compatible with a whole ecosystem approach and how both localism and internationalism are necessary components of an overall, holistic approach to global environmental protection.

International action alone is incapable of instituting a linkage paradigm. Traditional international law is unable to find adequate solutions to the myriad of problems that are global in scope, such as global warming, ozone depletion, overfishing, deforestation, marine pollution, and loss of biodiversity.[11] International cooperation tends to centralize environmental programs. This centralization strips power from local governments (and even from national governments) and places it in the hands of regional and global governing entities. These governing entities are not always the best political units to approach environmental degradation. A holistic system of environmental protection requires a balancing of global policies with local differences. There is a need to balance an international framework without depriving communities of their innovation. It requires acknowledgment that one solution does not fit all situations.

While the trend towards globalization appears to recognize the interconnectedness of ecosystems and the transboundary nature of environmental degradation, international action cannot alone solve environmental problems from a whole ecosystem approach.[12] The lack of community involvement and local empowerment will frustrate even the most global and noble of policy approaches. Those at the local level are best able to identify the problems and tailor solutions to the individual conditions of their environment.

Perhaps the biggest danger in overemphasizing international solutions is that as environmentalism becomes more global and international, its approach to environmental protection becomes more fragmented and piecemeal. A whole ecosystem approach requires both international and local action to solve environmental degradation and the environmental insecurity it causes. Such an integrated approach is best able to identify linkages between environmental issues. This allows policymakers at all levels to make sound policy choices.

Roots of Localism

The appeal of localism is evident in many modern political philosophy writings. When Alexis de Tocqueville visited America, he touted the benefits of civic associations. For Tocqueville, centralized rule making was a danger to the health and character of a nation. Local democracy was able to involve the people, and while it

> does not give the people the most skillful government . . . it does produce what the ablest governments are frequently unable to create; namely, an all-pervading and restless activity, a superabundant force, and an energy which is inseparable from it, and which may, however unfavorable circumstances may be, produce wonders. These are the true advantages of democracy.[13]

Tocqueville advanced the notion that involvement in the decision-making process forces citizens to consider the complexities of governance. It essentially creates citizenship. The words and wisdom of Tocqueville are just as important today as they were 150 years ago. His political writings have influenced many political theorists. For example, L. T. Hobhouse, writing almost one hundred years later, witnessed the partial transition to centralized control of government and argued for devolution in his writings on liberalism.[14] While Hobhouse justified the modern welfare state, he did not foresee the loss of localism that it has produced.

Another political philosopher, F. A. Hayek, also touted the value of local self-government, for

> it is only where responsibility can be learned and practiced in affairs with which most people are familiar, where it is awareness of one's neighbor (or environment) rather than some theoretical knowledge of the needs of other people which guides action, that the ordinary man can take a real part in public affairs because they concern the world he knows.[15]

Hayek promoted decentralized power because it was necessary to reduce the absolute amount of power.[16] It was for this very reason that the political revolutionary Karl Marx promoted centralization; the market forces of capitalism were too great to overcome without "the revolutionary dictatorship of the proletariat."[17] The debate about centralization versus decentralization continues today. Some favor a global governance approach to environmental protection while others tout the benefits of a local approach.

Many observers conclude that global environmental protection requires truly international cooperation.[18] Those who study the transboundary nature of pollution deduce, "therefore, it would appear only reasonable that the solutions to such problems should be sought in the international arena. Transboundary problems merit international solutions."[19] On the other hand, in response to the growing internationalization and westernization of environmental protection, a new movement is emerging. This movement recognizes the benefits of community empowerment and engagement. It realizes that those closest to the problem frequently know best how to fix it. It calls not for revolution but rather for devolution.[20]

The Move towards Localism

Environmental issues have risen to the top of many legislative and policy agendas. As environment degradation worsens, calls for government involvement increase. More often than not, this emphasis on involvement has translated into a push at the federal and international levels for control and guidance over environmental policies and programs. This push, however, is being met with backlash and resistance at the local level in many places throughout the world.[21] This resistance is justifiable. A centralized approach ignores the linkages between different levels of actors. The struggle for local control and autonomy has resurfaced in areas such as Latin America, Africa, and Asia. These areas, which contain the high concentrations of biodiversity, are inhabited by long-term occupant communities that exercise community-based conservation efforts.[22] As a result, localism is gaining considerable strength (despite the trend towards international governance) in the last couple of years both nationally and internationally.

For example, the U.N. Convention to Combat Desertification was signed by more than 125 governments. The convention emphasized local participation in land reclamation activities and specifically targeted the involvement of women.[23] Closer to home, local governments are fighting for increased power within the United States.[24] Adding fuel to this struggle is a recent Supreme Court decision that has called into question the authority of many federal statutes ranging from environmental to bankruptcy laws.[25] The landmark Supreme Court decision is part of a larger trend of curbing Congress's power to pressure states.[26] The Supreme Court "is reviving the doctrine that states are sovereign governments and have powers that Congress cannot contravene." [27] The Court formally exhumed this doctrine of "dual sovereignty" in 1995 when it ruled that a federal law that made it a federal crime to possess guns near schools exceeded Congress's power under the interstate commerce clause.[28]

The Supreme Court is not the only agent fueling the localism movement within the United States. The 1994 GOP Congress made decentralization one of its top legislative priorities. States were asked to take on everything from welfare to environmental protection and many state leaders felt that they were in a better position to make decisions than those in Washington, D.C.[29] Additionally, the inflexible nature of current environmental regulations is pushing some local leaders to argue for nullification of specific federal environmental provisions.[30] At the annual meetings of state governors, governors are embracing new policies that attempt to reclaim state power from federal bureaucrats.[31] The 2000 meeting will be devoted entirely to federalism issues. States are now organizing to take over environmental regulations and local governmental entities are taking initiatives to clean up the environment.[32] According to one congressional spokesperson, local solutions and voluntary participation will be the defining characteristics of environmental protection in the years to come.[33] These calls for localism are not new. In 1929, President Herbert Hoover suggested local involvement through community ownership of federal lands:

> the federal government is incapable of the adequate administration of matter which require so large a measure of local understanding. We must seek every opportunity to retard the expansion of federal bureaucracy and to place our communities in control of their own destinies. . . . Western states have long since passed from their swaddling clothes and are today more competent to manage much of their affairs than is the federal government.[34]

U.S. environmentalists need to shift their focus to give people and communities more power in protection of the environment.

Some signs indicate the beginning of this shift.[35] Calls for localism can be found in editorial pages.[36] Examples such as the Quincy Library Group, which is attempting to manage 2.4 million acres surrounding national forests in the timber town of Quincy in northern California, the Friends of the Cheat River, a West Virginia coalition working to restore a waterway damaged by mining runoff, the Applegate Partnership, which hopes to restore a watershed in southwestern Oregon while keeping timber jobs alive, and Envision Utah, which tries to foster consensus about how to manage land in and around Salt Lake City, are being touted as a new approach to conservation that centers on community efforts.[37] Localism can bring together diverse peoples to engage in real debate over environmental issues. Such efforts provide a glimpse of the future. One poll in the United States found that 72 percent favor state and local action to control air pollution and 65 percent believed that "state or local government would do a better job than the federal government in dealing with environmental concerns."[38]

Researchers are also taking note of the benefits of local action. The scientific community is increasingly focusing on community-based conservation.[39] Bill Adams, a researcher with the Department of Geography at Cambridge University, explains that policymakers would do well to look at a variety of local, "small-scale solutions."[40] Jeremy Swift, a specialist on desertification concurs that it is "very dangerous to generalize" when it comes to solutions for environmental scarcities.[41] Consider the words of one researcher: "[A]n effort must be made to empower local communities in the decision making process. Approaches based on grassroots development schemes together with help from NGOs deserve top priority, allowing local people to use indigenous farming knowledge and inherent natural resource management skills."[42] Although the environment is interconnected, the use of community specific indicators of environmental quality can help communities measure ecological health. For example, in Seattle the number of wild salmon in local streams is an indicator of sustainability whereas in the San Francisco Bay area, the striped bass count helps to measure ecological health.[43]

Local involvement is crucial for even the most global problems such as global warming. At first glance the ability to affect global warming appears beyond local control. In reality, communities and individuals are key players in the effort to reduce greenhouse gases.[44] In 1998, a national teleconference was held on local solutions to global warming. It concentrated on individual and community action such as changing the ways we design our buildings, communities, and transportation and industrial systems. Similar efforts are under way.

Fifty U.S. cities and counties, representing 25 million people, participated in the International Council for Local Environmental Initiatives' Cities for Climate Protection Campaign. Each of the local governments passed a resolution committing itself to act to protect the climate, set greenhouse gas emission reduction targets, and develop local plans to meet those targets. If we are to solve global warming, cities must make greenhouse gas emission reductions a part of their everyday decisions from their choice of lightbulbs to tax structures.

The Buildings for the Twenty-First-Century Program is a partnership with the building design, construction, and investment industries and communities across the country. The program formed to create a new generation of energy-efficient and sustainable residential and commercial buildings. Through such programs, communities and local governments can work to reduce greenhouse gas emissions through more efficient building systems, reduced energy use for transportation, changes in land use and community systems, and decreases in the amount of waste produced.

The national conference concluded that "[c]learly, many of the most effective solutions to the global warming problem are being arrived at locally. Experience from the work of local governments, businesses, and citizens suggests that aggressive targets and timetables for greenhouse gas emissions reductions are realistic and achievable."[45] While such local solutions and innovations are important, communities still need to work together and share ideas and programs. This is but one role of global frameworks in which localities can compare notes and achieve common objectives.

Sustainable Communities Movement

Currently, environmental protection focuses on international efforts. While this is an important component of an integrated approach, it is time to take a second look at local governments. Just as all politics are local, so too, "all pollution is local." While international conferences such as the Rio Earth Summit serve to rally environmentalists worldwide, local governments are the ones that must carry out the day-to-day task of protecting the environment. Public awareness and concern about environmental degradation can only be raised if it is felt locally; "when environmental problems are localized, our local institutions will respond more readily."[46] The appeal of localism is based, in part, on the perception of the problem. People are most concerned about whether the building they work in will make them sick or whether the lake where they recreate is polluted.

Many environmentalists now believe that the key to combining environmental protection lies in extending to local communities the power and ability to control and manage their own natural resources. Additionally, local practices are important. Although sometimes they need to be upgraded and modernized, they must be respected.[47] It is time to realize that local institutions and indigenous forms of knowledge of using natural resources in a sustainable way are more effective than many "modern" techniques. Localism changes the role of the central government from one of central policymaker to one of evaluator of environmental claims and disseminator and conduit of information and ideas.

The well-known environmental scholar Thomas Homer-Dixon believes that "most of the ingenuity that is going to be particularly useful in solving scarcity and food production problems is going to be locally generated, by people familiar with local geography, social relations, and resources."[48] He advocates increased funding for local research to improve the situation of environmental degradation in the less-developed world. He is not alone.

The Brundtland Commission (formally known as the World Commission on Environment and Development), in 1987, developed several principles for environmental protection and sustainable development. Unfortunately, few states have acted upon these principles, and even fewer have incorporated them into their core value systems. The Brundtland report has, however, spawned developments at the local level. The Ontario Roundtable on Environment and Economy is one such development. It seeks to actualize the Brundtland report's recommendations for achieving sustainability. The Roundtable seeks to improve decision making by acknowledging that an environmentally literate society is a necessity, not a luxury, to good policy decisions. The Roundtable addresses individual responsibility. It explains that, "in both a legal and moral sense, it is difficult to hold responsible any person or entity unaware of environmental problems and the consequences of the given action. However, the rights and freedoms of individuals and organizations in a democratic society must be balanced with the need to safeguard present and future generations and the world in which we live."[49]

A movement toward localization has the ability to spur vast networks of local nongovernmental organizations. Such a network facilitates global environmental governance based on local-international action systems. A global network of organizations may evolve into a reliable and meaningful governance system on a global scale because "[i]n contrast to many other global interests, environmental problems have the great advantage of being tied to specific locales."[50]

Signs of community-based environmental activism are emerging as a part of a greater movement called the sustainable communities movement. This form of local environmental action has surfaced throughout the United States and the world. Jeffrey Barber, the director of the Integrative Strategies Forum in Washington, D.C., explains, "although not fully acknowledged by the media, the movement may emerge as one of the most important social forces during the transition to the 21st century."[51] The goal of the sustainable communities movement is to:

> create communities that are able to sustain and improve the quality of life of their population and environment without undermining the sustainability and quality of life of other communities, human and

nonhuman. Whereas the concept of sustainable development refers to a process or means to an end, the concept of a sustainable community refers to a specific settlement of humans working to satisfy their needs equitably and in harmony with the biological community of which they are a part.[52]

One goal of sustainable communities is economic self-reliance. This does not, however, mean isolation from global society. The transboundary nature of pollution means that no community can avoid considering the flow of products, raw materials, investment capital, jobs, people, pollution, and waste. The sustainable communities movement recognizes that communities need to understand and address the possible impact of their decisions on not only future generations, but also on other communities, including those in other countries. Global frameworks can help communities make this realization.

Manifestations of the sustainable communities movement[53] can be found in a number of places. For example, in September of 1995, the U.S. Department of Commerce conducted a two-day National Teleconference on Sustainable Communities. The teleconference was sponsored by the National Oceanic and Atmospheric Administration (NOAA), the Economic Development Administration (EDA), and the Minority Business Development Agency (MBDA). It "was to provide 'an opportunity for local communities to share their experiences, ideas, and suggestions with us as our Nation begins to pursue a more sustainable future.'"[54]

The movement is not limited to the United States; a recent conference in Dakar, Senegal, entitled the Third International EcoCity Conference, illustrates the global dimension of the sustainable communities movement. A quick glance yields a number of gatherings during the past few years that have drawn together community activists, government officials, scholars, and business leaders to "discuss their visions and strategies for building sustainable communities."[55] These events include: the First International EcoCity Conference (1990, Berkeley), the First National People of Color Environmental Leadership Summit (1991, Washington, D.C.), meetings across the country of the Sustainable Communities Task Force and six working groups of the President's Council on Sustainable Development (1993-1995), the Defining Sustainable Communities Conference (1994, Oakland), the World Conference on Local Initiatives for Sustainable Cities (1995, Yokohama), the UN Conference on Human Settlements (1996, Istanbul), and the National Teleconference on Global Warming (1998).[56]

According to Maurice Lim Miller of the Asian Neighborhood Design, the sustainable communities movement meshes together the environmental movement and the social justice movement at the local level. Thus, action at the community level is not only able to clean up pollution, but is also able to promote social justice and the eradication of poverty and racism.[57] Those involved with the promotion of sustainable communities argue that a new value system is needed. They criticize the value of "unqualified growth and competition while affirming the need for greater democratic participation and a sense of community responsibility and stewardship."[58] These calls echo the calls for a change in ethics advocated by the linkage paradigm. Elizabeth Kline, director of the Tufts University Center for Regional Sustainability, has identified four characteristics of sustainable communities: ecological integrity, economic security, quality of life, and empowerment with responsibility. These four ideals are crucial to the development of global environmental solutions.

In 1994, a conference was held in Oakland, California, entitled Defining Sustainable Communities. It brought together 350 people representing organizations and individuals involved with various aspects of defining, building, and protecting sustainable communities throughout the United States. The participants stressed that "it is not enough to think globally and act locally. We must think and act globally while maintaining roots in a community. Because of the overwhelming complexity of crises at the global level, there is a great tendency to keep community organizing work focused on the community 'at home,' excluding the global interconnections."[59]

Those participating in the conference identified a number of fundamental principles governing sustainable communities:

- Recognition of ecological limits
- Equity and justice (especially regarding the redistribution of wealth)
- Pluralism, inclusiveness, and community-based decision making
- Decentralization of power, decision making, and economic relationships
- Cooperation, not competition, as the basis of economic, political, and social relationships
- Redefinition of prosperity and the ways in which it is measured
- Redefinition of work
- Identification, measurement, and payment of "real costs"[60]

The participants recommended various policies for realizing these principles. They focused on tax reforms, redefining prosperity and growth, reinvestment and increasing access to capital, increasing attention to land use and natural resource planning, improving transportation and health care, and campaign reform.

Those in the sustainable communities movement believe that it is essential to address the linkages between places, between decisions made in local communities (for example, in oil refinery sites such as Richmond, California, or Wilmington, Delaware), and between distant communities and ecosystems (for example, Alaska's North Slope or Ecuadoran rain forests).[61] Current environmental policies are either legal/regulatory or economic/incentive based. Neither of these modes is very democratic in structure. The command and control or regulatory model involves endless political negotiation between regulators, environmental groups, and courts. The economic model is akin to a technocratic system in which cost-benefit analyses are handed down to waiting subjects.[62] Localism, by contrast, is able to involve the actual community in the protection of the environment. People subsequently take more interest in policies. Additionally, the process is inherently more open. When community leaders actually make the decisions they are more accountable. It is also more driven by what citizens actually see and experience.

At the Rio Earth Summit in 1992, an agreement called Agenda 21 was adopted by the governments of the world. The agreement stated that "by 1996 most local authorities in each country should have undertaken a consultative process with their populations and achieved a consensus on a local Agenda 21 for the community." Despite this international call for action, it is rare "to find an American citizen or even a municipal official who has even heard of 'local Agenda 21,' much less been a part of a consultative process."[63] By comparison, a recent survey in England found that 70 percent of local authorities have committed themselves to the process of developing a local Agenda 21 plan.[64] Although local Agenda 21 plans have not lived up to expectations, other local programs are progressing.

The U.N. Conference on Human Settlements (Habitat II) took place in Istanbul in June of 1996. It brought together leaders and NGOs to agree on a Global Plan of Action. The conference led to a nationwide dialogue within the United States and a statement entitled, "A Call for a Just and Sustainable United States." The call was presented at the Habitat II conference and has circulated around the U.S. It lists eight priorities for action:

- Support sustainable livelihoods
- Commit to justice—social, economic, environmental, and gender
- Enable civic engagement and local governance
- Build just and sustainable communities
- Institute new indicators/measures of progress and success

- Promote sustainable production, consumption, and trade
- Reallocate resources
- Redefine national security[65]

The Call for a Just and Sustainable United States contributed to the policy deliberations in Instanbul and has influenced the President's Council on Sustainable Development.

The President's Council on Sustainable Development[66] (PCSD), composed of leaders in the fields of industry, environment, and government, recently capped three years of policy discussions. The PCSD set up three task forces to spur follow-up activities at the local, state, national, and international levels. The state and local task force is working on a proposal by the National Association of Counties and U.S. Conference of Mayors to establish a Joint Center on Sustainable Communities. According to John Bullard, a former mayor of New Bedford, Massachusetts, and director of the Commerce Department's Office of Sustainable Development, the joint center "would look at how to help local officials with these issues on their terms. . . . You can't really get a sustainable America until you do it one community at a time."[67] In his statement announcing the conclusion of the three-year council, President Clinton described the final report as an outline for a new direction in environmental policy. He reinforced in his State of the Union address that the "era of big Government is over."[68] Clinton further explained that "citizens must work together to tackle the challenges of a new century. We must reach across the lines that divide us to find common ground."[69]

Local leaders throughout the United States have commended the work of the President's Council on Sustainable Development. According to Norman Rice, former mayor of Seattle and president of the U.S. Conference of Mayors, the report is a "visionary blueprint for the future of the United States and a valuable tool for city officials as we continue to pursue local sustainable development initiatives."[70] The report emphasizes the redevelopment and strengthening of local communities. Instead of providing a detailed road map to the future, it recognized the need for communities to develop unique and sustainable solutions to address their local situations. It also called for greater coordination and sharing of information between localities, which is a critical step for environmental protection.

President Clinton, in his 1996 State of the Union address, stated that the era of big government is over. He emphasized the need to move toward a new, smaller government whereby citizens are empowered to work together "to tackle the challenges of a new century."[71] This empowerment, however, appears to be occurring without any nudging from above. Local communities throughout the United States have found inspiration to act in the face of strains on local populations. For example, in response to booms in population in Denver and other cities, the sustainable communities movement has found increased appeal.[72] Ray Studer, director of the Urban and Regional Planning Program at the University of Colorado at Denver, states that the movement is "an old concept that's fashionable again."[73]

This fashionable movement encompasses three trends, which have emerged to resist top-down, global governance. They are: community-based democracy, community-based development initiatives, and community-based conservation.[74]

Community-Based Democracy

The surge in localism discussed thus far is due, in part (especially in the less-developed world), to what scholar Michael Shuman describes as community-based democracy. This local form of governance is sweeping the planet and calls into question the ideals of centralization.[75] By bringing the government to the people, it fosters democratic values. Armed with new outlooks of government, communities demand local democracies, which in turn demand democracy at the state and international levels. Democracy has increased in Asia, Latin America, Eastern Europe, and the republics of the former Soviet Union.[76] It could even be said that with decentralization, community-based democracy has increased in the Western world as well. As community-based democracy increases, so too does the chance for local environmentalism. Local governance is essential to both the creation and implementation of environmental policy.

Community-Based Development Initiatives

Community-based development initiatives (CDIs) are an outgrowth of community-based democracy and the sustainable communities movement. Though frequently dismissed by governments and foreign policy officials, "community development initiatives constitute a new layer of international civil society that is becoming an important autonomous actor."[77] CDIs link activists in wealthy developed countries with their counterparts in the less-developed world. These initiatives frequently involve environmental and development objectives. Many activists favor CDIs because they are not "more rich Northern Hemisphere countries making things worse for less well-off Southern Hemisphere countries."[78] Michael Shuman, in a recent book on the subject, describes the failure of top-down "solutions" to solve environmental problems. He highlights the vast amount of good that individuals are doing throughout the world.[79]

Shuman describes the technique of preferential purchasing by which a locality can bestow economic rewards on corporations or governments that behave well in North-South relations. It can also impose punishments on those that perform poorly. One example of the impact of preferential purchasing can be found in the Netherlands where more than 300 communities and eleven of the twelve provincial governments are buying "solidarity coffee."[80] This type of coffee is procured from small-scale, environmentally responsible producers in the South at a slightly higher price. The Dutch Campaign has yielded an extra $4 million of income per year for low-income coffee farmers and has increased international awareness about the inequalities facing producers of raw commodities in the South.[81] In lieu of the interference of large-scale global governance, similar community-based development initiatives are emerging throughout the world. Perhaps the most successful local policies are those carried out under the umbrella of community-based conservation.

Community-Based Conservation

Community-based conservation efforts empower localities to protect their natural resources while providing for the basic needs of the community. Such programs are natural conduits for grassroots activism because they can better incorporate local concerns than top-down approaches. Instead of forced educational efforts, individuals learn by becoming involved in citizen-initiated environmental protection. In almost every region of the world, community-based conservation efforts are proving themselves to be effective and efficient, engaging and extensive.

In October of 1993, a group of sixty people from twenty countries met to reconsider environmentalism. Under the auspices of the Claiborne-Ortenberg Foundation, the individuals met at the Airlie House near Washington, D.C. The group included, among others, anthropologists, field biologists, and tribal leaders. The approach developed by these environmental activists was based on a series of case studies from around the world. The primary feature of the "view from Airlie" was positive local participation. The group sought ways to make local communities the custodians of conservation efforts. Their report concluded that previous efforts to protect public goods, which were based on exclusion and enforcement, were not viable over the long term because they ignored communal use rights and systems of tenure.[82]

When local communities lack standing in the decision-making process, they lack incentives to manage for sustainability. Such communities thus consider only short-term interests and immediate gain. The "view from Airlie" found this to be true in both the United States and around the world. The report concluded that "[i]t's time for community-based conservation and for rethinking environmentalism."[83] The conference at Airlie is not alone;

local governments are hosting a number of international conferences on the environment and coming to similar conclusions.

Three conferences in Japan recently drew representatives from over 200 local entities. While the three conferences focused on different themes (conservation and management of lakes, climate change, and "environment-friendly cities and lifestyles"), they all addressed the role of local governments in the protection of the environment. The participants at the conferences realized that, "as all areas of society become increasingly subjected to the tide of globalization, endeavors to improve the environment could not succeed by viewing the condition of local environments separately from that of the entire world."[84] For example, when individual localities cut back on the use of natural resources and energy, they contribute to the preservation of forests and the curbing of global warming.

The conference on global warming was a significant step towards cutting the emission of greenhouse gases. Representatives of more than 200 local entities agreed to take action on the worldwide problem. They were able to share approaches of combating air pollution and because they are closer to residents and businesses than national or international governments, participants were better able to implement the emission reductions. Likewise, the conference on the preservation and conservation of lakes was able to stimulate conversations between local governments about different approaches to environmental protection. The local governments also discussed the problem of acid rain and its relationship to the health of lakes. They agreed to reduce pollutants responsible for acid rain. All three conferences agreed that decentralization and local autonomy were necessary for environmental protection.[85] Thus through community-based democracy, community development initiatives, and community-based conservation efforts, the sustainable communities movement is going a long way towards strengthening our communities and developing local solutions to environmental degradation.

Conclusion

Community empowerment is an essential ingredient to any scheme of environmental protection. The next chapter exemplifies how local solutions can solve even some of the most difficult environmental problems. However, even though localism is an essential component to any approach to environmental protection, localism alone can not solve environmental degradation and conflict. The next chapter also illustrates that many local initiatives are only successful when they operate within global frameworks.

Notes

1. John R. Beaumont, "A New World Order and Managing the Environment," *Futures* (March 1993): 200.

2. Gerald B. Thomas, "U.S. Environmental Security Policy: Broad Concern or Narrow Interests," *Journal of Environment and Development* 6, no. 4 (Dec. 1997): 397.

3. David Adamson, *Defending the World: The Politics and Diplomacy of the Environment* (New York: I. B. Tauris & Co., 1990), 225.

4. Unfortunately, the case studies also illustrate the high degree of issue isolation that characterizes international responses to environmental degradation. According to Maurice Strong, international responses must deal with the synergistic linkage between environmental issues to be successful. Maurice F. Strong, in *Global Accord: Environmental Challenges and International Responses* (Cambridge: The MIT Press, 1993), xiii.

5. Oran R. Young, *International Governance: Protecting the Environment in a Stateless Society* (Ithaca: Cornell University Press, 1994), 22.

6. Beaumont, "A New World Order and Managing the Environment," 199.

7. Richard Falk, in *Cosmopolitan Democracy: An Agenda for a New World Order*, ed. Daniele Archibugi and David Held (Cambridge: Polity Press, 1995), 169.

8. Scott Hoffman, *A New World Order: Can It Bring Security to the World's People*, ed. Walter Hoffman (Washington: World Federalist Association, 1991), introduction.

9. David Held, in *Cosmopolitan Democracy: An Agenda for a New World Order*, ed. Daniele Archibugi and David Held (Cambridge: Polity Press, 1995), 113.

10. Thomas Homer-Dixon, "War and Peace: The Ominous Trends around the World," *Maclean's* (January 9, 1995): 19.

11. Gregory F. Maggio, "Recognizing the Vital Role of Local Communities in International Legal Instruments for Conserving Biodiversity," *UCLA Journal of Environmental Law and Policy* 16 (1997/1998): 179

12. This book will not discuss at length the existence of an environmental crisis; many authors have explored the issue in numerous volumes of work. The scientific certainty that humans are degrading the environment is accepted by most people. Thus, questions concerning environmentalism no longer center on the existence of a problem (the what and why); rather, the question has become one of who and how: Who should act to abate environmental degradation and how should they go about it? These are the questions this book seeks to address.

13. Alexis de Tocqueville, *Democracy in America*, ed. Richard D. Heffner (New York: Penguin Books, 1984), 110.

14. L. T. Hobhouse, *Liberalism* (New York: Oxford University Press, 1964), 127.

15. F. A. Hayek, *The Road to Serfdom* (Chicago: The University of Chicago Press, 1994), 258.
16. Ibid., 160.
17. Karl Marx, *Selected Writings*, ed. Lawrence H. Simon (Indianapolis: Hackett Publishing Company, Inc., 1994), 328.
18. Sheldon Kamieniecki, "Emerging Forces in Global Environmental Politics," in *Environmental Politics in the International Arena: Movements, Parties, Organizations, and Policy*, ed. Sheldon Kamieniecki (Albany: SUNY Press, 1993), 4.
19. Lettie Wenner, "Transboundary Problems in International Law," in *Environmental Politics in the International Arena: Movements, Parties, Organizations, and Policy*, ed. Sheldon Kamieniecki (Albany: SUNY Press, 1993).
20. There are different forms of localism and different points in its evolution. At the most developed form, localism would include a network of largely self-sufficient communities. Citizens would incorporate a biocentric view in which an ethic of voluntary simplicity and local autonomy dominate. Through their proximity to nature, people and the environment become bonded in a spiritual nature.
21. Take for instance the Wise Use movement, which has gained a popular following backed by some very wealthy individuals and large corporations.
22. Gregory F. Maggio, "Recognizing the Vital Role of Local Communities in International Legal Instruments for Conserving Biodiversity," *UCLA Journal of Environmental Law and Policy* 16 (1997/1998): 179.
23. Judith Achieng, "Environment-Africa: Desertification Still a Nagging Problem," *Inter Press Service* (June 18, 1998).
24. The chapters on localism do not concentrate solely on the United States of America. Rather it will use the U.S. as an example of the fight for local control and then show how community-based conservation efforts are succeeding throughout the entire world. The relation to global governance is clear: if national control is being shunned in favor of localism, how can one argue for increased international and global governance?
25. *Seminole Tribe v. Florida*, 517 U.S. 44 (1996).
26. "'States' Rights: Supremes Limit Lawsuits against States," *Greenwire* (March 28, 1996).
27. Robert A. Rankin, "Huge Power Shifts: States Rights, Line-Item Veto," *The Record*, 31 March 1996, 1.
28. *United States v. Lopez*, 514 U.S. 549 (1995). See also David Savage, "High Court Curbs Federal Lawsuits against The States; Law: The 5-4 Decision Offers Bold Support Of States' Rights at the Expense of the U.S. Government. Ripples from Indian Reservation Gambling Case Will Be Widely Felt, Experts Say," *Los Angeles Times*, 28 March 1996, A1.

29. Kevin Kelly et al, "Power to the States," *Business Week* (August 7, 1995): 49.
30. Philip M. Burgess and Mike Kelly, "New Constitutional Life for States' Rights," *Washington Times*, 22 August 1995, A15.
31. "Governors Cheer States' Rights Agenda," *Times-Picayune*, 29 July 1995, A6.
32. "States' Rights: Meeting Is 'High-Water Mark' For Movement," *Greenwire* (October 25, 1995): section, Society and Politics; Jane S. Shaw, *Real Estate News* 21, no. 1 (April 1996): 4-9.
33. Jeff Barnard, "A Grass-Roots Effort to Save Salmon in Oregon; Environment: Fishermen Rebuild Habitat, Restore Streams; Protection Could Hinge on Local Solutions," *Los Angeles Times*, 29 October 1995, B4(BE).
34. Quoted in Robert H. Nelson, "Public Land Federalism: Go Away and Give Us More Money," in *Environmental Federalism*, ed. Terry L. Anderson and Peter J. Hill (New York: Rowman & Littlefield Publishers, Inc., 1997), 25.
35. Steven Teles, "Think Local, Act Local; Civic Environmentalism," *New Statesman* 126, no. 4348 (Aug. 22, 1997): 28.
36. "Conservation: OP-EDS Examine New Approaches," *Greenwire* (Oct. 13, 1998): Natural Resources section.
37. Charles C. Mann and Mark L. Plummer, "A Look at New Approaches to Conservation: Grass-Roots Seeds of Compromise," *Washington Post*, 11 October 1998, C3.
38. Terry L. Anderson and Peter J. Hill, "Environmental Federalism: Thinking Smaller" in *Environmental Federalism*, ed. Terry L. Anderson and Peter J. Hill (New York: Rowman & Littlefield Publishers, Inc., 1997), xi.
39. See Kathleen A. Galvin, "Traditional Peoples and Biodiversity Conservation in Large Tropical Landscapes," *Bioscience* 2, no. 48 (Feb. 1998): 131.
40. Dipankar De Sarkar, "Africa-Environment: Avoiding Simplistic Explanations of Conflict," *Inter Press Service* (July 4, 1997). See Greg Lashutka, "Columbus Defining New Localism in Environmental Policy: Combines Sound Science with Citizen Participation," *Nation's Cities Weekly* 19, no. 10 (Mar. 11, 1996): 3 ("Too often, however, the top-down, 'one-size-fits-all' rules and reporting requirements for these national strategies had a predicable result at the home town level: unfunded mandates and the imposition of a regulatory straightjacket that stifled local creativity in solving environmental problems.")
41. De Sarkar, "Africa-Environment: Avoiding Simplistic Explanations of Conflict."
42. Mario Giampeitra and Kozo Mayumi, "Another View of Development, Ecological Degradation, and North-South Trade," *Review of Social Economy* 56, no. 1 (Mar. 22, 1998): 20.

43. See "UC Berkeley Indicators of Sustainable Communities Topic of Environmental Roundtable," *PR Newswire* (Feb. 20, 1995): State and Regional News section.

44. "Global Warming: Local Solutions," Issue Paper from the Renew America's Earth Day 1998 National Town Meeting. Available from http://solstice.crest.org/sustainable/renew_ america/issue98.htm; Internet.

45. Ibid.

46. Scott McCallum, "Trade and the Environment: Local Action in a New World Order," *Environmental Law Review—Northwestern School of Law of Lewis & Clark College* 23 (winter 1992): 621.

47. Eddie Koch, "Environment: New Vision Vital to Novel World Order," *Inter Press Service* (May 6, 1992).

48. Janet Raloff, "The Human Numbers Crunch: The Next Half Century Promises Unprecedented Challenges," *Science News* 149, no. 25 (June 22, 1996): 396.

49. Edwin R. McCullough, "Through the Eye of a Needle: The Earth's Hard Passage Back to Health," *University of Oregon Journal of Environmental Law and Litigation* 10 (1995): 389.

50. See John D. Aram, book review of *Global Civil Society and Global Environmental Governance: The Politics of Nature from Place to Planet*, *Journal of Socio-Economics* 26, no. 5 (Sept. 19, 1997): 553.

51. Jeffrey Barber, "The Sustainable Communities Movement," *Journal of Environment and Development* 5, no. 3 (September 1996): 338-348.

52. Ibid.

53. Ibid. There is no official single definition of what constitutes a sustainable community. However, there are a number of common themes or principles: (1) sustainability (social as well as environmental), (2) justice (both social and environmental), (3) civic engagement and participation, (4) new definitions and measures of wealth, and (5) economic localization (also decentralization, local self-reliance).

54. Ibid.
55. Ibid.
56. Ibid.
57. Ibid.
58. Ibid.
59. Ibid.
60. Ibid.
61. Ibid.

62. Steven Teles, "Think Local, Act Local; Civic Environmentalism," *New Statesman* 126, no. 4348 (Aug. 22, 1997): 28.

63. Barber, "The Sustainable Communities Movement," 338-348.

64. Ibid.
65. Ibid.

66. President's Council on Sustainable Development, *Sustainable America: A New Consensus for Prosperity, Opportunity, and a Healthy Environment* (Washington, D.C.: U.S. Government Printing Office, 1996) (in particular, see chapter 4).

67. "PCSD: Presidential Panel Spurs Still More Activity," *Greenwire* (October 25, 1996).

68. "Statement on the Report of the President's Council on Sustainable Development," *Weekly Comp. Pres. Doc.* 32 (March 7, 1996): 446.

69. Ibid.

70. Norman Rice, "Council Report, President's Endorsement Signal Progress on Sustainable Development in the United States," *U.S. Newswire* (March 11, 1996).

71. William Clinton, "Statement by the President," *M2 Presswire* (March 8, 1996).

72. According to one report, the "growth has thrust the Denver-Boulder area into the forefront of the 'sustainable communities' movement, a holistic approach to coping with the boom that originated in the Northwest." Guy Kelly, "Population Boom Spawns Backlash Poll by News Indicates Most Think Metro Area Is Growing Too Fast, Favor Developer Fees," *Rocky Mountain News*, 5 November 1995, 56A.

73. Ibid.

74. For primary information on the sustainable communities movement, see, among others, C. Church, *Towards Local Sustainability* (London: UNA-UK/Community Development Foundation, 1996); Executive Order No. 12852, 3 C.ER (1993); "What Are Sustainable Communities," paper submitted at the Defining Sustainable Communities Conference, Oakland, CA.

75. Michael H. Shuman, "Foreign Policy: What Role for Local Voices?" *Orlando Sentinel Tribune*, 24 May 1992, G1.

76. Sheldon Kamieniecki, "Emerging Forces in Global Environmental Politics," in *Environmental Politics in the International Arena: Movements, Parties, Organizations, and Policy*, ed. Sheldon Kamieniecki (Albany: SUNY Press, 1993), 14. For an article promoting the idea of civic environmentalism, see Steven Teles, "Think Local, Act Local; Civic Environmentalism," *New Statesman* 126, no. 4348 (Aug. 22, 1997): 28.

77. Francis Fukuyama, "Towards a Global Village: International Community Development Initiatives," *Foreign Affairs* (summer 1995): 132.

78. J. Baldwin, "Towards a Global Village," *Whole Earth Review*, no. 86 (September 22, 1995): 42.

79. Michael Shuman, *Towards a Global Village* (Boulder: Pluto Press, 1994).

80. Ibid.

81. Ibid.

82. John A. Baden, "Community-Based Conservation Works," *Seattle Times*, 3 January 1996, B5.
83. Ibid.
84. "Local Governments Key to Environment," *Daily Yomiuri*, 23 October 1995, 6.
85. Ibid.

8

Everyone Else Is Doing It

The previous chapter alluded to the wide array of local initiatives to protect and preserve the environment. The world is witnessing an explosion of community-based efforts to conserve and preserve the environment.[1] Examples can be found from Zambia to the United States, from Peru to India, and from Indonesia to Kenya.[2] Local social, legal, and political institutions are essential to an integrated approach of environmental protection. The challenge is to tap local ingenuity and utilize the resources of international cooperation. The case studies explored in this chapter illustrate how local efforts can effectively complement international and national environmental policies.

United States

In response to years of federal control over environmental protection in the form of laws such as the Safe Drinking Water Act and the Comprehensive Environmental Response Compensation and Liability Act (CERCLA, otherwise known as "Superfund"), communities are attempting to reshape the nature of environmental protection in the United States.[3] Many local governments now feel that federal regulations are too inflexible for their communities and too detached from the people. Proponents of community-based conservation in the United States point out that well-informed citizens, who want and try to do the right thing, are unable to do so.[4] The increasing centralization and top-down nature of environmental protection efforts only further frustrate people. But there is hope: a renewal of the concept of community-based conservation. Groups such as the multi-county Great Smoky Mountains Alliance of Communities, the Tuckaseegee Alliance, the Western North Carolina Alliance, and others around the country are comprised of citizens, business executives, civic leaders, and scientists. Their members are overcoming their differences through dialogue and action at the local level.[5]

One recent account of the changing times is the building of trust and respect in the West. Conflict is tragically moving people of the rural West toward both resentment and confrontation. Fortunately, community-based conservation is improving the situation by overcoming the barriers to building trust and mutual respect. Take for instance the focus at the annual meeting of the Greater Yellowstone Coalition in West Yellowstone, Montana. The Coalition did not emphasize increased governmental regulation and agency reform; rather, it endorsed a shift in the prevailing conventional wisdom toward localization and harmonization. Policymakers, community leaders, and concerned individuals acknowledged the failure of top-down regulatory controls to restore, enhance, and preserve environmental quality. According to one observer, this new vision of community-based conservation fosters the long-term solutions needed for environmental protection; for "if the 'New West' is to flourish, trust among neighbors, environmentalists and loggers is essential."[6] This trust is best developed through community action and activism.

Community-based conservation has been applied in the less-developed world for many years (see the following sections). This has led many to advocate such an approach in the American West. However, not all environmentalists are ready to cede control to an area that is home to the Wise Use Movement and where logging and grazing interests seem to overwhelm those of the ecologically minded. Groups such as the Sierra Club have expressed skepticism over redistributing power to the rural communities of the West. They point out that large corporate and industrial entities have disproportionate economic and political power. Furthermore, such entities are ultimately responsible to stockholders and not to local or environmental interests.[7]

While opponents to community-based conservation believe that there are few environmental voices in the rural west, recent action in a rural Montana valley suggests that this stereotype of rural communities is outdated and undeserved. The valley illustrates the link between the environment and the economy. It shows how environmental degradation eventually catches up with the economy. As a result, loggers, retirees, hunting guides, tourism business owners, and small sawmill operators have begun meeting to address the problems stemming from the decline of the resource-based economy in Montana's Swan Valley. Long-term residents are not the only ones attending these strategy sessions; representatives from the U.S. Forest Service, Plum Creek Timber Company, and the University of Montana also attend. Through constructive engagement, anger and polarization have been significantly dampened. The community building has fostered "connection and commitment to both people and place."[8]

Many of the participants have dedicated their time and effort to develop and implement plans for grizzly bear recovery and forest-restoration projects. They work closely with the U.S. Forest Service and others who have traditionally been foes instead of friends. Plans are also under way for a learning center to educate the community about the valley's complex forest ecosystem. Residents of Swan Valley appreciate the opportunity to have a voice in federal land management. In one committee member's words, "People are more accepting of road closures when they feel listened to. Acceptance and understanding occurs when people come to the table and talk. This is real progress."[9] The example of Swan Valley illustrates the ability of rural areas to think and act "locally" with respect to the environment.

Another example is found in the town of Quincy in northern California. A longtime timber town, Quincy is the example of a community recognizing the need for conservation in the face of powerful business interests. After approaching the Forest Service for help and discovering it largely dysfunctional, the town developed its own plan for community conservation. The group took its plan to their congressional representative. The Quincy plan for reformation of the three national forests that surround the town passed overwhelmingly in the U.S. House of Representatives before it was blocked in the Senate under pressure from big environmental lobbies. The Quincy group attempted to work with groups such as the Wilderness Society, the Natural Resources Defense Council, and the Sierra Club but found them too centralized and bureaucratic.[10]

But not all large environmental groups are so skeptical of localism. Some large environmental groups are realizing the benefits of community-based conservation. The Nature Conservancy recently made a strong commitment to community-based conservation. It learned that a neighborhood barbecue can be more effective in wildlife protection than years of lobbying the federal government. Thus the national environmental nongovernmental organization has shifted its focus from lobbying to empowering localities to make a difference. The group "recognizes that community-based conservation is the critical ingredient to long-term conservation success."[11] It works with local communities to promote a prosperous future and the preservation of natural resources. The Nature Conservancy recently launched the Center for Compatible Economic Development (CCED), which helps integrate economic development with conservation at the local level.[12] It now plans to use the CCED as a vehicle for multiplying its efforts on an international scale.

The Nature Conservancy has been particularly involved in Texas where it found that its most successful projects are those that involve the community. In East Texas, sustainable forestry projects have been developed while rice farmers on the Texas coast have adopted community-based conservation to enhance rice fields for wintering waterfowl. In Texas City, local action has been critical to the conservation of habitats for a wide variety of birds, including the endangered Attwater's Prairie Chicken. Additionally, private landowners have helped to create habitat corridors to link the now isolated areas of habitat for the ocelot and the jaguarundi in the Rio Grande Valley. According to one Texan involved with community-based conservation efforts:

> Building on Texans' long-standing respect and love for the land is at the heart of community-based conservation. Community conservation is more complicated, time consuming and expensive than simply owning land. But, ultimately, community-based conservation is the only way to conserve this state's magnificent natural heritage. Texans expect—and deserve—nothing less.[13]

The goal then is to tap this long-standing respect in creating and implementing our global environmental policies.

The Nature Conservancy learned something that many others are now realizing: the community must be involved and that community-based conservation is a foundation for successful environmental protection. The success of community-based conservation is not unique to Texas. Many localities throughout the U.S. are now reaping the benefits of community action.

The Nature Conservancy recently announced a $1 million grant to community-based conservation efforts along the Great Lakes shoreline. The grant is an investment from the Dow Chemical Company and two private foundations in community-based conservation. The Nature Conservancy works with businesses and residents in rural communities along an eighty-mile stretch of Great Lakes shoreline. According to Kent Gilges, project director in the Conservancy's Upper Peninsula office, "once people realize the important role these preserves play, they begin to act as ambassadors for them in the larger community. They begin talking to their neighbors. They start to take ownership. That is the key to developing the kind of long-term land ethic that will protect natural communities."[14] The project has led to new partnerships between government, environmentalists, industry, and private citizens. It has also created a new vision along the Great Lakes, one of local stewardship and long-term sustainability.[15] In short, it is implementing the personal level of the linkage paradigm. It is changing individual attitudes and personal codes of ethics. Such change at the moral level is imperative if we are to have real change at the policy level.

The Mattole River valley area in northern California is another example of community-based conservation at work. At one time, the valley was home to ranching, logging, mining, and salmon fishing. State and federal agencies struggled to ensure the biodiversity of the region. Only local organizations were able to fill the void and integrate the interests of various parties (loggers, environmentalists, ranchers, and so forth) by articulating mutually acceptable ideas about environmental management and preservation of natural resources to stabilize employment prospects.[16]

Three hundred miles north of the Mattole watershed is the urbanized Anacosta River in metropolitan Washington. It has been called one of the country's most polluted rivers, degraded by channelization, riparian and wetland loss, forest removal, sewer overflows, and other pollution.[17] Though separated by hundreds of miles, restoration efforts are bringing people together to rebuild their watersheds and revitalize their communities. The community-based efforts to restore each of these watersheds are among thirteen restoration case studies documented by the American Fisheries Society. The effort illustrates the effectiveness of "vesting communities with an interest in conservation."[18]

Community-based conservation is working in Columbus, Ohio. The city formed an Environmental Science Advisory Committee to provide independent, technical advice to city hall on the scientific rationale, relevancy, and benefits of current environmental programs at all levels of government. A second aspect of the community effort includes a two-year study to identify and rank environmental risks within Columbus. After identifying thirty environmental problems, the study developed 192 recommendations to reduce the risks.[19]

Community-based conservation efforts have also proven themselves successful in Iowa, where grassroots activism led to closer communities and greater environmental protection.[20] In Alaska, community-based conservation in the Kanai River watershed has been critical to preserving the local ecosystem.[21] In the Cannon River Valley in Minnesota, community-based conservation set a new standard for ecosystem preservation in that state.[22] In Tennessee, Lockheed Martin and the Nature Conservancy supported a community-based conservation initiative called the Southern Appalachian Rivers Initiative.[23] The conservancy worked to improve the Clinch River in Hancock County and the Conasagua River near Chattanooga. Together, the rivers provide a critical habitat for many threatened species.[24] Community-based conservation efforts have been successful in preserving the Mackinaw River in Illinois,[25] maintaining the Waccamaw National Wildlife Refuge in South Carolina,[26] setting aside open space in Utah,[27] conserving electricity in Colorado, restoring the Everglades in Florida, and reducing agricultural chemicals in Iowa.[28] From Virginia to California and from North Dakota to Texas, community-based conservation is spreading throughout the United States.[29]

These examples of local action are part of the considerable research that indicates that local governments are an effective way to address environmental degradation in the United States. In his testimony before the United States Congress, Randy Johnson, the third vice president of the National Association of Counties, used an analogy to describe how the process of environmental protection currently works: "each federal agency [views a city] by looking through a soda straw, taking a very detailed look at a specific subject, such as landfills, or underground storage tanks, or stormwater runoff. Such tunnel vision does not allow them to see how each regulation affects the others, nor do the agencies understand the cumulative impact and cost at the local level."[30] In other words, the federal government fails to recognize linkages.

Johnson is not alone in his criticism of federal environmental regulations that attempt to micromanage the environment.[31] The Environmental Protection Agency was created in 1970. While the agency was appropriate at the time when pollution blackened the skies, and waterways were so polluted that the Cuyahoga River in Cleveland caught on fire,[32] the dynamics of environmental protection have changed.[33] However, what is needed is not less environmental protection, but rather less federal control. The National Academy of Public Administration recently completed a thorough study of Congress and the EPA and now recommends that the Environmental Protection Agency clarify its mission and trust state and local governments to set and follow their own environmental priorities.[34] Even the EPA administrator, Carol Browner, recognizes that the agency must move beyond traditional standards and command and control regulations; for, "environmental improvement only works when the public believes their problems are being solved."[35] The EPA and its counterparts in other countries have an important role to play. They are the link between local ingenuity and international action. By assuming the role of facilitator and disseminator, their importance to our overall scheme of environmental protection increases, rather than decreases.

By adopting such a role, it is possible to avoid the danger of national (and international) programs stifling local initiatives and community-based conservation efforts.[36] Currently, national programs tend to take power away from state and local governments and replace them with inflexible regulations that separate individuals from the land. Additionally, they risk one of the principles upon which this nation was founded: federalism. When state and local jurisdiction is usurped, the concept of federalism is undermined.[37]

Some issues, such as waste management[38] and water purification,[39] have been traditionally dealt with by local governments. Additionally, most planning and zoning is now, and has been, done at the local level. In fact, local government authority for land-use planning was affirmed by the U.S. Supreme Court in 1926.[40] Many other pollution issues can and should be addressed at the local level; "most pollution is local and can be handled locally."[41] Such pollution includes agricultural waste,[42] automobile emissions,[43] water pollution,[44] and air pollution.[45] Many even advocate local control over species protection, property takings, and wetland preservation.[46]

In fact, wetlands protection and preservation has become a rallying cry for the localism movement as national and international governmental responses prove to be inept. In the words of Robert Kasten, former U.S. senator from Wisconsin and chairman of the Center on Regulation and Economic Growth at the Alexis de Tocqueville Institution, "[n]o environmental issue has caused as much populist revolt."[47] Federally micromanaged wetland regulations frustrate landowners who must navigate through endless bureaucratic red tape. This has led many to conclude that the U.S. federal government should not be in the business of wetland protection.[48] Such sentiments, however, need to be tempered. Local protection may not be enough, as a central authority is needed to ensure that localities are equipped with the necessary research and to oversee local action in order to avoid a race to the bottom.

Despite the calls for local activism, many still feel that an international or global response is needed for such environmental issues as stratospheric ozone depletion, acid rain, and global climate change. But to disregard the role of local action is irresponsible. Even "global problems" require community involvement. Such issues occupied the talks at Omiya, Japan (discussed previously), in which 200 local entities from around the world agreed to take proactive steps to cut the emission of global warming gases. As CFCs and the depletion of stratospheric ozone layer become a states' rights issue,[49] many are already arguing for localities to assume responsibility for tropospheric ozone pollution. Dr. Kenneth Chilton and Christopher Boerner maintain that clean air policies need to be customized to each region to produce the most efficient and effective policies.[50]

The challenge is to foster local action by utilizing effective international frameworks. In other words, the goal is to create an integrated approach to environmental protection. Localities in the United States are not alone in their ability to implement global environmental protection policies. The next sections examine community-based conservation programs throughout the world.

Africa

Perhaps the best examples of community-based conservation are found in the continent of Africa, where localism has proven to be an effective complement to national and international efforts. Lessons learned from these efforts need to be incorporated into our global environmental protection efforts. During colonial and postcolonial decades, wildlife preservation policies tended to place animals above people. This drew deep hostility and resistance. Tourists and foreign hunters were allowed to enter wildlife areas and even kill wild animals, while villagers were totally excluded from the land on which they once lived.[51] By returning the land to communities, community-based conservation has done much to alleviate such hostilities. For example, the United States Agency for International Development (U.S.A.I.D.) sponsors four African Wildlife Foundation projects: Tanzanian Park Agency (TANAPA) in Tanzania, the "Cobra" project in Kenya, and the Lake Mburo and Bwindi Forest projects in Uganda. These projects specifically focus on community-based conservation. They seek to empower local communities to benefit from wildlife protection within the communal lands and other protected areas. The projects show that communities will tolerate the costs associated with cohabitating with wildlife only when they benefit from conservation. Rural conservation has been successful by providing rural people the opportunity to secure rights to resources and to defend their gains against encroachers.[52]

The elephant is a highly visible symbol of African wildlife. Half of the world's population of elephants is found in the southern African states. Environmentalists discovered that elephant populations were dwindling even as centrally managed protectionism increased. This "protectionism" was carried out by white African governments that took wildlife from the historic control and effective stewardship of self-governing tribal bodies and placed the animals into open-access commons.[53] The policies forced native Africans to poach wildlife to prevent crop destruction, to provide meat for the village, and to trade in skins, horn, and ivory. The wildlife was not only the enemy, but it was also a symbol of the hated white rule.[54]

The traditional system for managing wildlife is no longer appropriate for countries where people are largely dependent on natural resources and where acute poverty runs rampant. The first effort to involve local people in wildlife protection was in Amboseli in the early 1970s. Given the opportunity to earn income from tourism, the Maasai quickly responded by discouraging poachers. As a result, wildlife numbers recovered markedly in the following decade.[55] These local initiatives, however, succeeded because of international support and pressure. Thus, while local action is necessary, it is rarely enough.

Current efforts to save the elephant population of southern Africa are based on self-regulation and local involvement. Until recently, elephants were not viewed as good neighbors. They trampled crops, destroyed grazing areas, and even killed villagers. According to David Western, former director of international programs at the Wildlife Conservation Society and former chairman of the African Elephant and Rhino Specialist Group, however, "coexistence has a place in most traditional societies, but also has enormous potential to improve the lives of rural communities and the status of wildlife."[56] When the benefits from wildlife are devolved to communities and landholders, the wildlife provides local communities with the financial resources to develop themselves. No longer are communities dependent on the patronage of foreign donors. Reminiscent of the civic society Alexis de Tocqueville found when he visited America, decisions are made democratically in public meetings. Not only is wildlife protected, but also an effective system of grassroots democracy is introduced. Communities begin to do things for themselves and overcome the crippling sense of dependency and helplessness. The process becomes sustainable because everyone has a vested interest in the long-term survival of the wildlife. The end result is "more wildlife, more democracy, more economic development and people with a greater sense of self-worth."[57] Community efforts involve more than just wildlife protection. Studies are under way to determine, for example, whether building an oat-processing plant could help farmers make more money and resist the pressures to sell their land to large developers.[58] Community-based conservation along with grassroots democracy have spread throughout Africa and provide important lessons for national, international, and global governance.

As community-based democracy spreads and local people clamor for the right of self-rule, centrally devised management plans are no longer viable; experience has shown that if environmental protection does not benefit the people, it will be circumvented.[59] Conservation must address the link between the needs of wildlife and those of the people. Take for instance the environmental problems in the Sudan. After examining the impact of ecological degradation and the failure of the state to address this degradation, one researcher concluded that "[l]asting peace will . . . depend on (1) land reform . . . (2) assisting the peasants and pastoralists to rehabilitate their natural habitat, (3) direct agricultural production . . . (4) . . . implementing sustainable development policies . . . (5) achieving far reaching democratization in all walks of life as well as . . . empower[ing] the people [so that] they will green the land."[60]

Perhaps one of the most successful manifestations of community-based conservation is the Communal Areas Management Program for Indigenous Resources (CAMPFIRE).[61] The program secures community claims to wildlife and engages "local villagers in the sustainable harvest and economical marketing of wildlife products to benefit, in a word, the very people who must pay, on a daily basis, the conservation price of putting up with less-than-benign wild neighbors."[62] CAMPFIRE earns over 2 million dollars a year for local people. This revenue is divided by communities and partially reinvested into conservation efforts. The program also connects communities with the global market and allows them to participate on equal footing. Most importantly, however, the program changes rural attitudes towards wildlife.[63] Wildlife is now highly valued and protected. Another benefit of the program is that it is bringing communities together and creating a type of civic democracy and environmentalism.

Related to community-based conservation efforts are integrated conservation and development projects (ICDPs). ICDPs establish formal partnerships between conservation organizations and development agencies. The projects are concerned with individual sites and tailor their design to its specific problems and prospects. ICDPs emphasize community-based conservation while taking an integrated approach to environmental protection by utilizing international expertise. More than one hundred ICDPs have been described, including more than fifty in at least twenty countries of sub-Saharan Africa.[64] The following examples of community-based conservation efforts from throughout Africa illustrate how these benefits are being realized by hundreds of communities.

Kenya

Kenya is a prime example of the success of community-based conservation in Africa.[65] The most famous of Kenya's local success stories is the greenbelt movement. Started in 1977 by Kenya's National Council of Women, the program enlists rural peoples to plant trees in the fight against desertification and soil erosion. The reforestation efforts meet the demands for firewood and fruit while contributing to community development. Local communities have established tree plantations on open spaces, school grounds, and land near roadways. By 1990, ten million native trees had been planted. According to one observer, this effort has done more to reverse desertification than any U.N. environmental program.[66] One important facet of the program is that women continue to be the backbone of the greenbelt movement, the benefit of which is discussed in chapter 10.

Another flourishing environmental project at the local level is called "Cobra." Sponsored by the African Wildlife Foundation, it seeks to build community conservation capacity in the Kenya Wildlife Service. After a militant government temporarily stifled the greenbelt movement, Cobra attempted to increase government tolerance of pastoralism through recognition of the role of this traditional way of protecting wildlife.[67] Additionally, the technique of game cropping, whereby local populations shoot wildlife to get protein-rich food, allows the community to directly profit from the wildlife and thus encourages long-term sustainability and preservation. When people can make money building tourist lodges and leading safaris near their villages, people consider wildlife valuable instead of nuisances.[68] The result of all these programs has been both community development and environmental protection.[69]

Results from a four-year-old program in Kwale specifically illustrate the success of community-based conservation. The Duruma people of Kenya now coexist with elephants after decades of fighting with them. As a result of empowerment and "ownership," the community now jealously guards elephant herds. With the help of the Eden Wildlife Trust and the Kenya Wildlife Service, the residents of the Mwalughanja came to accept the idea of setting aside almost 60,000 acres of land adjacent to the elephant zone. The project has not only increased elephant populations, but has also significantly increased the community's income.[70]

In Amboseli, Kenya, community-based conservation has been particularly successful. The Kenyan government established the Amboseli National Park in 1974. The park, however, protects only one-tenth of the ecological system. The surrounding areas are owned by approximately 20,000 Maasai. Although they do not regularly hunt wild animals, the wildlife competes with their livestock for forage. This conflict lasted almost twenty years until community-based conservation was introduced. In 1990, the Kenya Wildlife Service assumed management of the park and was allowed to raise and retain its own revenue. This revenue was subsequently shared with the Maasai, who now have a stake in the protection and preservation of the wildlife. Although the revenue sharing initially hampered conservation efforts, the active participation guarantees long-term success for both the Maasai and the wildlife.

By many accounts, Kenya once again favors community-based conservation.[71] In fact, many now refer to Kenya as a model for wildlife protection through local empowerment.[72] Wildlife preservation has been returned to community control.[73] These examples from Kenya illustrate the ability of communities to successfully protect and conserve the environment. It should be remembered, however, that local efforts were only successful when the national government placed a high priority on halting environmental degradation. Additionally, nongovernmental organizations were very active in promoting the protection of the environment.[74] These lessons need to help the global community shape its approach to environmental protection.

Uganda

In Uganda, the African Wildlife Foundation works with communities in and around Lake Mburo National Park and in the Bwindi Forest. Phase two of the Mburo project began in 1995 and was completed in 1998. It helped ease conflicts between the park and the local communities by empowering local communities in the name of environmental protection.[75] A similar community-based project enlists locals in Uganda in a battle to save the gorilla.[76] Both projects were successful only because they combined elements of community-based conservation with global support.

Malawi

Malawi's government has adopted community-based conservation and development.[77] This, however, was not always the case. In 1975, government officials moved many of the villages in and around the Nyika National Park off of the high, cool, and productive plateau into a marshy and mosquito-infested plain. Though the government intended to expand the park and improve wildlife habitat, it caused many villagers to die of malaria. The program caused resentment and in the end the area became infested with poachers.[78] In response to tension between preservation and human needs, leaders in Malawi turned to community-based conservation. The government handed over the authority to manage natural resources, including the land and the wildlife, to the local people. Communities now benefit legally from both subsistence and commercial use of wild species. The programs in Malawi have won global recognition and are supported in part by assistance from the United States. Vice President Al Gore wrote, "one of the most effective ways to encourage market forces to work in environmentally benign ways is to give concerned citizens a better way to take the environment into account when they purchase goods or make other economic decisions."[79] For Malawi and other African states, this "better way" is community-based conservation.

Namibia

In a remote corner of newly independent Namibia, community-based conservation helps to protect both a selection of spectacular wildlife and the traditional semi-nomadic lifestyles of the local Himba people. While unarmed local herdsmen guard against poaching, local Himba communities play an increased role in managing local resources. The approach led to an increase in wildlife populations and a decrease in militarism.[80] The new Namibia government embraces conservation and plans to extend this community-based approach to guard against poachers in other parts of the country. The programs also foster a new type of rural democracy and sense of community.[81]

Another remote area of Namibia is Nyae Nyae, formerly Eastern Bushmanland. The area is home to one of the world's last remaining groups of Jauhoan people (also known as !Kung or Bushmen), who are traditional hunters and gatherers. The Juahoansi have lived there for at least 11,000 years. Prior to 1990, the South African government ruled Nyae Nyae. The government squeezed the Juahoansi into an area called Bushmanland as part of an attempt to segregate ethnic groups in order to capture natural resources. Although the people of Nyae Nyae still primarily depend on the natural environment for their food, the diminished territory is unable to support the current population.[82]

Over the past two decades, conservationists and developers clashed over what was best for the Jauhoansi and the wildlife of Nyae Nyae. Too often, these debates took place without any input from the Jauhoansi. Now, the Namibian government is attempting a new approach that incorporates community-based conservation. This approach recognizes that the Juahoansi coexisted with wildlife for millennia and highly value it. The Juahoansi community is one of seven Namibian communities involved in the Living in a Finite Environment (LIFE) project sponsored by the Namibian Ministry of Environment and Tourism. This project allows local communities to manage their own wildlife and generate income through tourism.[83] Hopefully, the project will be able to accomplish what thirty years of central control could not: preservation of the wildlife and the human life.[84]

South Africa

Another program, with the same acronym, but different focus, is the worldwide Local Facility for Urban Environment (LIFE) program, which was recently launched in South Africa. The U.N. Development Program, as part of the 1992 Earth Summit in Rio de Janeiro, established LIFE as a pilot program. The program focuses on community-based approaches to solving the consequences of environmental degradation and urban development. It has been launched in thirteen countries, which include Brazil, Egypt, Jamaica, Pakistan, Senegal, Tanzania, and Thailand. LIFE is described as "a response by the international community to the growing challenge of urbanization in developing countries and the need for local initiatives to deal with the linkages between urban poverty and environmental degradation."[85] The program is an example of an integrated approach whereby localism operates within a global framework.

South Africa is a place in which community-based conservation also improves social, racial, and political tensions. The apartheid state was authoritarian and secretive. It excluded black people from any meaningful political participation. The government protected conservation areas at the expense of local communities and to the exclusion of communities from the management and benefits of conservation. LIFE now hopes to equip and empower underresourced and previously excluded communities so that they can decide the best way to protect their own environment.[86] It allows individuals who were excluded from participatory democracy in the past a chance to actually effectuate change in their communities.

Zimbabwe

Two projects in Zimbabwe have received international recognition for their emphasis on community-based conservation. The Organization of Rural Association of Peasants (ORAP) is a movement that grew out of women's groups. ORAP groups engage in "income-generating projects and 'service projects' promoting environmental improvement and restoration, especially related to water and sanitation."[87] The grassroots, self-help nature of such groups is evident in their names: Siyazenzela ("We're doing it for ourselves") and Vusanani ("Support each other to get up"). The programs bring communities together and facilitate for community-based democracy.

CAMPFIRE is another program that embodies the tenets of community-based conservation.[88] The program has been quite successful, due in large part because of its international support.[89] In Zimbabwe, villagers are given control over the safari trade. Instead of proceeds going to a distant, detached national trust, the money goes directly to the community. People have a vested interest in the preservation of local wildlife. By involving the villagers in the future of environmental protection, they have an incentive to carefully guard their resources. In the past, poaching and government corruption made elephant protection very difficult. Since Zimbabwe adopted community-based conservation, the elephant population has doubled from 32,000 to 66,000. The community was given a stake in taking care of the natural resource base, which included the elephant. More than 3,000 elephants are born each year and about one hundred are allowed to be hunted.[90] Permits are granted and strictly regulated by the community. Because the community has a stake in the process, the elephant is assured long-term survival. Additionally, villages benefit economically from tourism related to their wildlife reserves.[91]

Tourism is the not the only way communities are protecting wildlife in Zimbabwe. By 1990, three out of four ranchers in areas too dry to support crop production had shifted, at least in part, to wildlife ranching. Ranchers realized a four-time gain in profit per acre as opposed to ranching cattle. Groups of ranchers also combined to form "conservancies" of five to twenty-five properties. This not only brought communities together, but also led to the reintroduction of far-roaming, yet economically valuable, species such as the elephant and cape buffalo.[92] Other animals are also thriving on private ranches. Black and white rhinos have made a dramatic comeback as have leopards, which were once regarded as vermin by ranchers, who used to fear for the well-being of their livestock.[93] Again, community-based conservation benefits both the community and the wildlife. However, these programs are made possible by international support. CAMPFIRE operates in numerous countries with the support of the international community. Such global frameworks are essential because they allow communities to share and disseminate information and ideas enabling them to benefit from a vast network of resources.

Mali, Tanzania, Zambia, Botswana, and Senegal

The trend towards community-based conservation is spreading throughout Africa. Mali is now giving local communities a voice after years of environmental degradation.[94] In Tanzania, the African Wildlife Foundation is working to build a community outreach program. It has already created a new government benefit-sharing policy and trained community wardens. The revenue supports digging wells, building schools, and staffing health clinics. The environment is protected and the community is able to meet the needs of its people.[95] In Zambia,[96] the World Wildlife Fund established the Zambian and Kilum mountain projects, which work

150   *Rethinking Environmental Protection*

with local inhabitants and enhance indigenous methods of combining wildlife conservation with economic development.[97] In Sough Luangwa, a village in Zambia, villagers own the wildlife, which is then sold to rich safari hunters. Since the wildlife is now a community resource, the elephant population has doubled from 1993 to 1998.[98] Another program that attempts to incorporate community-based conservation in Zambia is the Administrative Management Design for Game Management Areas. The program channels profits from trophy hunting to wildlife management and community development while increasing wildlife numbers.[99]

In Botswana, the central government gave wildlife areas to villages for their exclusive control. Though controlled hunting has increased, poaching has decreased, and the wildlife is rebounding.[100] Community-based conservation efforts have also fueled reforestation efforts in Senegal. Groups called "women's gardening clubs" (even though men participate) have become a major force in efforts to overcome desertification. They plant gardens and trees "and engage in projects that protect the environment while reducing the work of rural women involved in subsistence agriculture."[101] Community-based conservation has proven successful throughout Africa, and the continent now serves as a model for community-based conservation efforts elsewhere. In many cases, these local projects depended on international agencies for the necessary start-up and mobilization social capital, illustrating how global frameworks are necessary to assist community-based conservation efforts.

Asia

After decades of centrally managed wildlife protection efforts, authorities in some of Asia's developing countries are beginning to realize that it is impossible to protect nature without the help of the local people. A conference on Community-Based Conservation Policy and Practice (sponsored by the U.N. Educational, Scientific, and Cultural Organization) brought together eleven south and central Asian states. A background note to the conference explained that "communities which were once in control of their immediate surroundings are once again gaining center-stage after having been sidelined for decades, in some cases, centuries."[102] Countries in Asia are realizing that it is impossible to exclude local people even from the most strictly protected areas.[103]

State wildlife departments, frequently overworked and understaffed, realize that local communities can help them with their labor and knowledge. Ashish Kothari, a well-known Indian conservationist, explains that "all over the world, but especially in developing countries, it is being realized that central agencies are simply not able to carry out this task, being understaffed, underfunded, ill-trained, and ill-equipped [to handle] the myriad threats that habitats and species face."[104] A quick trip around Asia illustrates how local efforts, when assisted by national and international entities, are improving environmental protection.[105]

India

Community-based forest management schemes have achieved notable success in India.[106] This success is due, in part, to India's long history of community and woman environmental activism. On World Earth Day, 1979, women gathered in Tehri, India, with empty water pots to protest water scarcity and the failure of water supply projects. Subsequent years found peasants protesting the damming of the Ganga and Narmada Rivers, waterways whose shores and valleys were home to thousands, while others refused to sell milk from their cows in a sign of protest over social conditions. In 1987, rural inhabitants, who were mostly women, blockaded mining operations that were destroying forests and streams in Doon valley. Despite being beaten by two hundred men hired by the quarry contractor, the blockade continued. Each of these events was a manifestation of a movement called Chipko Andolan (literally, "hugging-the-trees-movement").[107] The movement incorporates Hinduism, Jainism, and Buddhism and promotes biospheric equality. Members regard species as possessing intrinsic worth separate from whatever value they may hold for humans.[108] For the Chipko activists, the defense of nature takes on a religious-moral duty.

Originally, the Chipko movement concentrated on the exploitation of forest resources by outside contractors; by 1975 three hundred villages in the hill districts of Uttar Pradesh faced severe erosion and landslides due primarily to deforestation by nonlocal commercial interests. After widespread, organized protests, the government adopted a new strategy that utilized local labor and forest contractor cooperatives. Notwithstanding this victory, the focus of the local movement has broadened to include mining, the damming of India's rivers, and control over dairy production.[109] The Chipko movement illustrates how community efforts can implement the linkage paradigm at the personal level by effectuating changes in morals. The challenge for the international community is to answer the calls of communities for greater control of natural resources and to recognize that communities can be better protectors of the environment.

Pakistan

Grassroots initiatives are emerging in Pakistan to provide services and solutions for the community. For example, the Orangi Pilot Project created a series of community-based organizations to improve urban services and infrastructure in Orangi Township, Karachi's largest squatter settlement. The project serves as a model for effective grassroots development. The community participates in the creation, financing, operation, and maintenance of an expanding sanitation system as well as housing, health, and welfare.[110] It illustrates the knowledge and ingenuity a community can bring to such issues.

Southeast Asia

Southeast Asia exemplifies both the positive results and negative repercussions of community-based conservation. Ecotage has become one of the primary mechanisms utilized by local peoples to disrupt unecological practices of national and international governments and to fight for control over local land. The Malaysian state of Sarawak has witnessed numerous battles between local tribes with spiritual attachments to the land and an unsympathetic Malaysian government bent on continued logging. The Penan, the last nomadic, hunter-gatherers in Southeast Asia, have fought since 1987 to end the destruction of their tropical hardwood forests on which their spiritual and physical existence depends. The war, however, appears to have been lost.

Another Sarawak tribe, the Iban, were more successful. They were able to keep their land free from loggers, in part, through ecotage. In 1982, the tribe blew up twenty-five bulldozers and logging trucks, having to repeat the feat four years later.[111] Although the battle was ultimately successful, they and the Penan exemplify the struggle of many native peoples to secure their land from outside intrusion and to overcome destructive national environmental policies.

The actions of the Penan and Iban, and other local initiatives, gained worldwide notice and interest. The International Union of the Conservation of Nature selected Sabah, Malaysia, to host its Conservation Forum in 1998. The Forum highlighted the integrated and localized efforts in Sabah, such as the Malaysian-German Sustainable Forest Management Project, which started in 1989, and serves as a model to others for forest reserves.[112] The Forum also addressed local wildlife protection efforts and bilateral agreements between Malaysia and the Philippines to address problems of nesting and foraging grounds of marine turtles in both countries.

In the Philippines, a community-based conservation project is working on Mt. Makiling to develop an area of the rain forest for ecology-walking in an effort to showcase the biodiversity and values of the mountain. The project is a joint effort between the Los Banos Science Community and farmer organizations in Mt. Makiling.[113] Such community efforts are gaining the support of the Philippine government. In 1995, Philippine Executive Order No. 247 instituted participation in the form of equitable sharing as a legal obligation for prospecting biological resources.[114]

Community-based efforts in Thailand have garnered less support. In 1988, opponents of the Nam Choan Dam in Thailand were beaten and arrested. Many protesters were killed as a result of conflicts over resource utilization and conservation. The Nam Choan Dam was to be the largest hydroelectric dam in the country. The Electric Generating Authority of Thailand slated the dam to be built in the Thung Yai Naresuan Wildlife Sanctuary. It was projected to flood 200 square kilometers in the middle of the biologically diverse sanctuary. The dam construction became a contentious issue throughout the country, resulting in debate among the forestry department, urban students, academicians, and nongovernmental organizations.[115]

Philip Hirsch, author of *The Political Ecology of Environment in Thailand*, wrote that the Nam Choan Dam campaign "provided lessons and a level of confidence for actors at various levels, but in part the politics of environment have continued to reflect an emerging political economy based on increasingly diverse and fluid coalitions of interests, together with continued tensions and opportunities arising from the incorporation of peripheral areas and their populations into national structures and discourses."[116] A decade later, a small group of protesters is attempting to halt the Yadana gas pipeline's passage through virgin forest. Unfortunately, this small group has gone relatively unsupported, despite the sixty-two nongovernmental organizations and sixteen conservation groups that are officially in a coalition in opposition to the pipeline. While both campaigns were similar in that there was active participation from local residents, the Nam Choan incident allowed people in the area much more time to get organized and galvanize support. The Nam Choan campaign illustrates the need for popular support from different levels of society. It highlights the need for "a division of labour—a local network which alerts the public about environmentally harmful projects, and academics and non-governmental organisations to disseminate information and convince people to take action."[117]

One issue that was able to garner support at the local level in Thailand was commercial logging. Before commercial logging, tribal peoples in both

Myanmar and Thailand practiced sustainable and ecologically sound logging techniques. As the demand for lumber increased and the forests became a profitable natural resource, commercial logging started to destroy the forests. As the degradation worsened, a coalition of peasant hill farmers, students, and intellectuals fought to return more sustainable methods. The grassroots efforts achieved victory in 1989 when the government banned all commercial logging. Unfortunately, this victory of local environmentalism would prove to be a major setback for similar efforts on the other side of the border in Myanmar.

Ever since Myanmar gained its independence from British colonial rule in 1948, the tribal peoples have fought a guerrilla war to regain their traditional lifestyles against outsiders invading their ancestral territories. Revenue from selective rebel logging was used to purchase arms and ammunition. The rebels logged carefully, for they viewed their forest as "'their heritage, the only home they had ever known. Parents . . . plant teak trees as a kind of living inheritance for newborn children, who, despite the fighting [grow] up believing that the forest is eternal.'"[118] The fight for community control of the forests was seriously set back when commercial logging was banned in Thailand. The Myanmar government sold the rebel land to the Thailand government. Thus, the efforts in Thailand, while good for the local people, inevitably hurt other local peoples and resulted in a zero-sum gain in environmental protection. While local action is critical to our overall environmental policy, it fails when communities simply export their environmental problems. Global frameworks are thus needed to ensure that community action results in real solutions to environmental degradation, not simply its transport from one locale to another.

China

China has started to realize the benefits of community-based conservation. As provincial and local regions grow wealthier, they replace the center as the primary initiator and financial sponsor of environmental protection policies. Thus, while state capacity may be diminished in some respects (see chapter 3), other elements of the state emerge to respond more effectively to regional resource demands.[119]

Take one recent case study for instance. During China's "Great Leap Forward," the government drained the water in Cao Hai, a freshwater wetland in southwestern China. The intent was to create a huge new area for agriculture. When the entire lake was drained, what resulted was a vast sweeping dust bowl. After a change in policy, the area is once again a wintering area for tens of thousands of migratory birds, including hundreds

Everyone Else Is Doing It   155

of black-necked cranes, an endangered species that breeds in the remote highlands of Tibet. However, serious issues remained, such as what to do with the 20,000 people living inside the reserve.[120] When the central government told farmers they could no longer reclaim the wetland for growing crops and their fishing was restricted, farmers resisted. In the face of such resistance, a new approach took form; the first sustained community-based conservation project in China was born. The strategy consisted of six prongs: (1) undertaking community-based conservation and development activities, (2) zoning Caohai Nature Reserve into both core and buffer areas, (3) developing ecotourism, (4) diversifying financial sources, (5) enhancing infrastructure and facilities, and (6) improving the capacity of the Caohai Nature Reserve office.[121]

Communities were given loans to start small businesses such as raising pigs, guiding tourists in boats on the lake, making stoves from oil drums, and selling food products in the market. Villagers now participate in setting conservation guidelines. Villagers patrol the reserve and decide on limits to prevent overfishing. Local support for the natural reserve is higher than ever before. Huang Mingjie of the Guizhou Environmental Protection Bureau notes that "[t]he lesson from our project is we should connect nature conservation with rural development."[122] The project also illustrates the benefits of an integrated approach to conservation. The project recognized that the villagers and their living base, the Caohai Nature Reserve, cannot be separated. It recognized that villagers must use and manage natural resources of the reserve. The project also acknowledged that the villagers within the reserve area are poor and still live on subsistence, and thus to preserve the environment, human needs must be met. Caohai Nature Reserve has ultimately been successful because it has incorporated local action with national and international assistance and expertise, which has been critical in solving issues such as zinc melting and sewage pollution problems.[123]

On the heals of the success of the Caohai Nature Reserve project, community-based conservation efforts are surfacing in Tibet. The major rivers of India, China, and Vietnam originate in Tibet. Thus, the need for protection there is especially critical. Additionally, Tibet occupies a very fragile ecosystem, one that takes more time to recover because of its high altitude and dryness. Even more important, climate changes in Tibet are likely to affect the monsoon patterns in the entire Himalayan region.[124] Currently, the Chinese government is instituting large hydroelectric schemes and other ecologically disturbing activities. In response, community-based conservation efforts are forming. One such effort has empowered groups of villagers and monks to patrol an area of 5,000 acres to discourage illegal logging. Additionally, monks are ordaining trees and wrapping them in cloth in an effort to dissuade loggers from cutting them down.[125]

Elsewhere in China, a community-based conservation management program is under way with the support of the Canadian International Development Agency to implement community-oriented field training in habitat protection and species conservation in rural areas in China and Vietnam. Areas near mangrove and tropical forests are threatened by ecosystem degradation caused by overexploitation of natural resources, the use of new technologies, rapid population growth, and economic expansion. The program will attempt to train officials and academicians in techniques of conserving natural ecosystems, promoting sustainable use of natural resources in communities, and establishing networks to monitor results.[126] The lessons learned in China illustrate not only the success of community-based conservation, but also of an integrated approach to environmental protection.

Indonesia

The previous discussion of Indonesia in chapter 3 discussed the environmental insecurity arising from environmental degradation in Indonesia. Many view the rising insecurity the result of the government's inability to work with or listen to local communities. Indonesian policies are almost exclusively top-down—leading to the erosion of community management capabilities. Population pressures, combined with deforestation, create severe environmental scarcities and ripen the potential for violent conflict. Additionally, "[a]s conflicts grow more severe, the state may cut itself off from innovative solutions that might otherwise arise from local communities and other elements of civil society."[127]

Those who have spent time working with officials of the Indonesian government attest to the fact that there are untold numbers of them exploding with innovative ideas—both visionary goals and rudimentary practicalities—on how to better realize the goals of sustainable development, stability, and equity.[128] According to Charles Barber:

> If the combined ingenuity of the state and society can be unleashed from the outmoded and harmful structures, attitudes, and webs of special interests that have developed over the past thirty years, Indonesia will stand a good chance of surmounting the challenges of resource scarcity that all of humanity faces on the cusp of the twenty-first century.[129]

Unfortunately, after decades of top-down policies, many communities lack the capacity to organize, innovate, and act: "The problem is not so much the erosion of local resource management practices. Instead, the stunting of local institutions of social cooperation undermines ingenuity generation."[130] For these and other reasons, Indonesia is hard-pressed to supply this ingenuity. In Indonesia, the problem is the state. To overcome environmental problems, the national government must allow those with innovative ideas to act on them, yet another example where local action is possible only with national and international support.

Conclusion

Homer-Dixon advances the notion of ingenuity—ideas applied to solve practical and technical problems. In order to overcome resource scarcities, local communities must develop ingenious methods to counter the rising social disunity created by scarcity. While Homer-Dixon acknowledges the role of the state in developing ingenuity, he notes that much of the ingenuity needed to deal with natural resource scarcities must come from the bottom up; "[t]he ingenuity needed to adjust to resource scarcity . . . [and] many of the ideas needed for successful adjustment are produced at the community and household level as people learn, for example, how to reform local institutions to solve collective-action problems."[131]

The case studies provided in this chapter illustrate that given the opportunity, communities can develop ingenious methods to preserve the environment. Communities, however, frequently need the support and coordination offered by national and international bodies in order to realize this ingenuity. By combining global frameworks with local involvement, real environmental protection is possible. The following chapter illustrates how local communities can operate and thrive within an integrated approach as well as how international cooperation can best achieve its goals through community involvement and implementation.

Notes

1. Timothy Beatley, "The Visions of Sustainable Communities," in *Cooperating with Nature: Confronting Natural Hazards with Land-Use Planning for Sustainable Communities*, ed. Raymond J. Burby (Washington, D.C.: Joseph Henry Press, 1998) (describing the increase in the number of local sustainability initiatives in cities such as Seattle and Chattanooga).

2. See, for example, David Western, "Stewards of the Last Place," *Chicago Tribune*, 19 October 1997, C1. See also B. Goldstein, *Community-Based Conservation: An Annotated Bibliographic Database* (New York: Liz Claiborne

and Art Ortenberg Foundation, 1994); David Western et al., eds., *Natural Connections: Perspectives on Community-Based Conservation* (Washington, D.C.: Island Press, 1994).

3. Gerald A. Emison, "From Compelling to Catalyzing: The Federal Government's Changing Role in Environmental Protection," *William and Mary Environmental Law and Policy Review* 20 (spring 1996): 233. See also Terry L. Anderson and Peter J. Hill, "Environmental Federalism: Thinking Smaller" in *Environmental Federalism*, ed. Terry L. Anderson and Peter J. Hill (New York: Rowman & Littlefield Publishers, Inc., 1997), xi-xiii.

4. Brandon Loomis, "Regulations 'Fight Is On'—Environmental Issues Are up for Debate, Says Crapo Aide," *Idaho Falls Post Register*, 4 April 1996, C2.

5. Cindy Gray, "The Trouble with Environmentalists," *Asheville Citizen-Times*, 14 August 1996, A7.

6. Pete Geddes, "Building Trust and Respect in the West," *Seattle Times*, 3 July 1996, B5.

7. Jill Belsky and Barb Cestero, "Creating New Visions for the Rural West," *Seattle Times*, 25 September 1996, B5.

8. Ibid.

9. Ibid.

10. Charles C. Mann and Mark L. Plummer, "A Look at New Approaches to Conservation: Grass-Roots Seeds of Compromise," *Washington Post*, 11 October 1998, C3.

11. Robert J. Potts, "Community-based Conservation Draws on Texans' Stewardship," *Austin American-Statesman*, 6 May 1996, A7.

12. John C. Sawhill, "The Nature Conservancy; International Nonprofit Environmental Organization," *Environment* 38, no. 5 (June 1996): 43.

13. Ibid.

14. "The Nature Conservancy Announces $1 Million Grant to Community-Based Conservation Program in the Upper Peninsula," *PR Newswire* (August 29, 1996).

15. Ibid.

16. John D. Aram, book review of *Global Civil Society and Global Environmental Governance: The Politics of Nature from Place to Planet*, The *Journal of Socio-Economics* 26, no. 5 (Sept. 19, 1997): 553.

17. Michael P. Dombeck, Christopher A. Wood, and Jack E. Williams, "Focus: Restoring Watersheds, Rebuilding Communities," *American Forests* 103, no. 4 (Jan. 1, 1998): 26.

18. Ibid.

19. Greg Lashutka, "Columbus Defining New Localism in Environmental Policy: Combines Sound Science with Citizen Participation," *Nation's Cities Weekly* 19, no. 10 (Mar. 11, 1996): 3.

20. Larry Stone, "Efforts to Help Conservation Grow at Grass-Roots Level," *Des Moines Register*, 18 June 1995, 9.

21. "Around Anchorage," *Anchorage Daily News*, 6 March 1997, 2K.
22. Nelson French, "Community-Based Conservation Takes Root along Cannon," *Star Tribune*, 22 April 1995, 18A.
23. "Good Morning, East Tennessee; Something Special We'd Like to Call Your Attention To," *Knoxville News-Sentinel*, 18 June 1997, A2.
24. "Grins; A Look at Recent Events in the News That Please Us," *Knoxville News-Sentinel* (TN), 28 June 1997, A10.
25. Guy Fraker, "The Good Earth/As Earth Day Nears, We Ask: How 'Well' Is Our Planet?" *Pantagraph* (Bloomington, Il.), 19 April 1998, A1.
26. "Help Build Maccamaw Refuge," *Post and Courier* (Charleston, S.C.), 13 January 1998, A8.
27. Editorial, "How to Preserve Open Space," *Deseret News* (Salt Lake City, UT), 17 December 1997, A16.
28. DeWitt John, *Civic Environmentalism: Alternatives to Regulation in States and Communities* (Washington, D.C.: Congressional Quarterly Press, 1994).
29. The National League of Cities (NLC) maintains a database of over 3,000 local government sustainable development programs. For information, call the NLC Municipal Reference Services at (202) 626-3130. For a sample of some of the programs, see "NLC's Database Captures Localities Making Sustainable Waves," *Nation's Cities Weekly* 18, no. 16 (April 17, 1995): 13.
30. Randy Johnson, "Testimony of Randy Johnson, Vice-President of the National Association of Counties," *Federal Document Clearinghouse Congressional Testimony* (February 1, 1995).
31. Peter Overby, "The Politics Of Mining; Ronald Reagan and Ed Meese Left behind a Movement That Could Threaten Environmental, Health, and Safety Regulations," *Common Cause Magazine* (summer 1994): 13.
32. If a silver lining is to be had, it perhaps may be the Burning River Pale Ale, an excellent beer brewed by the Great Lakes Brewing Company.
33. Casey Bukro, "First EPA Chief: Change Overdue; Statutes 'Obsolete,' Says Ruckelshaus," *Chicago Tribune*, 25 December 1995, C1. See also Ralph K. M. Haurwitz, "Bush Ecology Policy Takes Shape; Governor's Environmental Stance Based on State's Rights, Science, Economic Concerns," *Austin-American Statesman*, 26 July 1995, A1.
34. Tom Arrandale, "Cleaning Up at the Polls," *Governing Magazine* (September 1996): 74. See also "Report: Congress Should Share Blame For Onerous Environmental Regulation," *Ground Water Monitor* 11, no. 8 (April 22, 1995).
35. "EPA Seen As Leader in Kindlier Government As Hearing Explores Regulatory Flexibility," *Pesticide and Toxic Chemical News* 21, no. 24 (March 6, 1996).
36. Steven Brostoff, "Report: Fed. Oversight Unwarranted," *National Underwriter, Life and Health* (December 21, 1992): 3; "C.A. Turns Down

Request to Modify Opinion on Unfair Competition Law," *Metropolitan News-Enterprise*, 8 July 1996, 3.

37. Thomas Dye, *American Federalism: Competition among Governments*, 1990, 40; Vincent Ostrom, *American Federalism*, 1991, 91. This argument in defense of federalism may, however, be an unwinnable one given the vast encroachment of the national government into almost every area of governance.

38. Robert Stickels, "Testimony of Robert L. Stickels, Administrator for Sussex County, Delaware on Behalf of the National Association of Counties, National League of Cities, U.S. Conference of Mayors, American Communities for Cleanup Equality, International City/County Management Association, National Association of Towns and Townships; Senate: Environment: Superfund," *Federal Document Clearinghouse Congressional Testimony* (April 24, 1996).

39. Alan Reed, *American City and County* (December, 1993): 14; Chris Collins, "Clinton Budget Aims $175 Million at Colonias," *Gannett News Service* (February 7, 1994); Beverly Cingler, *State and Local Government Review* (winter 1995): 57.

40. *Village of Euclid v. Ambler Realty Co.*, 272 U.S. 365 (1926); Zachary A. Smith, *The Environmental Policy Paradox* (Englewood Cliffs: Prentice Hall, Inc., 1995), 190.

41. Jane S. Shaw, *Real Estate Issues* 21, no. 1 (April 1996): 4.

42. James Walsh, "Rural Areas Grapple with Environmental Regulations," *Star Tribune* (Minneapolis, MN), 16 April 1995, 1B.

43. Sharon Fahrer, "Emissions Trading Programs Making Sense of the Options," *Chemical Engineering* 103, no. 3 (March 1996): 139.

44. Roger Meiners and Bruce Yandle, "Get the Government out of Environmental Control," *USA Today (Magazine)* 124, no. 2612 (May 1996): 70.

45. David Shoenbrod, *Power without Responsibility: How Congress Abuses the People through Delegation* (New Haven: Yale University Press, 1993), 147.

46. Jeff Barnard, "A Grass-Roots Effort to Save Salmon in Oregon; Environment: Fishermen Rebuild Habitat, Restore Streams. Protection Could Hinge on Local Solutions," *Los Angeles Times*, 29 October 1995, 4; Jane S. Shaw, *Real Estate Issues* 21, no. 1 (April 1996): 4.

47. Robert Kasten, "It's a Tough Competition for the Worst Regulation," *The Washington Times*, 13 July 1996, A19.

48. Meiners and Yandle, "Get the Government out of Environmental Control," 70; Jane S. Shaw, *Real Estate Issues*, 4; Gary S. Guzy, "Testimony of Gary S. Guzy, Deputy General Counsel of the Environmental Protection Agency: Senate: Environment," *Federal Document Clearinghouse Congressional Testimony* (July 12, 1995); Michael Davis, "Testimony of Michael Davis, Chief of the Regulatory Branch of the U.S. Army Corps of Engineers: Senate: Environment," *Federal Document Clearinghouse Congressional Testimony* (July 12, 1995).

49. "CFC Production a States' Rights Issue in WA," *Ozone Depletion Network Online Today* (February 5, 1996).

50. Kenneth Chilton and Christopher Boerner, "Smog in America, Integrity of Air Quality and Public Health; Social Science and Public Policy," *Society* 33, no. 5 (July 1996): 51.

51. David Western, "Stewards of the Last Place," *Chicago Tribune*, 19 October 1997, C1.

52. R. Michael Wright, "Africa's Environment: The Final Frontier; Statement of R. Michael Wright, President, the African Wildlife Foundation, before the Sub-Committee on Africa House Committee on International Relations," *Federal Document Clearinghouse Congressional Testimony* (July 17, 1996).

53. Karl Hess Jr., "Wild Success; African Wildlife," *Reason* 29, no. 5 (Oct. 1997): 32.

54. Ibid.

55. Western, "Stewards of the Last Place," C1.

56. Betty Spence, "Getting Along with Elephants," *Christian Science Monitor*, 11 February 1998, 14.

57. Mohamed Suliman, "Civil War in Sudan: The Impact of Ecological Degradation," *International Project on Violence and Conflicts Caused by Environmental Degradation and Peaceful Conflict Resolution* (Dec. 1992). Available from http://ifaa.org/encop1.html; Internet.

58. Rocky Barker, "'Power to Control, Responsibility to Protect;' Yellowstone's Neighbors Take Small Steps to Preserve Grizzly Habitat," *Idaho Statesman*, 18 August 1998, 1A.

59. Brian Child, "The African Elephant Conservation Reauthorization Act of 1997; Statement of Dr. Brian Child to the Subcommittee on Fisheries, Wildlife and Oceans of the Committee on Resources of the U.S. House of Representatives," *Federal Document Clearinghouse Congressional Testimony* (March 13, 1997).

60. Mohamed Suliman, "Civil War in Sudan: The Impact of Ecological Degradation," *International Project on Violence and Conflicts Caused by Environmental Degradation and Peaceful Conflict Resolution* (Dec. 1992). Available from http://ifaa.org/encop1.html; Internet.

61. See Gregory F. Maggio, "Recognizing the Vital Role of Local Communities in International Legal Instruments for Conserving Biodiversity," *UCLA Journal of Environmental Law and Policy* 16 (1997/1998): 179.

62. Karl Hess Jr., "Wild Success, African Wildlife," *Reason* 29, no. 5 (Oct. 1997): 32.

63. Ibid.

64. Peter Alpert, "Integrated Conservation and Development Projects: Examples from Africa," *BioScience* 46, no. 11 (Dec. 1996): 845.

65. Spence, "Getting Along with Elephants," 14.

66. Bron Taylor et al., "Grass-Roots Resistance: The Emergence of Popular Environmental Movements in Less Affluent Countries," 79-80.

67. R. Michael Wright, "Africa's Environment: The Final Frontier; Statement of R. Michael Wright, President, the African Wildlife Foundation, before the Sub-Committee on Africa House Committee on International Relations," *Federal Document Clearinghouse Congressional Testimony* (July 17, 1996).

68. See David E. Graham, "UCSD Professor in Battle for His Kenya Wildlife Post," *San Diego Union-Tribune*, 27 June 1998, B-1.

69. Yvonne Baskin, "There's a New Wildlife Policy in Kenya: Use It or Lose It; Encouragement of Wildlife-Based Business to Preserve Range Lands," *Science* 265, no. 5173 (August 5, 1994): 733. See also Leslie Crawford, "Survey of Kenya," *Financial Times*, 10 May 1994, 7.

70. Njuguna Mutonya, "Kenya; Far-Fetched Dream Now a Jumbo Success," *Africa News* (Oct. 28, 1998): News section.

71. Kirimi Kaberia, "Kenyan Conservation Chief Finds Refuge in Communities' Support," *Washington Times*, 24 November 1994, A12.

72. Jack Bettridge, "The Kenya Example; Zoologist David Western," *Travel-Holiday* 177, no. 7 (Sept. 1994): 27.

73. "Kenya: New Wildlife Head Backs: Community-Based Conservation," *Greenwire* (May 10, 1994).

74. Christoph I. Lang, "Environmental Degradation in Kenya As a Cause of Political Conflict, Social Stress, and Ethnic Tensions," *ENCOP Occasional Paper No. 12* (Center for Security Policy and Conflict Research: Zurich, 1995). Available from http://www.fsk.ethz.ch/fsk/encop/12/en12-con.htm; Internet.

75. "Africa Wildlife Foundation Boss Visits Uganda," *Xinhua News Agency* (August 21, 1995).

76. Rachel Nowak, "Uganda Enlists Locals in the Battle to Save the Gorillas," *Science* 267, no. 5205 (March 24, 1995): 1761.

77. Karl Hess Jr., "Wild Success; African Wildlife," *Reason* 29, no. 5 (Oct. 1997): 32.

78. Rocky Barker, "'Power to Control, Responsibility to Protect'; Yellowstone's Neighbors Take Small Steps to Preserve Grizzly Habitat," *The Idaho Statesman*, 18 August 1998, 1A.

79. Albert Gore, quoted in Matthew Matemba, "Prepared Statement of Matthew Matemba, Coordinator, SADC Wildlife Technical Coordination Unite Director, National Parks and Wildlife Management, Malawi; Before the House Resources Committee, Subcommittee on Fisheries, Wildlife and Oceans," *Federal News Service* (June 20, 1996).

80. "Chinese Dissident and Russian Environmentalist among Seven Grassroots Heroes Named to Receive Fourth Annual Goldman Environmental Prizes," *Canada NewsWire* (April 19, 1993).

81. Chrispin Inamabao, "Namibia; Conservancies Give Muscle to Democracy in Rural Areas," *Africa News* (June 18, 1997).
82. Victoria Butler, "Bushmen at a Crossroads; Kung Bushmen," *International Wildlife* 27, no. 4 (July 1997): N20.
83. Ibid.
84. For an additional example of success in Zambia, see Peter Alpert, "Integrated Conservation and Development Projects: Examples from Africa," *BioScience* 46, no. 11 (Dec. 1996): 845.
85. Gumisai Mutume, "South Africa-Development: LIFE Tackles Urban Decay," *Inter Press Service* (March 3, 1997).
86. Ibid.
87. Bron Taylor et al., "Grass-Roots Resistance: The Emergence of Popular Environmental Movements in Less Affluent Countries," in *Environmental Politics in the International Arena: Movements, Parties, Organizations, and Policy,* ed. Sheldon Kamieniecki (Albany: SUNY Press, 1993), 80.
88. CAMPFIRE and community-based natural resource management (CBNRM) can be found in South Africa, Namibia, Botswana, Malawi, Mozambique, and Zambia. Karl Hess Jr., "Wild Success; African Wildlife," *Reason* 29, no. 5 (Oct. 1997): 32.
89. Stephen Kasere, "Prepared Testimony by the Campfire Association of Zimbabwe before the Senate Committee of Environment and Public Works, Subcommittee on Drinking Water, Fisheries and Wildlife. Re: The U.S. Endangered Species Act and Rural Communities in Africa," *Federal News Service* (July 20, 1995).
90. Some take exception to the hunting of wildlife. An amendment in the U.S. House of Representatives, which was defeated 267-159, would have defunded any portion of CAMPFIRE that dealt with or promoted hunting as a conservation tool. See Rudy Rosen, "Hunting Crucial to Saving Africa Wildlife," *Asbury Park Press* (Neptune, N.J.), 9 September 1997, A22.
91. Rocky Barker, "Njabula Zonda Has Found His Niche in Zimbabwe's New Wildlife Economy," *Idaho Statesman*, 17 August 1998, 7A.
92. Karl Hess Jr., "Wild Success; African Wildlife," *Reason* 29, no. 5 (Oct. 1997): 32.
93. Ibid.
94. "Mali Gets $20 Million Loan to Manage Its Resources," *World Bank Watch* 2, no. 31 (August 24, 1992): 6.
95. R. Michael Wright, "Africa's Environment: The Final Frontier; Statement of R. Michael Wright, President, the African Wildlife Foundation, before the Sub-Committee on Africa House Committee on International Relations," *Federal Document Clearinghouse Congressional Testimony* (July 17, 1996).
96. See Kema Kasalada and Kelvin Shimo, "Zambia; WWF Calls for Conservation of Nature," *Africa News* (April 9, 1998): News section.

97. Paul Wapner, *Environmental Activism and World Civic Politics* (Albany: State University of New York Press, 1996), 93.

98. Rocky Barker, "Conservation That Pays Its Own Way; Idaho Could Learn from Villagers Who Now Protect Wildlife Neigbors," *Idaho Statesman*, 16 August 1998, 1A.

99. Peter Alpert, "Integrated Conservation and Development Projects: Examples from Africa," *BioScience* 46, no. 11 (Dec. 1996): 845.

100. Karl Hess Jr., "Wild Success; African Wildlife," *Reason* 29, no. 5 (Oct. 1997): 32.

101. Bron Taylor et al., "Grass-Roots Resistance: The Emergence of Popular Environmental Movements in Less Affluent Countries," 80.

102. Mahesh Uniyal, "Environment—Asia: Greater Say for Locals in Conservation," *Inter Press Service* (February 11, 1997).

103. For example, two-thirds of protected areas in India have human settlements.

104. Taylor et al., "Grass-Roots Resistance: The Emergence of Popular Environmental Movements in Less Affluent Countries," 80.

105. While local people are now being asked to join in conservation efforts, there is concern that in the male-dominated Asian culture, the voice of women will be excluded. Efforts in Africa and elsewhere have illustrated the importance of women's involvement in any successful community-based conservation effort. This highlights the need for international involvement and the fostering of community-based democracy.

106. Gregory F. Maggio, "Recognizing the Vital Role of Local Communities in International Legal Instruments for Conserving Biodiversity," *UCLA Journal of Environmental Law and Policy* 16 (1997/1998): 179.

107. Taylor et al., "Grass-Roots Resistance: The Emergence of Popular Environmental Movements in Less Affluent Countries," 72.

108. It is very similar to the deep ecology movement in the West. For a study of the effect that this movement has had on American environmental politics, see Phillip F. Cramer, *Deep Environmental Politics: The Role of Radical Environmentalism in Crafting American Environmental Policy* (Westport: Praeger Press, 1998).

109. Ibid., 75-76.

110. Peter Gizewski and Thomas Homer-Dixon, "Environmental Scarcity and Violent Conflict: The Case of Pakistan." Available from http://utl1.library.utoronto.ca/www/pcs/eps/pakistan/pak3.htm; Internet.

111. Bron Taylor et al., "Grass-Roots Resistance: The Emergence of Popular Environmental Movements in Less Affluent Countries," 76-77.

112. Joseph Bingkasan, "Sabah Shows the Way in Efforts to Conserve Natural Resources," *New Straits Times-Management Times*, 17 Oct. 1998, Emerging Markets Datafile.

113. "Agri Bits," *Business Daily*, 15 July 1998, Emerging Markets Datafile.

114. Executive Order No. 247 of 1995, "Prescribing Guidelines and Establishing a Regulatory Framework for the Prospecting of Biological and Genetic Resources."

115. Atiya Achakulwisut, "Testing Times," *Bangkok Post*, 20 Feb. 1998.

116. Ibid.

117. Ibid.

118. Taylor et al., "Grass-Roots Resistance: The Emergence of Popular Environmental Movements in Less Affluent Countries," 78.

119. Elizabeth Economy, "The Case Study of China: Reforms and Resources: The Implications for State Capacity in the PRC," *Occasional Paper, Project on Environmental Scarcities, State Capacity, and Civil Violence* (Cambridge: American Academy of Arts and Sciences and the University of Toronto, 1997). Available from http://utl1.library.utoronto.ca/www/pcs/state/china/china1.htm; Internet.

120. "Community-Based Strategy for Conservation of Caohai: Villagers Can Be Protectors and Beneficiaries or Destroyers and Sufferers," *The Asian Manager*, 3 Oct. 1997, Business section.

121. Ibid.

122. Lou Waters and Gary Strieker, "Environmental Conservation Scores Unlikely Victory in China," *CNN Today* (April 22, 1998, 1:46PM Eastern Time), Transcript #98042205V13.

123. "Community-Based Strategy for Conservation of Caohai: Villagers Can Be Protectors and Beneficiaries or Destroyers and Sufferers," *The Asian Manager*, 3 Oct. 1997, Business section.

124. Dalai Lama, "Earth: A Conservation District in the Universe; Dalai Lama interview," *Whole Earth*, no. 91 (Dec. 22, 1997): 38.

125. Ibid.

126. "Bradshaw Announces the University of New Brunswick's Participation in a Community Environmental Conservation Program in China and Vietnam," *Canada NewsWire* (Oct. 24, 1997): Domestic News section.

127. Charles Victor Barber, "The Case Study of Indonesia." Available from http://utl1.library.utoronto.ca/www/pcs/state/indon/indonsum.htm; Internet.

128. Ibid.

129. Ibid.

130. Ibid.

131. Thomas Homer-Dixon, "The Ingenuity Gap: Can Poor Countries Adapt to Resource Scarcity?" *Population and Development Review* 21, no. 3 (Sept. 1995): 591.

9

Putting It All Together

The previous chapters highlight the ability of local communities to protect the environment. But even the most ardent proponents of local action realize that localities cannot do it alone. This book proposes a synergistic linkage paradigm as a means to solve environmental degradation. A synergistic linkage paradigm views nature as nature views itself—an interconnected web of life. When we approach nature, we must do so likewise. Environmental problems interrelate much like species in an environment do. When one problem is exacerbated, others are also affected. Similarly, when we address a single environmental issue, others are affected, often in negative ways. Thus, to solve environmental degradation, we must adopt a holistic approach. Implementing such an approach is easier said than done.

To implement a holistic way of solving environmental degradation, we need an equally holistic approach. Such an integrated approach requires more than just international action. It requires utilization of the complete web of environmental actors from international regimes to community groups. On the surface, such a diverse group of actors appears to conflict with the ideals of holistic action. Community-based environmental action emphasizes local and isolated policies while international action touts the need for holistic responses. This inherent tension arises from the clash between centralized and local control; it would appear that a centralized system of policy administration could incorporate a whole ecosystem approach more easily than if attempted at the local level. Norma Myers explains that it is appropriate to split up the world into manageable packages such as states or communities so long as they remember the overriding rationale that they are but a part of a large, interconnected system. Unfortunately, Myers notes, each state or community inherently becomes more occupied with its own portion of the whole and loses sight of the larger perspective.[1] This emphasizes the need for global frameworks.

Governance from above has the ability to coordinate the efforts of peoples from around the world. It can bring in experts from various states and nongovernmental organizations that can help policymakers make the most informed decisions while being mindful of synergistic linkages. The difficulty in adopting a linkage paradigm at the local level lies in the fact that pollution does not respect borders and thus one community's pollution may quickly spill over into many other localities. Without control over the pollution from other communities, it is difficult for any single locality to protect its local ecosystem. Furthermore, though communities can coordinate with others, it is much easier to coordinate the efforts of 180 states than to bring together 100,000 communities.

But community action may be the key to a linkage paradigm. A whole ecosystem approach to environmental degradation increases local action. In order to incorporate linkages into daily life, people must be both aware and active. The examples of community-based conservation illustrate that this is most likely to occur at the local level. Large social structures, though able to bring people together, tend to detach humans from their natural environments. This detachment is partly responsible for the current non-linkage mind-set. The "sheer size of contemporary political, economic, and social organizations is responsible for present environmental dangers because large impersonal constructs diminish personal dignity and engender human dependence."[2]

If human society were to adopt a synergistic linkage paradigm, localism would be reborn because a synergistic linkage paradigm naturally spurs bioregionalism. Unlike political boundaries, bioregions are geographically defined ecoregions. They incorporate the natural characteristics of the ecosystem into the boundaries of human communities. Bioregionalism allows humans to live with the land instead of against it. Through recognition of the linkages between various environmental problems as well as between the environment and society, community action is inspired and garnered. A whole ecosystem approach begins (and perhaps ends) with community involvement and community-based conservation. While authors such as Myers feel that communities will lose sight of the larger environmental picture, the examples explored in this book indicate otherwise when global frameworks are involved. The slogan of "think globally, act locally" is perhaps more appropriate today than it was thirty years ago.[3] As people begin to think globally in a linkage mind-set, they realize that they must act to preserve the Earth. These actions will inevitably occur at the community and substate levels.

Integrated conservation and development projects (ICDPs) attempt to embody the ideals of a linkage paradigm. They focus on both biological conservation and human development. More than one hundred ICDPs have been described, including more than fifty in at least twenty countries in sub-Saharan Africa. These projects stress the linkages between the environment and development. Additionally, they seek to empower local communities. They seek to promote inherent local self-interest in conservation while spreading public awareness, removing disincentives, and galvanizing community action.[4] ICDPs provide empirical evidence of how a linkage paradigm can promote and preserve localism.

A synergistic linkage paradigm asks the individual to become aware of his or her surroundings. It forces international and national governments to educate and empower their people. It makes state governments realize that they are perhaps not the best actors for environmental protection. It asks people to recognize the linkage between their own well-being and that of the environment. It asks each of us to change our values and to take action in defense of our future and the futures of generations to come. Thus, it is able to inspire local action and community-based conservation efforts. Just as a patchwork makes a much larger quilt, bioregionalism makes a healthy biosphere.

Linkages via an Integrated Approach

Linkages do not have to be ignored when the world is split up into manageable compartments.[5] The very fact that they are indeed manageable means that an integrated approach is the only way to incorporate a linkage paradigm. Problems may only be observable at the global level but only be manageable at the local level. Perhaps the greatest impediment to the adoption of a whole ecosystem approach lies in the vast nature of the problem. The variables facing the international policymaker are so numerous that the task appears to be overwhelming. How is one to balance the needs for development with the strains of population growth, ethnic problems, and environmental concerns? A linkage paradigm is not possible solely at the international level when so many interest groups are in a constant state of competition.

At the local level, a linkage paradigm is a less daunting concept. However, the need for a linkage paradigm is also less evident. This is why an integrated approach is so important. While a community can come together to address common concerns, it first needs to understand why it must come together. Global frameworks can spur such actions. They allow communities to discover the relationship between their various problems and implement policies that are community, and not issue, oriented. Both point and nonpoint sources of pollution can be addressed at the local level in such a manner that it is possible to recognize the human component and the linkages between the different environmental issues. Furthermore, through community-based conservation, people learn new sets of values, values that are more ecocentric and less anthropocentric. Localism builds a constructive relationship to the land. No longer is environmental protection a shell value; rather, it moves into the core.

Linkages require a basic shift in people's perception of environmental protection. Some feel that this broad-scope shift is not likely to occur until there is massive buildup of signals from the economy, "triggering a creeping revolution in institutional systems."[6] Localism is a necessary component in the implementation of a linkage paradigm. Community-based conservation intrinsically causes individuals to think within a linkage mind-set. The examples discussed in this book attest to the positive relationship between localism and linkages. The idea of community is enlarged to incorporate the environment (thus linking development with the environment). Community becomes an ecology of life forms: energy and information webs that include humans as dependent members.[7] At the community level, humans learn that they must respect and uncover linkages or risk their own survival and sustainability. The benefits of such thinking are numerous; "the instability of human relations with the environment can be used to explain both cultural and ecological transformation . . . once we begin to think about . . . ever-changing environments, we are led to consider how economic institutions, political and gender relations, intellectual leadership and moral imperatives may have been involved in the process of environmental adaptation."[8] Environmentalism depends on incorporating human needs into environmental protection and human needs depend on incorporating environmental protection into humanism.[9]

Richard Falk discusses the global governance implications of environmental protection in his doctrine of humane governance. He notes that the challenge of humane governance is to connect development with the stewardship of nature in such a manner as to ensure social and economic justice for all peoples while maintaining the spiritual connection between people and the land.[10] The following section illustrates how an integrated approach to environmental protection that incorporates global frameworks and local solutions is able to fulfill Falk's vision.

Examples of an Integrated Approach

A synergistic linkage paradigm is presently emerging within an integrated approach. Research has begun that attempts to understand the interactions between various actors at the local, regional, and global levels.[11] This research is being followed by changes in policy that incorporate actors at all levels in a web of integrated action. Recent international agreements reflect a change in perspective on the status and utilization of local communities in facilitating environmental protection.[12]

At the Earth Summit in Rio de Janeiro, the states of the world stressed the need for local action within an international framework. Principle 10 of the Rio Declaration provides that:

> [e]nvironmental issues are best handled with the participation of all concerned citizens, at the relevant level. At the national level, each individual shall have appropriate access to information concerning the environment that is held by public authorities, including information on hazardous materials and activities in their communities, and the opportunity to participate in decision-making processes by making information widely available.[13]

Principle 22 of the Rio Declaration expands on this concept and explains that:

> [i]ndigenous people and their communities and other local communities have a vital role to play in environmental management and development because of their knowledge and traditional practices. States should recognize and duly support their identity, culture and interests and enable their effective participation in the achievement of sustainable development.[14]

To effectuate such policies, the international community created and endorsed a plan of action called Agenda 21.[15] Chapter 28 of Agenda 21 emphasizes local initiatives. It explains that "[b]ecause so many of the problems and solutions being addressed by Agenda 21 have their roots in local activities, the participation and cooperation of local authorities will be a determining factor in fulfilling its objectives."[16] Additionally, "[a]s the level of governance closest to the people, they play a vital role in educating, mobilizing and responding to the public to promote sustainable development."[17] The chapter directs local authorities to undertake a consultative process with their populations and calls for the international community to initiate a consultative process aimed at increasing cooperation between local authorities.[18]

The chapter also directs local authorities, in connection with citizens, local organizations, and private enterprises, to develop and adopt a local Agenda 21.[19] It calls for partnerships between relevant organs and organizations such as the U.N. Development Programme, the United Nations Centre for Human Settlements and the United Nations Environment Program, the World Bank, regional banks, the International Union of Local Authorities, the World Association of the Major Metropolises, Summit of Great Cities of the World, the United Towns Organization, and other relevant partners. The goal of this partnership is to increase international support for local programs and initiatives.[20] Agenda 21 significantly embodies an integrated approach that creates an international framework for local action. Unfortunately, the international community has been slow to implement Agenda 21, although some positive signs are emerging.[21] Conferences such as the Local Government Association Conference Local Agenda 21 are springing up throughout the world.

There are other signs of integrated approaches emerging throughout the world. For example, President Clinton participated in an environmental roundtable in the spring of 1998 in which he was joined by five leading environmental experts from the continent of Africa. Two of the themes that emerged from the dialogue included the linkage between poverty and environment and the importance of engaging communities in managing natural resources and protecting the environment.[22] The U.S. is also spending $80 million a year for environmental assistance in Africa, much of which is appropriated for community-based natural resource management. Additionally, a relatively new program called Green Communities for Africa attempts to provide additional tools for local communities in Africa to take environmental considerations into account when making decisions.[23] NASA is also participating in international efforts designed to provide local communities in Africa with scientific information so they can protect their environment.

These efforts followed international action on desertification, which continues to be a large problem in Africa caused by overgrazing, from agricultural practices such as monocropping, overutilization of limited water supplies, and drought.[24] The Desertification Convention[25] contains innovative provisions that encourage local governments and communities to become involved in efforts to fight the spread of desertification.[26] Article 5 of the convention calls on the parties to "promote awareness and facilitate the participation of local populations . . . in efforts to combat desertification and mitigate the effects of drought."[27]

The Desertification Convention is not the only international effort that embraces an integrated approach. The Convention on International Trade in Endangered Species,[28] otherwise known as CITES, is an international effort to conserve the planet's biodiversity. The recent evolution of the treaty illustrates the move toward an integrated approach to environmental protection.[29] The executive director of the United Nations Environment Program explains that "[y]ou need an international framework of law and regulation, but if we're going to have meaningful change, we've got to change people's attitudes and behaviors. You don't necessarily do that by simply trying to police them."[30] The director points to the example of Costa Rica where local people were trained to conduct biodiversity studies. Species protection works because the people understand the value of biodiversity and the biodiversity, people, and income stays within the community.[31]

Some groups, however, criticize CITES because it allows communities to make decisions regarding wildlife management. The Humane Society is one group that expresses concern over the trade in species.[32] In response to such criticism, CITES is spurring a high degree of cooperation and solidarity among southern Africa community groups and nongovernmental organizations, which have formed a group called Southern African Forum for Communities and Nongovernmental Organizations (SAFCAN). The group hopes to develop common positions on the need for sustainable utilization of natural resources. One of the driving factors that led to the formation of the group was the perception that animal rights groups were blocking efforts of community-based conservation and development.[33] The group illustrates how an integrated approach to environmental protection can work by bringing together actors at all levels.

Another species conservation treaty, the Convention on Biological Diversity,[34] also attempts to involve community-based conservation efforts. The preamble to the convention notes "the close and traditional dependence of many indigenous and local communities embodying traditional lifestyles on biological resources."[35] Although the convention does not explicitly include local communities as beneficiaries of the equitable sharing, the IUCN commentary on the convention indicates that local communities are by implication among the beneficiaries.[36] Article 8(j) of the convention calls for the respect and preservation of indigenous and local knowledge, innovations, and practices. The article also requires the parties to promote "wider application [of indigenous and local knowledge, innovations, and practices] with the approval and involvement of the holders of such knowledge, innovations and practices and encourage the equitable sharing of the benefits arising from the utilization of such knowledge, innovations and practices."[37] Although scholars are divided about the extent to which the Convention on Biological Diversity embodies community-based conservation, the convention does illustrate the emergence of local participation in the protection of biodiversity. Consider the words of the Philippine Secretary of the Environment and Natural Resources at the first follow-up meeting to the convention:

> We are . . . concerned with the rights of our indigenous peoples, farmers and local communities are being disregarded in the guise of intellectual property rights. We therefore consider it imperative for the conference of the Parties to find a mechanism, in the context of implementing the Biodiversity Convention, to recognize and respect the rights of these sectors. We emphasize particularly the need to ensure that indigenous and local communities give their prior informed consent to any biodiversity prospecting and the imperative that the benefits be shared not only with the state but with these communities.[38]

More and more, calls for an integrated approach to environmental protection are being answered. The Framework Convention on Climate Change includes provisions for the promotion and facilitation at the national and subnational level for "(i) the development and implementation of educational and public awareness programmes on climate change and its effects; (ii) public access to information on climate change and its effects; and (iii) public participation in addressing climate change and its effects and developing adequate responses."[39]

Policymakers and researchers must now engage in an effort to link the local with the global. To this point, most of the research concerning climate change has been top-down. For example, the Intergovernmental Panel on Climate Change (IPCC) amassed years of research and developed approaches to abate global warming.[40] Policymakers, however, are beginning to realize that actions to abate greenhouse gases are never global, and most are not even carried out at the national level. Real change in the level of greenhouse gas accumulation occurs when individuals and organizations modify their behavior, change their activities, and employ different technologies.[41] All of these decisions are ones best made at the local level.

One major example of such a bottom-up approach is a project in which many regional organizations and universities are sharing their scientific competence and local knowledge to determine the linkages between individual localities and global climate change. The project is sponsored by the Mission to Planet Earth program of the National Aeronautics and Space Administration through the Association of American Geographers. The project is determining how local places contribute to global change and what control local institutions have to accomplish mitigation and adaptation policies.[42]

Research is also under way throughout the United States to estimate local contributions to changes in land use and atmospheric conditions. Localities are developing new methods for measuring greenhouse gas emissions. The results of these studies are being used to demonstrate the many "ways in which local emissions (and their evolution over time) differ from those of states, provinces, and nations, and thus argue for incorporating local knowledge in global change research."[43]

One of the earliest local efforts to measure and affect climate change was the International Council for Local Environmental Initiatives (ICLEI). The ICLEI is an international environmental agency established to assist local governments. It now serves as a clearinghouse on environmental protection policies, programs, and techniques being implemented at the local level by local institutions. In 1990, the ICLEI launched a project that fosters local reductions to greenhouse gas emissions. The project started with twelve North American and European cities that pledged to reduce emissions. In 1995, ICLEI established the Cities for Climate Protection Campaign to include the growing number of local governments committed to reducing greenhouse gas emissions.[44] Participants were given case studies, handbooks, and specialized software for quantifying emissions and emissions reduction efforts. The U.S. Environmental Protection Agency also sponsored a series of workshops in which participants shared their experiences and received training in the implementation of local efforts. In a speech to the United Nations General Assembly, President Clinton remarked that:

> The science is clear and compelling. . . . No nation can escape this danger or evade its responsibility to confront it. We must all do our part—industrial nations that emit the largest quantities of greenhouse gases, and developing nations whose emissions are growing rapidly. Here in the United States, we must do better. . . . We must create new technologies and develop new strategies. In order to do our part, we must first convince the American people and the Congress that the climate problem is real and imminent.[45]

To convince the American people and the Congress, local communities must become involved. They are the link to changing individual perceptions and attitudes necessary to implement real action on global climate change. This is but one benefit of an integrated approach: local communities who are closest to the people are able to develop and implement plans with the resources from national and international bodies.

When the international community met in Kyoto to discuss international efforts on global climate change, ICLEI surveyed participants in the Cities for Climate Protection Campaign about their progress. It found that numerous cities had completed emission inventories, adopted emissions reduction targets, and implemented measures to reduce carbon dioxide and methane.[46] In addition, local governments did not just let their results speak for themselves. Just as the states gathered in Kyoto to discuss "international" approaches to global climate change, so too did the leaders of over 130 local governments. The conference brought local leaders together a month before the high-profile U.N. Conference on Global Climate. It was the fourth such local leaders' summit on climate change.[47] The conference illustrates how local communities can operate within international frameworks to benefit both the local and international communities.[48]

The World Bank is also beginning to realize that global change can best be affected by local initiatives. The global problem of greenhouse gas emission is also a local health problem. The World Bank is redirecting its efforts by finding ways to demonstrate the global and local external costs arising from air pollution. The Bank and others helped to develop an environmental assessment tool that through satellite imagery can depict greenhouse gas and acid rain "hot spots" to local regulators throughout Asia.[49]

An integrated approach is also developing with respect to the protection of coral reefs. The U.S. Coral Reef Task Force is a national program chaired by the secretary of the interior and the deputy secretary of commerce. The Task Force is designed to bring the management, policy, and scientific expertise from certain United States agencies to coral reef conservation and management efforts around the world. The strength in the program lies in its approach to "encourage the empowerment of local communities so that they can manage their own resources through open, participatory, and democratic processes. Local communities, national governments, and private businesses must work together to develop appropriate, sustainable resource practices."[50]

A report by the World Resources Institute found that 58 percent of the world's coral reefs are potentially threatened by human activities. In addition to U.S. efforts to create an integrated approach, the international community formed the International Coral Reef Initiative (ICRI). The initiative raises global and local awareness of the threats to coral reefs and encourages action at all levels to address those threats. In 1995, the ICRI issued a "Call to Action" for the conservation of coral reefs as well as a "Framework for Action" to mobilize local, regional, and international action on the problem of coral reef destruction.[51] The integrated approach combines the benefits of local ingenuity and international resources.

Water is another issue that requires an integrated approach to resolve both environmental insecurity and degradation. A recent international conference in Germany concluded that water can be used as a catalyst for regional cooperation and local empowerment instead of conflict. Experts came from Europe, southern Africa, the Middle East, and Asia. They agreed that the availability of water and access to its use were critical to both the economic and environmental well-being of entire regions. Water is a problem particularly adaptive to local action because the effects of pollution and shortages personally affect millions, if not billions, of individuals. Eighty percent of illnesses and one-third of deaths in developing countries are due to polluted water.[52] Water represents an issue that requires an integrated approach. Because rivers and watersheds are rarely confined within a single state or community, regional and international assistance is required. On the other hand, local communities are best able to implement plans of action. This is exemplified by the number of river and lake projects described in chapter 8. It is time for policymakers at all levels to support international partnerships between international agencies, states, localities, nongovernmental organizations, and private business to address water issues.[53]

Examples of an integrated approach are also emerging at the regional level. An interdisciplinary group that included anthropologists, biologists, environmentalists, historians, agriculturists, and lawyers, issued the Baguio Declaration.[54] The declaration acknowledged the need for broad-based structural reforms at the national and international levels to facilitate the operation of community-based conservation efforts.[55] The declaration called for the development of new and innovative community-based resource management systems as an alternative to state control. The conference is an example of an integrated approach whereby experts from many different fields from many different countries come together to create frameworks within which local governments may effectively operate.[56]

The examples throughout this chapter illustrate the potential of an integrated approach to environmental protection. Furthermore, they show how coordinated local and international action can overcome the most serious environmental threats facing humanity.

Conclusion

Even though global environmental problems are common issues for all of humankind, the solution to them is not. Only an integrated approach is able to implement a synergistic linkage paradigm by combining local ingenuity with international resources. This chapter illustrated some preliminary attempts to incorporate an integrated approach into environmental protection. The following chapter explores barriers to further implementation. However, it also highlights the benefits an integrated approach brings not only to environmental protection, but also to the social, political, and moral well-being of the world community.

Notes

1. Norma Myers, "The Question of Linkages in Environment and Development," *BioScience* 43, no. 5 (May 1993): 302.

2. Paul Wapner, *Environmental Activism and World Civic Politics* (Albany: State University of New York Press, 1996), 34.

3. Perhaps a more appropriate slogan would be, "think linkages, act locally."

4. Peter Alpert, "Integrated Conservation and Development Projects: Examples from Africa," *BioScience* 46, no. 11 (Dec. 1996): 845.

5. Myers, "The Question of Linkages in Environment and Development," 302.

6. Ibid.

7. C. A. Bowers, *Education, Cultural Myths, and the Ecological Crisis: Toward Deep Changes* (Albany: SUNY Press, 1993), 167.

8. Gregory Maddox, James L. Giblin, and Isaria N. Kimambo, *Custodians of the Land: Ecology and Culture in the History of Tanzania* (Athens: Ohio University Press, 1996), 1-2.

9. Raymond E. Grizzle, "Environmentalism Should Include Human Ecological Needs," *BioScience* 44, no. 4 (April 1994): 263.

10. Richard Falk, *On Human Governance: Toward a New Global Politics* (University Park: The Pennsylvania State University Press, 1995), 252-253.

11. Jill Jager, "The Human Side of Global Change; the 1997 Open Meetings of the Human Dimensions of Global Environmental Change Research Community," *Environment* 40, no. 1 (Jan. 11, 1998),: 25.

12. See, e.g., Non-Legally Binding Authoritative Statement of Principles for a Global Consensus on the Management, Conservation and Sustainable Development of All Types of Forests, 31 I.L.M. 881 (1992), United Nations Commission on Human Rights Sub-Commission on Prevention of Discrimination and Protection of Minorities: Draft United Nations Declaration on the Rights of Indigenous People, 34 I.L.M. 541 (1994). See also Gregory F. Maggio, "Recognizing the Vital Role of Local Communities in International Legal Instruments for Conserving Biodiversity," *UCLA Journal of Environmental Law and Policy* 16 (1997/1998): 179.

13. Rio Declaration on Environment and Development, June 13, 1992, princ. 10, 31 I.L.M. 874, 878.

14. Ibid., princ. 22, 31 I.L.M. 874.

15. Nicholas A. Robinson, ed., *Agenda 21: Earth's Action Plan: Annotated* (New York: Oceana Publications, Inc., 1993).

16. Ibid., para. 28.1.

17. Ibid., para. 28.1. Some criticize the entire notion of sustainable development as nothing but a guise for business as normal. They explain that the rhetoric is deceptively used in order to achieve greater profits in a gentler way. Ronald E. Purser et al., "Limits to Anthropocentrism: Toward an Ecocentric Organization Paradigm?" *Academy of Management Review* 20, no. 4 (Oct. 1995): 1053.

18. Nicholas A. Robinson, ed., *Agenda 21: Earth's Action Plan: Annotated* (New York: Oceana Publications, Inc., 1993), Para. 28.2(a)-(d).

19. Ibid., para. 28.3.

20. Ibid., para. 28.4.

21. "Working Together to Create Sustainable Local Communities," *M2 Presswire* (January 15, 1998). For information on how the World Bank is attempting to incorporate the same, see Charles E. Di Leva, "International Environmental Law and Development," *Georgetown International Environmental Law Review* 10 (winter 1998): 501 ("To the extent that the Rio Conference underscored the fundamental need for broad-based public participation in environmental and social issues, the Bank's environmental assessment policy serves to implement these same principles. Perhaps here the Bank can have the most impact toward allowing the poorest citizens an opportunity for involvement in the development projects which affect their lives.")

22. David Sandalow, "Transcript of Press Briefing by David Sandalow, National Security Council Director of Environmental Affairs," *U.S. Newswire* (March 31, 1998).

23. Ibid.

24. Ibid. Also note that desertification, while a problem within and of itself, is also the expression of other environmental problems such as global warming. Attempts to combat desertification are beginning to incorporate an integrated approach.

25. United Nations Convention to Combat Desertification in Those Countries Experiencing Serious Drought and/or Desertification, Particularly in Africa, June 17, 1994, 33 I.L.M. 132.

26. David Sandalow, "Transcript of Press Briefing by David Sandalow, National Security Council Director of Environmental Affairs," *U.S. Newswire* (March 31, 1998).

27. United Nations Convention to Combat Desertification in Those Countries Experiencing Serious Drought and/or Desertification, Particularly in Africa, June 17, 1994, 33 I.L.M. 132, 1335.

28. Convention on International Trade in Endangered Species of Wild Fauna and Flora, Mar. 3, 1983, 27 U.S.T. 1087, 993 U.N.T.S. 243.

29. However, nothing in the text of the CITES addresses the issue of local community harvesting and consumption of wildlife for domestic subsistence or commercial purposes. Of the pre-CITES broad-based wildlife conservation regimes, only the 1968 African Convention on the Conservation of Nature and Natural Resources, Sept. 15, 1968, 1001 U.N.T.S. 3, acknowledged the role of local populations in conservation efforts. See Gregory F. Maggio, "Recognizing the Vital Role of Local Communities in International Legal Instruments for Conserving Biodiversity," *UCLA Journal of Environmental Law and Policy* 16 (1997/1998): 179.

30. Elizabeth Dowdeswell, "Interview: UNEP's Dowdeswell Discusses Species Issues," *Greenwire* (November 17, 1994), Focus section.

31. Ibid.

32. Morris Nyakudy and Lewis Machipisa, "Environment-CITES: Shifting from Restrictions to Rewards?" *Inter Press Service* (June 20, 1997).

33. Emmanuel Koro, "Zimbabwe: CITES Harare Conference Dubbed Most Difficult," *Inter Press Service* (June 13, 1997).

34. Convention on Biological Diversity, June 5, 1992, 31 I.L.M. 818 (1992).

35. Ibid., at prmbl., para. 12.

36. See Gregory F. Maggio, "Recognizing the Vital Role of Local Communities in International Legal Instruments for Conserving Biodiversity," *UCLA Journal of Environmental Law and Policy* 16 (1997/1998): 179.

37. Convention on Biodiversity, at art. 8(j).

38. Philippine Secretary of Environment and Natural Resources, "Ensuring the Diversity of Life: A Call for Partnership between States, Peoples, and Communities," text on file at World Resources Institute, Washington, D.C.

39. Framework Convention on Climate Change, May 9, 1992, 31 I.L.M. 849, Art. 6.

40. Robert W. Kates and Ralph D. Torrie, "Global Changes in Local Places," *Environment* 40, no. 2 (March 1998): 5.

41. Ibid.

42. Ibid.

43. Ibid.

44. Ibid.

45. William J. Clinton, "UN General Assembly Is Told Man-Made Greenhouse Gas Have Reached Highest Concentrations in 200,000 Years," *M2 Presswire* (June 30, 1997).

46. Robert W. Kates and Ralph D. Torrie, "Global Changes in Local Places," *Environment* 40, no. 2 (March 1998): 5.

47. "International Local Government Leaders Open Climate Forum," *BBC Summary of World Broadcasts* (Nov. 7, 1997): Asia-Pacific section.

48. See "UN General Assembly Is Told Man-Made Greenhouse Gas Have Reached Highest Concentrations in 200,000 Years," *M2 Presswire* (June 30, 1997). The report includes statements made at the General Assembly by representatives from over fifty countries on the status of their efforts to combat greenhouse gas emissions. For example, Oscar Ceville, the vice minister of the presidency of Panama describes how Panama is carrying out its plans within a local and international framework. It also includes a call from the representative of Korea for implementation of Agenda 21 through the development of a sense of common responsibility by the international community.

49. Charles E. Di Leva, "International Environmental Law and Development," *Georgetown International Environmental Law Review* 10 (winter 1998): 501.

50. "U.S. Coral Reef Task Force to Strengthen International Action to Protect Coral Reef," *M2 Presswire* (Oct. 21, 1998) (quoting David Hales, the deputy assistant administrator of USAID for the Global Environment Center).

51. Ibid.

52. Ramesh Juara, "Environment: Conference Urges Water As Catalyst for Cooperation," *Inter Press Service* (Mar. 5, 1998) (citing a study circulated at the conference).

53. Ibid.; John Brodribb, "Mission Earth," *New Scientist* (Dec. 13, 1997).

54. See Baguio Declaration, NGO Workshop on Effective Strategies for Promoting Community-Based Forest Management: Lessons Learned from Asia and other Regions, Villa la Maja Inn (May 19-23, 1994) (transcript available at Center for International Environmental Law, Washington, D.C.)

55. Gregory F. Maggio, "Recognizing the Vital Role of Local Communities in International Legal Instruments for Conserving Biodiversity," *UCLA Journal of Environmental Law and Policy* 16 (1997/1998): 179.

56. It is also important to realize that community-based conservation does not have to exclude national actors. Take for instance the American Heritage Rivers Initiative. The initiative was proposed by President Clinton and was approved by the U.S. Conference of Mayors. The program will provide federal assistance to community-led river association and revitalization programs. Ten rivers have been selected to serve as models for community-based conservation efforts in the future. "U.S. Conference of Mayors Approves Resolution Supporting American Heritage Rivers Initiative; American Rivers Applauds Mayors in Boosting Local Economies through River Restoration," *PR Newswire* (June 24, 1997).

10

Getting Past the Hurdles and Reaping the Rewards

Times of crisis tend to bring individuals, peoples, and communities together. The threat of environmental security is starting to bring both international and local communities together. Coming together, however, is just the first step. Although the world came together at the Rio Earth Summit, there has been little advance on many issues since then.[1] This failure can be traced, in part, to a lack of effectiveness. As global efforts fail to achieve their stated goals, policymakers at both the local and national levels become disillusioned. This disillusionment is but one of the barriers that stands in the way of creating an integrated approach to environmental protection. Other obstacles include ethical, ideological, political, economic, and logistical barriers.[2] These impediments are evidenced in Jean-Jacques Rousseau's story of the stag hunt. Rousseau describes the situation:

> If it was a matter of hunting a deer, everyone well realized that he must remain faithfully at his post; but if a hare happened to pass within the reach of one of them, we cannot doubt that he would have gone off in pursuit of it without scruple and, having caught his own prey, he would have cared very little about having caused his companions to lose theirs.[3]

The primary difference between this anecdote and the environmental problems that face the world today is that it is no longer a question of hunting a deer or a hare, but rather a question of making the environment safe for all future deer and hare. For unless everyone stands faithfully at the post, there will no longer be any deer, much less a hare.[4]

Ethical Barriers

Ethics play an important role in the formation and implementation of environmental policy. Ethical barriers exist at two levels: a personal level and a policy level. Presently, thinking about the environment is centered on human needs and human concerns. Anthropocentrism is the belief "that there is a clear and morally relevant dividing line between humankind and the rest of nature, that humankind is the only principal source of value or meaning in the world."[5] Anthropocentrism is used to justify policies that exploit the social and natural environment. Such attitudes are closely tied with the Lockean view of the environment where land is seen as potential real estate, an idle resource that is without value until it is "used" by humans.[6] Psychologists note that an anthropocentric viewpoint creates egocentric orientation and organizations that have difficulty in understanding and perceiving that they are "nested within biological ecosystems and interconnected with biogeochemical cycles."[7] In other words, humans are unable to observe the most basic linkages, the linkages in which they are a part.

Anthropocentric views tend to be accentuated by monotheistic religions such as Judaism, Christianity, and Islam.[8] Genesis provides the mandate of "dominion"[9] and Psalm 8 explains "[w]hat is man that thou art mindful of him? Thou has made him a little lower than the angels and put everything else underneath his feet."[10] Some interpret these religions to encourage humans to view themselves as "special" creatures of God, distinct from the environment in which they operate. They feel religion charges them with replenishing and subduing the earth by having dominion over all living things.[11] This belief holds that the "universe was created for mankind's benefit."[12] This view has legitimized exploitation of nature for improvement of human life.[13]

Such views have also frustrated attempts to tackle problems of rapid and unsustainable population growth. In October 1999 the world's population reached 6 billion. In his book, *Juggernaut: Growth on a Finite Planet*, Lindsey Grant, the former Department of State coordinator for the Global 2000 Report to the President, explains that the population growth juggernaut is devastating to human societies at every level. For example, "[p]oor nations endure famine and destruction of their resources. Emerging nations struggle with the problems of industrialization. Affluent countries face joblessness, failing social structures, growing disparities between the rich and poor, ethnic conflict, and environmental degradation."[14] A faith in growth perspective "ignores the fact that our growth curve in key areas, such as agriculture, forestry, fisheries, and biodiversity, has stopped or begun to decline."[15] Humans must learn to view the Earth as a unified ecosystem and humankind as a part of that system rather than its master. Such a view is consistent with Judeo-Christian views, and in fact, many argue that they are mandated by such views.

In fact, as environmental degradation has spread, Christianity, Islam, and Judaism have increasingly emphasized the importance of a harmonious relationship between humans and other natural entities. For example, the National Council of Churches has urged ratification of a global warming treaty. The Central Conference of American Rabbis has declared that the survival of the redwood-dominated Headwaters Forests in California is "part of the convenant with the Creator."[16] Religion may even assist in the creation of a linkage paradigm. It provides a framework for global action at the local level. Religion has the ability to bring millions, if not billions, of people together for a common purpose. Then, at the local level, churches can carry out the ecological mandate through community programs. Religious institutions are already active at the local level. The Community Lutheran Church in Sterling, Virginia, established a habitat trail with 300 native plants while the Jewish Temple Beth El in East Amherst, New York, helped organize local residents to create a pesticide registry.[17] Religion can and should be a positive force in implementing an integrated approach to environmental protection that transcends both the personal and policy levels.

Other obstacles remain, however. Anthropocentrism is embedded at the international policy level. For example, the Rio Declaration at the Earth Summit asserted the claim that "[h]uman beings are at the centre of concerns."[18] Ethics are inextricably intertwined with the search and implementation of any solution to environmental degradation. Often, the prevailing ethical systems do not incorporate a synergistic linkage paradigm; rather, they are dominated by anthropocentric values.[19]

In order to adequately address the global environmental crisis we must incorporate ethical considerations into our international environmental policy.[20] Many environmentalists "are now calling for a moral revolution that would incorporate ecological values into our culture."[21] Lynton Caldwell, in this book *International Environmental Policy*, makes the suggestion that the breakdown of the world's ecology is causing a shift in environmental sensibilities tantamount to a second Copernican revolution.[22]

In the first Copernican revolution, the belief that our planet was the center of the universe, or geocentricism, was rejected. We now look back at those who resisted the revolution with a scornful eye for their ignorance and failure to accept the scientific facts.

Now, Caldwell suggests, the time has come for yet another Copernican revolution, even more important than the first. We must reject the belief that humans are at the center of the "moral universe" or biosphere. Humanity has reached a critical moment according to some in the environmental movement. They call for a totally new outlook on life. Rachel Carson, in *Silent Spring*, stated over thirty years ago:

> We now stand where two roads diverge. But unlike the roads in Robert Frost's familiar poem, they are not equally fair. The road we have long been traveling is deceptively easy, a smooth superhighway on which we progress with great speed, but at its end lies disaster. The other fork of the road—the one "less traveled by"—offers our last, our only chance to reach a destination that assures the preservation of our earth. The choice, after all, is ours to make.[23]

Rachel Carson's fork in the road requires that humans do a virtual somersault in how they see the earth. It calls for tempering the humanist anthropocentric mind-set.[24] An integrated approach that stresses linkages between humans and environment is a necessary first step. Through community empowerment and action, people can come to recognize that their fate is tied to that of the environment and realize that they are a part of the overall web of life.

North-South Barriers

Overcoming the ethical barrier, however, is not enough. Other barriers still exist. For example, the North/South divide will continue to hamper environmental protection efforts. This divide is shorthand for the differing conditions between more developed countries and their less developed brethren. Differences in standard of living and economic development affect cultural values. The Rio Earth Summit exemplified these values. The North sought to place the environment at the center of the conference while the South wanted to place human beings at the center, a position that eventually won out (as stated in Principle 1 of the Rio Declaration).[25] Environmental interdependence makes the North increasingly dependent upon the South. The South, however, is likely to refuse cooperation with the North unless the North is willing to pay for it. Unfortunately for the South, however, environmental scarcity and insecurity will likely affect developing countries first since by definition these countries are not well equipped to handle these problems.[26]

The past three decades have taken quite a toll on most, if not all, less-developed countries. These countries have witnessed massive deforestation, soil erosion, and desertification. Moreover, they have become all-too familiar with the problems that floods and droughts bring to an area already plagued with high population growth and urbanization, in which the "development of vast shanty-towns, in which human life has attained a degree of squalor probably unprecedented outside Hitler's concentration camps."[27] This destruction can be linked to relations between the North and South. Tony Blair, the prime minister of Great Britain, has commented that until the North changes and takes environmental protection seriously, the South cannot be expected to protect the environment or limit their consumption.[28] "If [the South] can export nothing else, the poor can export their misery through migration, crime, terrorism, and disease. This coupling of destinies means that there are no separate solutions, one for the South and one for the North."[29] Thus, while environmental scarcity and conflict may prevent the South from amassing any substantial military threat (though the possibility of nuclear proliferation is significant), the North would be wise not to "rely on impoverishment and disorder in the South for its security."[30]

The perception of these destinies is also very important. When the North concentrates on universal concerns such as biodiversity, the South perceives this as just a ploy to stunt its own development through the imposition of northern environmental (and human) priorities. The North concentrates on population control while the South seeks assistance to relieve the poverty of its people.[31] The South wants to alleviate poverty, hunger, and disease by pursuing the same development tract the North used to gain its standard of living. The North, on the other hand, seeks to "educate" the South about the shortsighted nature of such a course and encourage a more enlightened approach to development. North/South issues will remain a contentious issue within environmental policy. Most explain that only a global solution can solve North/South problems.[32] But a global solution will never work unless local communities support it. The goal must be to devise those plans of actions that are best able to overcome and improve North/South relations. An integrated approach is a good place to begin.

Institutional Inertia and Statism

Institutional inertia is another significant barrier to an integrated approach of environmental protection. Current environmental policy may be compared to a fully loaded supertanker. Once a supertanker achieves full speed, it requires literally hours, if not an entire day, of full-reverse engines in order to bring it to a stop.[33] Such strong inertia is also characteristic of current environmental policy. Mainstream environmental organizations have a stake in preserving their power and the traditional methods of environmental action. Meanwhile, national governments wish to maintain their sovereignty and power. Both resist calls for devolution. At the international level, parties frequently concentrate on centralized policymaking and the traditional, state-centric model for international obligations.

The prevailing structural framework at the international level revolves around the concept of realism. Realism is a set of ethical decisions and positions that includes, among others, the notion of sovereignty.[34] It focuses on states as rational maximizers of power in an anarchic system. This emphasis on the state divides the world into territorially distinct and mutually exclusive countries. Realism also tends to de-emphasize transboundary environmental problems.[35] Realism manifests itself at the domestic level as well. Many state governments are suspicious of community-based conservation efforts and the devolution of control, particularly where they involve indigenous communities that might also be seeking greater autonomy over their internal affairs.[36]

In addition to how states perceive their own power are problems related to how nature perceives states. Environmental conflict is caused, in part, by the artificial political boundaries we know as states. This happens two ways—either a state occupies more than one ecoregion or two or more states occupy parts of a single ecoregion. Each of these situations can lead to difficulties for both environmental protection and environmental security. For example, in the Horn of Africa, the desert and arid ecoregion inhabited by the Somali nomadic pastoralists is now divided into four states (Ethiopia, Somalia, Kenya, and Djibouti). This division was the basis for the interstate war in the late 1970s between Somalia and Ethiopia when environmental decline and scarcity in northern Somalia led Ishaq Somali pastoralists to move into Ogaden in Ethiopia, precipitating tensions between Ishaq and Ogaden Somali pastoralists.[37]

Additionally, one state may occupy a diverse ecoregion. For example, Sri Lanka comprises wet and dry zones. The wet zone, in the southwest of the country, is inhabited by most of the Sinhalese ethnic groups, while the dry zone, in the east and north, is occupied mainly by the Tamil. This multi-eco-geographical situation contributed to the civil war.[38]

The inclusion of environmental issues in the security agenda of states helps to entrench the top-down approaches to environmental protection. Environmental security works to maintain the state and its national security organizations as the dominant providers and recipients of security.[39] There is a need to change the narrow view of environmental security in order to look both at the broad issues surrounding the environment, such as environmental values and localized solutions to environmental protection. This book has attempted to illustrate how these two changes are intertwined, for changes in environmental values necessitate a localized approach.

Overcoming the Barriers

A synergistic linkage paradigm that changes attitudes at both the policy and personal levels is best able to overcome these barriers. First, it is able to overcome certain ethical barriers. A change in ethics is an integral part in solving environmental degradation.[40] An ethical synergistic linkage paradigm can alter the impersonal and economic forces that cause environmental degradation. At the personal level, it alters the way in which we view our place within the environment. It also builds human relationships within communities through increased community involvement and empowerment. At the policy level, an integrated approach allows for common discussions and the sharing of information and knowledge.

An integrated approach can also go a long way towards overcoming divisive North/South issues. In order to overcome North/South problems it is important to recognize that globalism is no panacea for environmental protection. Environmental policies cannot be imposed in a top-down fashion (and be very successful); we are already witnessing a growing backlash at the local level. Additionally, such impositions exacerbate North/South tensions. What is needed is greater local autonomy and less global and national control over environmental programs. Local governments and communities can provide the innovation and creativity needed for better environmental protection and allow less-developed states to incorporate human needs into their environmental protection plans.

Global frameworks allow for increased interaction between local communities and global institutions. They allow all states to maintain peaceful and productive coexistence. An integrated approach may be our only hope to protect the environment while meeting human needs. Communication and information technologies allow for the decentralization of activities and will help the move toward small towns. "A new spirit of community is reinforced by more self-reliant production patterns (including decentralized renewable energy systems) and pride in local environments."[41] At the same time, the development of more appropriate international cooperation allows for greater communication and recognition of environmental linkages.

An integrated approach can also overcome institutional inertia and statism. An integrated approach spurs interaction between local and national governments. It encourages governments and peoples to share approaches to environmental protection with one another. They are inspired to be creative and innovative in their approaches. Furthermore, they are asked to form an international institutional family and to form linkages at the governmental level both vertically and horizontally. These linkages, in terms of their implications for global governance, are as important as those linkages between environmental issues. Such an approach is not only good for the environment, but it is also good for humanity. It increases community-based democracy and civic associations. Knowledge is shared; awareness is heightened; differences are spanned.

The adoption of a synergistic linkage paradigm, or a whole ecosystem approach, is necessary for the long-term survival of environmentalism, the environment, and humanity. In order to overcome institutional inertia, change occur at the rhetorical, institutional, and value levels. Rhetorical change is often associated with the beginnings of a policy shift. Unfortunately, these can also be merely alterations in official policy statements without much substance.[42] Institutional change embodies changes in the issues, priorities, and procedures of government institutions and the creation of new government institutions to implement the policy shifts described in the policy rhetoric. Finally, value change involves changes in actual beliefs, both of the political elites and the mass public. These occur when policy shifts become deeply ingrained in the organizational culture of government institutions and actors.[43]

An integrated approach is best able to achieve all three levels of change. We are already witnessing changes at the rhetorical level. The global community has started to emphasize the need for local action. This emphasis is beginning to translate into changes in institutional frameworks. Local Agenda 21s are being developed. Foreign assistance now targets community-based conservation projects. Although each level of change is more difficult to achieve than the one before it, the higher levels of change are also more difficult to reverse. A concerted effort to implement an integrated approach makes it possible to overcome current institutional and value frameworks and to usher in a period of enlightened and effective global environmental protection.

Critics of an Integrated Approach

An integrated approach is not without its critics. Many environmentalists view local efforts, within or devoid of global frameworks, with skepticism.

It is difficult for many environmentalists to accept the premise that communities should be empowered to recognize the link between protection of biodiversity and human resource use.[44] In an ironic twist, Arne Naess, the father of deep ecology, has written, "Whereas 'self-determination,' 'local community,' and 'think globally, act locally' will remain key slogans, the implementation of deep changes nevertheless requires increasingly global action in the sense of action across every border, perhaps contrary to the short-range interests of local communities."[45] Benjamin Barber is another skeptic of local action. He states, "the Green adage 'think globally, act locally' is contradicted by the reality that local action rarely can impinge on truly global problems."[46] Furthermore, even proponents of local action note the difficulty of local action in solving for the problems of the world. This is especially true when the need for environmental protection engulfs the developing world.

Paul Wapner identifies five possible problems with community-based conservation.[47] First, he questions whether all global threats stem from local instances of environmental abuse. While it may be true that pollution must start somewhere, the difficulty today lies in the degree to which environmental degradation has progressed. Can local governments solve problems that require immediate action? Wapner's second question asks if everyone is looking out for their own locality, who will pay attention to the health of the entire planet? While individuals may be able to control environmental degradation in specific areas, who looks out for the cumulative effect of pollution?

The third criticism of local environmental protection strategies states that human activity is becoming more global and less local is scope. The average U.S. meal travels more than 1,000 miles before it is eaten. Everything from our clothes to our automobiles is more likely to come from across the ocean than from across the street. How are local governments to respond? Moreover, will governments be willing to respond if it means relinquishing their authority over their territory?[48] Finally, are people really cooperative and ecologically mindful? So can an integrated approach really overcome each of these barriers? The answer is that it is our best hope of doing so.

Global institutions can assist local communities identify local instances of environmental abuse. Communities can mobilize quickly because of their closeness to the problem. Local empowerment and realization changes human viewpoints and helps to overcome institutional inertia. National governments realize that local action relieves the state of costly obligations and increases governing efficiency. As communities respond to their individual problems, global institutions can monitor the overall health of the world ecosystem.

Criticism, however, abounds. Many environmentalists fear a race to the bottom in which jurisdictions will ease environmental standards to attract businesses. Moreover, those localities that are currently more dependent upon businesses that extract resources or pollute heavily will be co-opted by such business interests. Some fear lay people will be unable to understand the complexity of environmental degradation. At the policy level, others predict personalization will creep into policymaking. "Losers" will become more obvious at the local level and thus have more incentive to organize to protect themselves.[49]

Additionally, even supporters of community-based conservation feel that this "new approach cannot address global problems like climate change [n]or should it be routinely accepted if a local group decides on irrevocable changes in areas of paramount national interest [such as] filling in the Grand Canyon."[50] Such uneasiness with the localism is exactly why an integrated approach is required. An integrated approach can best capture the advantages of localism while enjoying the benefits of worldwide monitoring and dissemination of information.

An integrated approach is also able to overcome another risk associated with local action: the possibility of private tyrannies. The political philosopher, Noam Chomsky, while supporting local democracy has voiced concern over just such a danger.[51] Local governments have, in some instances, resisted change and acted as private tyrannies. Additionally, Chomsky sees a real danger in the totalitarian power of private power.[52] Thus, federal and international involvement is needed to prevent such forces from running unrestrained. I do not take these criticisms of localism lightly. While I acknowledge some of the dangers inherent in local power, my research illustrates that the benefits far outweigh the dangers.[53]

Benefits of an Integrated Approach

Answering the Critics and Overcoming Barriers

Devolution does not have to result in relaxed environmental regulations. Speaking in favor of greater local control, former E.P.A. director William Ruckelshaus explains that "today we have a much different climate as relates to the environment. I don't think it is possible for states to slide back again. Environmental regulations will not go away."[54] In fact, evidence in the U.S. shows that many businesses will go beyond compliance when central regulatory structures are removed and their performance is measured strictly on results, which could involve ongoing negotiations and dialogue with local environmental groups instead of reporting requirements.[55] Additionally, it is time to move away from the belief that national governments or any large central government can alone solve most problems. Most of what needs to be done in terms of reshaping the environment must be done at *both* the local and national levels.[56] If government is to be effective, not only in the United States, but also throughout the world, it must not ignore its local roots.[57]

One primary advantage of local governments is their ability to carry out policy choices more efficiently and more effectively than national governments.[58] Even the leader of one of the largest central governments in the world has acknowledged the need for government to get closer to the people.[59] President Clinton states, "we need to help move programs down to the point where states and communities and private citizens in the private sector can do a better job. If they can do it, we ought to let them do it. We should get out of the way and let them do what they can do better."[60] Problems are more easily solved and identified at the local level. Because communities have a better grasp of the nature of the environment and better idea of the available resources, they are better administrators of environmental policy.[61] Additionally, local governments are frequently able to better enforce environmental regulations.

The power to police, a function reserved for local government (in the United States), can be used to protect the environment. Police officers know how to investigate and interrogate and have proven themselves to be an effective tool in safeguarding the environment.[62] Additionally, some observers in the United States note that the common law, as exerted by the decisions of independent state judges, produces more sensible principles than federal legislation designed to be "one-size-fits-all."[63] Another reason to favor localism is that it is popular; it is favored by a majority of people, both in the United States and abroad.[64] As it will be seen later, local governments are popular not only for the environmental regulations they produce, but also for the manner in which they produce regulations.

People are best able to form connections and attachment to the land at the personal level when they are connected to it at the policy level. People love the environment largely because they love particular places, whether it be the forests in which they walk or the streams in which they fish. Localism and community-based conservation engage the people.

An integrated approach has value separate from any benefit it produces for the environment. Citizens become involved in the political process.[65] Individuals feel that their voices and their actions can and do make a difference. People interact and learn from one another. Information is shared and distributed. Education is advanced. Creative solutions are derived.[66] Differences are discussed and bridged. In short, civic democracy is born. Community-based conservation also revitalizes communities. Like barn raisings from the eighteenth century, community efforts are able to reunite communities and reconnect citizens to each other as well as to the land that sustains them.

Local governments are also more accountable to the people and local action within a global framework is more accountable to the environment. Information is not classified at the local level as it is frequently by the national government.[67] If individuals do not like a policy, they are able to walk across the street, instead of across the country, to make their concerns heard. Individuals are able to get information firsthand. Their information is not governed by what the national media may feel glamorous enough to warrant attention. Instead of having to answer to special interests and large contributors, leaders must see those whom they represent every day and be able to answer for their actions.

Localities and communities are the hotbeds of innovation and creativity, especially when they have economic incentives to do so.[68] They are able to experiment with different environmental policies and tailor environmental programs to fit the needs of the local ecosystem. They are able to find the best solution for a particular set of circumstances. Furthermore, localities are able to share this information with others through global frameworks. For example, success in wildlife protection in Africa is making its way into the United States. In 1872, Yellowstone National Park was created. It has since been the model for conservation worldwide. Throughout the world, countries have created 25,000 parks and preserves, representing about 5 percent of the earth's total land mass.[69] This book illustrates that perhaps this model has overstayed its welcome and usefulness. Natural parks become isolated habitat islands. According to David Western, "[n]o park, no matter how big, could ever be a self-sufficient system. National parks, far from saving species, could become extinction traps if ecologically isolated by human activity."[70] For example, in Africa, migration is critical to the survival of many interdependent species, such as the elephant. This is why community-based conservation efforts have been so instrumental in protecting that species.

Examples of community-based conservation, especially those from Africa, present powerful reasons for the adoption of new approaches to environmental protection in the United States and elsewhere.[71] When villagers and ranchers in countries such as Zimbabwe are convinced to protect wildlife, it makes sense to take notice. Three million acres surrounding Yellowstone are privately owned, over one million of which has already been subdivided, leaving less land for bears or for the 93,000 elk, 300 bird species, 94 kinds of mammals, two dozen different reptiles and amphibians, and 125 other sensitive species that make their home in and around the park.[72] Learning from community-based efforts in Africa, local landowners in Idaho are demanding more local control. Even those associated with Yellowstone's management explain that "[t]he model in Africa is right. If you don't engage the people who live around the park in its mission, it will fail."[73] The model is beginning to take root around Yellowstone National Park.[74] In Ashton, a logging and farming community of 1,104, the community created a river foundation that draws enough tourists to help balance the loss of timber jobs.[75] Programs are also springing up in Montana, Nevada, and Colorado that enable landowners to earn money for protecting fish and wildlife habitat based on lessons learned from Africa.

The process of sharing also possesses intrinsic worth, for local foreign policies are able to promote democracy around the world.[76] While traditional international conservation efforts have bordered on paternalism, an integrated approach that includes local political, social, and legal institutions is able to overcome what Richard Falk and others refer to as "eco-authoritarianism."[77] The ability of localities to form their own international institutional family is yet another advantage of localism.

Women and Community-Based Conservation

Global frameworks that emphasize local action are able to improve the situation of women as well as include women in the identification and implementation of solutions. Local activism shares a special relationship with the empowerment of women. As illustrated in the case studies of community-based conservation in Africa, women are frequently the driving force in many of the local environmental protection efforts. Studies show that the most productive path toward population stability and reduction is through empowerment of women, which has been particularly successful in many developing countries.[78] Population control is a key element of ecological and human sustainability. It is also a critical aspect of any community-based conservation effort.

A. O. I. Gabriel has identified seven strategies for the betterment of rural women in developing countries. They include: raising the consciousness of women about their rights and responsibilities, mobilizing women for a better understanding and resolution of their problems through collective action, educating women on environmental sanitation, mobilizing women to seek leadership roles, and enlightening women on opportunities in their local government areas.[79] It is no coincidence that many community-based conservation efforts grew out of the women's movement. Greater autonomy for localities can lead to greater prosperity for women and greater autonomy of women can lead to increase prosperity for the environment. At the same time, international cooperation can ensure that successes are shared and communities do not exclude women. Not only does community-based conservation protect the environment, but it also frequently empowers women, which leads to societal betterment. An integrated approach that subsequently allows women to share their experiences through global frameworks transforms not only individual localities, but also the entire world community.

Local Foreign Policy

The roles of local governments are expanding throughout the world. Not only are they addressing local problems, but they are also coordinating efforts with one another to address transboundary issues. Some have even moved into the realms of foreign policy.[80] These are among the first signs of a movement toward an integrated approach that incorporates global frameworks with local action. Municipal foreign policy has exploded in recent years. For example, as of 1991, more than 900 localities have passed resolutions supporting a halt to the arms race; 197 demanded an end to nuclear testing; 126, plus 27 states, divested more than $20 billion from firms doing business in South Africa; 86 formed linkages to provide humanitarian assistance to Nicaragua; and hundreds of cities have formed sister-city relationships with foreign cities.[81] In the United States, all 50 states sponsor international programs, maintaining over 110 offices in 24 countries. Additionally, over 1,000 cities are engaged in long-term international activities.[82] These activities include providing sanctuary to Salvadoran refugees, penalizing companies for their employment practices in Northern Ireland, and establishing nuclear-free zones. States and localities are increasingly articulating their own foreign policies.[83] Many of these cities are engaged in environmental protection.

For example, one U.S. city convened a conference of two dozen American and Canadian municipal officials to draft a stratospheric protection accord to phase out ozone-depleting chemicals. According to Michael Shuman, director of the Institute for Policy Studies, "'[a]s international affairs become indistinguishable from local affairs, it's inevitable that communities and states will assert themselves in foreign policy.'"[84] This phenomenon of local internationalism is prevalent in Europe as well. Local governments there have been particularly active in providing aid, educational programs, and technical assistance to less-developed countries.[85] By establishing links with other local entities, communities are able to share knowledge about social and environmental problems.

Nowhere has this relationship proven more effective than on the U.S.-Mexican and U.S.-Canadian borders. Local governments on either side of the U.S.-Mexican border as well as those on the U.S.-Canadian border[86] have been quite successful in addressing mutual environmental concerns. Even before the passage of the NAFTA, states on both sides of the U.S.-Mexico border met to address common environmental and economic problems. The governors of the ten border states have met numerous times since 1963 to discuss common issues.[87] With the passage of the NAFTA, the federal government took a renewed interest in the often neglected border area. What it found was that counties and cities, with the assistance of state agencies, were already accomplishing a great deal of the necessary improvements.[88]

The state of Texas is particularly active in working with municipalities on the other side of the border.[89] It currently coordinates efforts to address water pollution in the Rio Grande and air pollution at Big Bend.[90] Additionally, border states and communities are very active in pursuing environmental protection, especially in the maquiladores area, while allowing for economic development and infrastructure development. According to James M. Strock, the California secretary for environmental protection, "'[s]tates along the border know best the challenges and opportunities that exist along it and together we have formed a cooperative working relationship to find solutions to our mutual problems and collectively urge action on environmental opportunities.'"[91] What is true for the localities on the U.S.-Mexico border is true for other border areas. James N. Rosenau described the phenomenon of local regionalism:

> It is noteworthy that some cross-border coalitions may involve local governments located near national boundaries that find it more expedient on a variety of issues to form coalitions with counterparts across the border than to work with their own provincial or national governments. Such coalitions may even be formed deliberately in order to avoid "unnecessary or premature attention from central authorities to local solutions of some local problems by means of informal contacts and good neighborhood networks.[92]

Though localism is associated with isolated community-based action, global and even regional frameworks allow communities to address regional and global environmental issues.

Implications for Global Governance

An integrated approach to environmental problems has profound implication on global governance. Localism, as the name signifies, implies a move away from global governance to local activism. On the other hand, talk of global frameworks implies a move towards global governance. Just as the processes that act at the global level affect local behaviors and local identities,[93] a local approach to environmental protection is not devoid of international implications. A closer look reveals cooperation and intercontinental relations between and among local governments, private citizens, small businesses, political subdivisions, universities, and nongovernmental organizations. While some international relations theorists refer to a bifurcated world, rarely do they recognize the potential and development of local entities as coordinated and coordinating actors in an international institutional family, a family based not on formal treaties but one created through people-to-people interactions. Just as patchwork makes a quilt, so too will the work of local communities create a system of global environmental protection.[94]

James N. Rosenau describes a process of global governance that forms as a result of increased interaction between smaller local entities tackling common problems.[95] Rosenau explains, "in terms of governance, the world is too disaggregated for grand logics that postulate a measure of global coherence . . . [thus] in order to acquire the legitimacy and support they need to endure, successful mechanisms for governance are more likely to evolve out of bottom-up than top-down processes."[96] The international relation theorist discusses how micro- and macroregions play an increased role in the processes of global governance. He concludes that "it seems clear, in short, that cities and microregions are likely to be major control mechanisms in the world politics of the twenty-first century."[97] Thus, according to Rosenau, rather than being a move away from global governance, localism may, paradoxically, be the appropriate mechanism for governance in the twenty-first century.[98] In his book on globalism and tribalism, Benjamin Barber discusses the battle between Jihad and McWorld. He notes that, "only at the local and regional levels where Jihad plays out this game can an alternative form of identity be won that can ultimately contain McWorld at the global level."[99] Thus, no longer is the relationship between localism and globalization a one-way street; rather, localism shapes globalization and globalization shapes localism.

Development of community approaches to environmental protection within international frameworks are able to lift everyone's economic boat while progressing toward higher environmental standards. For example:

Members of the world community need information to help them define problems and discover opportunities. The beauty of that truth is there is a wealth of available information—in state agencies, state universities, small businesses and individuals—available for retrieval and application. With the new worldwide political freedoms, people of the world community can talk to each other, access each other's data banks and shop at an environmental information smorgasbord that was previously inaccessible. Moreover, fragmentation of markets and dismemberment or redefinition of nation-states allows for a much more diverse system of environmentally-sustainable actions, fulfilling the ecological principle that a diverse system is, by definition, stronger than a monoculture.[100]

Frequently, global problems such as greenhouse warming are thought to need an exclusively international response. Such large problems, which require an understanding of multiple linkages and ecological sustainability, have proven to be too much for global governance; the best solutions are instead coming through incremental and local responses where private citizens and local governments have the potential and power to affect even the most transient of resources, such as the air. An integrated approach is able to provide citizens and local governments with the necessary power and ability.

This power allows for increased security at all levels. The ultimate source of environmental security lies not in international action but in lifestyle changes for a majority of the human population. In other words, "because the ultimate sources of environmental insecurity reside in the independent actions of billions of individuals, the broad interpretation of environmental security suggests that effective policies to deal with these problems must have bottom-up (nonhierarchical, noncentralized, nontechnocratic) as well as top-down components."[101] An integrated approach is best able to achieve this ultimate security by solving for environmental degradation and preventing environmentally induced conflict.

Conclusion

To borrow from the words of Aldo Leopold, an approach "is right when it tends to preserve the integrity, stability, and beauty of the biotic community. It is wrong when it tends otherwise."[102] An integrated approach that utilizes global frameworks to encourage localism holds great promise for not only advancing environmental protection, but also for fulfilling the vision of those who desire a more civil and humane world. It is able to combine global environmental protection with community economic development. It is able to overcome traditional paternal environmentalism and stifle environmental backlash movements. It is able to solve environmental problems and overcome institutional and ethical barriers.

Notes

1. Richard Sandbrook, "Environment: Water-Down Dream," *The Guardian* (London), 18 June 1997, 4.

2. Adam Schwarz, "Looking Back at Rio: 'Give Us Trade, Not Aid': Environmental Values vs. Economic Growth," *Far Eastern Economic Review* (Oct. 28, 1993): 50.

3. Jean-Jacques Rousseau, *A Discourse on Inequality*, trans. M. Cranston (New York: Penguin Books, 1984), 111.

4. A more difficult problem still is when some people do stand faithfully at their post but refuse to share any fruits of the hunt. As the concern over environmental security rises, so too does the role of intelligence agencies. These agencies bring with them protocols of secrecy that run counter to the perceived need of cooperation. Also contributing to the obstacles of environmental cooperation are skeptics and conspiracy theorists wary of any international effort that encroaches upon sovereignty. While such concerns are shared by many, some take it to the extreme, preaching the onset of worldwide socialism and malevolent world government that would emanate from environmental cooperation. For an interesting account of these fears see http://www.inforamp.net/~jwhitley. This web site includes an article entitled "Maurice Strong and the New World Order," which appeared in the May 1996 issue of *The New World Order Intelligence Update*. This "illuminating item" concentrates on Maurice Strong and his work towards global governance.

5. R. Eckersley, *Environmentalism and Political Theory* (Albany: State University of New York Press, 1992), 51. See Ronald E. Purser et al., "Limits to Anthropocentrism: Toward an Ecocentric Organization Paradigm?" *Academy of Management Review* 20, no. 4 (Oct. 1995): 1053. For a study of how radical environmentalism has attempted to displace anthropocentrism in American environmental policy, see Phillip F. Cramer, *Deep Environmental Politics: The Role of Radical Environmentalism in Crafting American Environmental Policy* (Westport: Praeger Publishers, 1998).

6. Ronald E. Purser et al., "Limits to Anthropocentrism: Toward an Ecocentric Organization Paradigm?" *Academy of Management Review* 20, no. 4 (Oct. 1995): 1053.

7. Ibid.

8. See Elizabeth Dodson Gray, "Come Inside the Circle of Creation: The Ethic of Attunement," in *Ethics and Environmental Policy: Theory Meets*

Practice, ed. Frederick Ferre and Peter Hartel (Athens: University of Georgia Press, 1994), 21-41.

9. Genesis 1:26.

10. Psalms 8:4-6.

11. David Browner, "Earth: A Conservation District in the Universe; Dalai Lama Interview," *Whole Earth*, no. 91 (Dec. 22, 1997): 38. Browner also explains how the Ten Commandments in the Judeo-Christain theology talk exclusively about how we should treat each other and do not mention how we should treat the Earth.

12. Andy Hines, "Population Growth: Two Warring Paradigms; Faith in Growth and Big Is Bad Paradigms," *Futurist* 32, no. 1 (Jan. 11, 1998): 68.

13. Additionally, the Baconian creed has further reinforced a view of technical development. The Baconian drive to enlarge the boundaries of human dominion marshaled in an imperial view of nature in which humankind would use the power of science to attain absolute power over the environment. See Mario Giampeitra and Kozo Mayumi, "Another View of Development, Ecological Degradation, and North-South Trade," *Review of Social Economy* 56, no. 1 (Mar. 22, 1998): 20.

14. Hines, "Population Growth: Two Warring Paradigms; Faith in Growth and Big Is Bad Paradigms," 68 (quoting Lindsey Grant).

15. Ibid.

16. Edward Flattau, "Science, Religion Agree on the Environment: Activists Can't Be Dismissed As Tree-Hugging Pagans," *Plain Dealer*, 24 Dec. 1998.

17. Ibid.

18. The United Nations Conference on Environment and Development (UNCED), "The Rio Declaration" (New York: United Nations, 1992).

19. Ibid., 459.

20. Henry Shue, "Ethics, the Environmental and the Changing International Order," *International Affairs* 71, no. 3 (July 1995): 547.

21. John Bellamy Foster, "Global Ecology and the Common Good," *Monthly Review* 46, no. 9 (Feb. 1995): 1.

22. Lynton K. Caldwell, *International Environmental Policy: Emergence and Dimensions*, 2d ed. (Durham: Duke University Press, 1990); Christopher Manes, *Green Rage: Radical Environmentalism and the Unmaking of Civilization* (Boston: Little, Brown and Company, 1990), 141.

23. Rachel Carson, *Silent Spring* (Greenwich: Fawcett Publication, Inc., 1962), 244.

24. Rodney Aitchtey, "The Ways of Decp Ecology," *Contemporary Review* 260, no. 1513 (Feb. 1992): 94.

25. See Lugi Campigloi et al., eds., *The Environment after Rio: International Law and Economics* (Boston: Graham & Trotman, 1994), 41.

26. Thomas F. Homer-Dixon, "On the Threshold: Environmental Changes As Causes of Acute Conflict," *International Security* 16, no. 2 (fall 1991): 76.

Available from http://utl.library.utoronto.ca/www/pcs/thresh/thresh1.htm; Internet.

27. Mario Giampeitra and Kozo Mayumi, "Another View of Development, Ecological Degradation, and North-South Trade," *Review of Social Economy* 56, no. 1 (Mar. 22, 1998): 20.

28. Interview of Tony Blair, "Gore Visits Earth Summit Plus Five," *All Things Considered;* NPR (June 23, 1997), Transcript No. 97062314-212.

29. Gliberto C. Gallopin and Paul Raskin, "Windows on the Future: Global Scenarios and Sustainability," *Environment* 40, no. 3 (Apr. 1998): 6.

30. Thomas F. Homer-Dixon, "On the Threshold: Environmental Changes As Causes of Acute Conflict," *International Security* 16, no. 2 (fall 1991): 76. Available from http://utl.library.utoronto.ca/www/pcs/thresh/thresh1.htm; Internet.

31. Ranee K. Panjabi, *The Earth Summit at Rio: Politics, Economics, and the Environment* (Boston: Northeastern University Press, 1997), 99.

32. Ibid.

33. Phillip F. Cramer, *Deep Environmental Politics: The Role of Radical Environmentalism in Crafting American Environmental Policy* (Westport: Praeger, 1998), 63-64.

34. Shue, "Ethics, the Environmental and the Changing International Order," 453, 456.

35. Thomas F. Homer-Dixon, "On the Threshold: Environmental Changes As Causes of Acute Conflict," *International Security* 16, no. 2 (fall 1991): 76. Available from http://utl.library.utoronto.ca/www/pcs/thresh/thresh1.htm; Internet.

36. Gregory F. Maggio, "Recognizing the Vital Role of Local Communities in International Legal Instruments for Conserving Biodiversity," *UCLA Journal of Environmental Law and Policy* 16 (1997/1998): 179.

37. Shin-wha Lee, "Not a One-Time Event: Environmental Change, Ethnic Rivalry, and Violent Conflict in the Third World," *Journal of Environment and Development* 6, no. 4 (Dec. 1997): 365.

38. Ibid.

39. Gerald B. Thomas, "U.S. Environmental Security Policy: Broad Concern or Narrow Interests," *Journal of Environment and Development* 6, no. 4 (Dec. 1997): 397.

40. Anak Agung Banyu Perwita, "Is Ecological Damage a National Security Issue?" *Jakarta Post*, 20 Sept. 1997, 4.

41. Gliberto C. Gallopin and Paul Raskin, "Windows on the Future: Global Scenarios and Sustainability," *Environment* 40, no. 3 (Apr. 1998): 6.

42. Thomas, "U.S. Environmental Security Policy: Broad Concern or Narrow Interests," 397.

43. Ibid.

44. John A. Baden, "Community-Based Conservation Works," B5. However, the former president of the Sierra Club has endorsed a self-termed concept of radical localism. See Eric Brazil, "Giving Activism the MTV Edge Young, Nervy; Sierra Club Leader's First Book Preaches 'Radical Localism,'" *San Francisco Examiner*, 6 October 1997, D1(SE).

45. Arne Naess and David Rothenberg, *Ecology, Community, and Lifestyle: Outline of an Ecosophy* (New York: Cambridge University Press, 1989), 31.

46. Benjamin R. Barber, *Jihad vs. McWorld: How Globalism and Tribalism Are Reshaping the World* (New York: Ballantine Books, 1996), 233.

47. Wapner, *Environmental Activism and World Civic Politics*, 36-38.

48. Additionally, Peter S. Wenz argues that utopian thinking based on the dissolution of the state must be rejected. He explains that while inspiration may be drawn from some indigenous societies, Western society cannot duplicate them. The national government will continue to be indispensable in the foreseeable future for most of its current functions. Additionally, state action is needed to create international treaties and worldwide agreements with respect to global environmental pollution. Peter S. Wenz, *Nature's Keeper* (Philadelphia: Temple University Press, 1996), 157.

49. Steven Teles, "Think Local, Act Local; Civic Environmentalism," *New Statesman* 126, no. 4348 (Aug. 22, 1997): 28.

50. Charles C. Mann and Mark L. Plummer, "A Look at New Approaches to Conservation: Grass-Roots Seeds of Compromise," *Washington Post*, 11 October 1998, C3.

51. Local governments have been inconsiderate and even hostile to minorities in need of protection from bigotry and discrimination. The resistance to school integration in many southern communities bears witness to this tendency.

52. Noam Chomsky, "You Say You Want a Devolution," *Progressive* (March 1996): 18-19.

53. Kevin Kelly et al., "Power to the States," *Business Week* (August 7, 1995): 49.

54. Casey Bukro, "First EPA Chief: Change Overdue; Statutes 'Obsolete,' Says Ruckelshaus," *Chicago Tribune*, 25 December 1995, C1.

55. Teles, "Think Local, Act Local; Civic Environmentalism," 28.

56. Michael Shuman, *Common Ground* (January 24, 1995).

57. Beverly Salas, "With Neighborhood Empowerment, Local Government Reaches Its Roots," *Nation's Cities Weekly* (February 13, 1995): 4.

58. Terry L. Anderson and Peter J. Hill, "Environmental Federalism: Thinking Smaller" in *Environmental Federalism*, ed. Terry L. Anderson and Peter J. Hill (New York: Rowman & Littlefield Publishers, Inc., 1997), xiv. Anderson and Hill provide the example of state forest management. They illustrate how Montana state forests earn $2.16 for every $1 they spend, while neighboring national forests earn only $0.51 for every $1 spent.

59. On Earth Day 1997 President Clinton announced a new strategy for environmental protection. He advocated empowering local communities through "right to know" legislation. He stated that knowledge is power, which communities need to take action in defense of the environment.

60. William Clinton, *Congressional Quarterly Weekly Report* (January 28, 1995): 300.

61. Jonathan Walters, *Governing Magazine* (August, 1996): 31.

62. Jerry Urban, "HPD Looks Out For Environment Full-Time; Unit Proves Its Worth with Crackdowns on Illegal Dumping, Pollution," *Houston Chronicle*, 12 August 1996, 17.

63. Roger Meiners and Bruce Yandle, "Get the Government Out of Environmental Control," *USA Today (Magazine)* 124, no. 2612 (May 1996): 70.

64. Mike Ivey, "Clinton Will Be Playing Environment Card Deftly," *Capital Times*, 7 Sept. 1996, C1.

65. John DeWitt, *Civic Environmentalism: Alternatives to Regulation in States and Communities* (Washington, D.C.: Congressional Quarterly Press, 1994), 273.

66. Lance H. Gunderson, C. S. Holling, and Stephen S. Light, "Barriers Broken and Bridges Built: A Synthesis," in *Barriers and Bridges to the Renewal of Ecosystems and Institutions*, ed. Lance H. Gunderson et al., (New York: Columbia University Press, 1995), 532.

67. Michael H. Shuman, "Foreign Policy: What Role for Local Voices?" *Orlando Sentinel Tribune*, 24 May 1992, G1.

68. Michael Shuman, *Foreign Policy* (spring 1992): 158.

69. Rocky Barber, "Conservation That Pays Its Own Way; Idaho Could Learn from Villagers Who Now Protect Wildlife Neigbors," *Idaho Statesman*, 16 August 1998, 1A.

70. Betty Spence, "Getting Along with Elephants," *Christian Science Monitor*, 11 February 1998, 14 (quoting David Western).

71. Karl Hess Jr., "Wild Success; African Wildlife," *Reason* 29, no. 5 (Oct. 1997): 32. Hess argues that the African model of communal rights can be applied to a wide array of American environmental issues. He explains that there is no reason why local councils could not take over control and management of federal lands. As support, he illustrates how in the Deep South logging companies are leasing millions of acres of prime deer habitat to the collective rule of thousands of hunter associations and how in the Bitterroot mountain range of western Montana and northern Idaho, environmentalists, ranchers, and loggers are communally trying to save the grizzly bear.

72. Rocky Barker, "'Power to Control, Responsibility to Protect'; Yellowstone's Neighbors Take Small Steps to Preserve Grizzly Habitat," *Idaho Statesman*, 18 August 1998, 1A.

73. Ibid.

74. David Western, "Stewards of the Last Place," *Chicago Tribune* 19 October 1997, C1.
75. Barker, "Conservation That Pays Its Own Way; Idaho Could Learn from Villagers Who Now Protect Wildlife Neighbors," 1A.
76. George Moffett, "Cities Dabble in Foreign Affairs," *Christian Science Monitor*, 8 February 1995, 3.
77. Richard Falk, *On Humane Governance: Toward a New Global Politics* (University Park: The Pennsylvania State University Press, 1995), 118.
78. R. J. A. Goodland, "South Africa: Environmental Sustainability Needs Empowerment of Women," in *Faces of Environmental Racism: Confronting Issues of Global Justice*, ed. Laura Westra and Peter S. Wenz (Lanham: Rowman & Littlefield Publishers, Inc., 1995), 218.
79. A. O. I. Gabriel, "A Better Life Program for Rural Women in a Developing Nation," in *Environmental and Economic Dilemmas of Developing Countries: Africa in the Twenty-First Century*, ed. Valentine Udoh James (Westport: Praeger Publishers, 1994), 199.
80. Earl H. Fry, "State and Local Governments in the International Arena," *Annals of the American Academy of Political and Social Scientists* 509 (May 1990): 119.
81. Shuman, "Foreign Policy: What Role for Local Voices?" G1.
82. Fry, "State and Local Governments in the International Arena," 119-124.
83. Jonathan Knee, "Confederacy of Dabblers: Local Foreign Policy," *Legal Times* (June 18, 1990): 19.
84. Moffett, "Cities Dabble in Foreign Affairs," 3.
85. Ibid.
86. See Alan Reed, *American City and County* (December 1993): 14.
87. Howard LaFranchi, "Border States Work for Better Ties," *Christian Science Monitor*, 21 February 1989, 8.
88. Reed, *American City and County,* 14.
89. Scott Pendleton, "Stetson-Size Agenda for Texas," *Christian Science Monitor*, 15 Dec. 1994, 2.
90. Ralph K. M. Haurwitz, "Bush Ecology Policy Takes Shape; Governor's Environmental Stance Based on State's Rights, Science, Economic Concerns," *Austin American-Statesman*, 26 July 1995, A1.
91. James J. Lee, "U.S./Mexico Border States Work Together on Clean-Up; Agree to a Series of Proposals for Joint Participation," *PR Newswire* (October 8, 1993).
92. James N. Rosenau, "Governance in the Twenty-first Century," *Global Governance* 1 (1995): 31.
93. Barrie Axford, *The Global System: Economics, Politics, and Culture* (New York: St. Martin's Press, 1995), 209.

94. Scott McCallum, "Trade and the Environment: Local Action in a New World Order," *Environmental Law—Northwestern School of Law of Lewis & Clark College* 23 (winter 1992): 621.

95. Rosenau, "Governance in the Twenty-first Century," 21.

96. Ibid., 16-17.

97. Ibid., 27.

98. It is interesting to note, however, that Rosenau, in another writing, states that environmental issues may be the one problem that lends itself to centralization instead of localization. He notes, "the centralizing tendencies inherent in the possibility of worsening environmental conditions in the years ahead ought not be underestimated. It is not inconceivable that if the processes of global warming and the widening of ozone gap—to cite only the more capricious of the many environmental threats that may gather momentum—continue to unfold at their pace, the tendencies toward a pluralist order will be substantially offset by the evolution of shared norms that attach even greater value to forms of governance without government which reinforce a cooperative global order." James N. Rosenau, "Citizenship in a Changing Global Order," in *Governance without Government: Order and Change in World Politics*, ed. James N. Rosenau and Ernst-Otto Czempiel (New York: Cambridge University Press, 1992), 294.

99. Benjamin R. Barber, *Jihad vs. McWorld: How Globalism and Tribalism Are Reshaping the World* (New York: Ballantine Books, 1996), 288.

100. Scott McCallum, "Trade and the Environment: Local Action in a New World Order," 621.

101. Gerald B. Thomas, "U.S. Environmental Security Policy: Broad Concern or Narrow Interests," *Journal of Environment and Development* 6, no. 4 (Dec. 1997): 397.

102. Aldo Leopold, *A Sand County Almanac with Essays on Conservation from Round River* (New York: Ballantine, 1970), 262.

11

Rewarding the New Century with a New Approach

When policymakers discuss security issues, they often focus on threats such as rogue dictators and bothersome neighbors. As we welcome in the twenty-first century, it is time to reexamine our traditional notions of security. Security must encompass society's overall well-being and safety. In the years to come, society's well-being will be directly tied to the integrity and sustainability of the environment. Ecological degradation and marginalization occur with striking regularity around the planet, affecting hundreds of millions of people.[1] This degradation brings with it new threats to the security of our planet. These security threats take many forms: food scarcity, resource depletion, inundation of land, desertification, water contamination, well salinization, and so forth.

One of the most severe manifestations of environmental insecurity is environmentally induced conflict. Case studies from around the world show the direct relationship between environmental degradation and interstate and intrastate conflict. Such conflict is likely to catch the eyes of many policymakers as environmental degradation breaks down world order and international relations. Although environmentally induced conflict is as old as civilization itself, the world is witnessing it on a scale never before imagined.

Environmental conflict is not limited to just the poorest, or the most resource dependent, or even the least politically stable countries; rather, every continent, every region, and almost every country will feel the effects of environmental degradation. Instances from around the world exemplify how states and peoples already struggle with environmental degradation and the insecurity it brings. In these states, environmental issues have contributed to the collapse of legal, social, and political institutions. Such collapse spurs economic instability and violent conflict. To avoid and overcome such dire consequences, it is time to reexamine how we approach environmental degradation. Although conflict may be the harm, environmental degradation is the root cause. To address environmental degradation is to solve the conflict, instability, and social decay it causes.

In this book I have proposed an integrated approach to environmental protection. This approach builds on the synergistic linkage paradigm and its scientific framework for environmental solutions. The linkage paradigm teaches us that numerous environmental issues are interrelated. When we attempt to solve one problem, we often exacerbate others because of a failure to take into account the synergistic reactions between ecological components. Only an approach that recognizes the interconnectedness of the environment and addresses environmental degradation from a whole ecosystem approach can effectively begin to solve environmental degradation.

To implement such an approach, change must occur at both the policy and the personal levels. At the policy level, we need to learn from our past efforts. Traditional, centralized, command-and-control regulatory action has outlived most of its usefulness. It is time to mold a solution that is able to recognize linkages between environmental issues as well as between environmental actors. Any approach to environmental protection should utilize a full array of actors to capture the benefits of local, national, and international expertise. As communities are given more responsibility and people learn to live with the land, change at the personal level is possible. After all, policy changes are not enough. Individual outlooks must be altered to achieve a truly integrated approach to environmental protection.

To be successful, an integrated approach must begin by building global frameworks that can assist local and national environmental protection efforts. The international community is already well on its way in building the global frameworks needed to ensure the success of an integrated approach. Such construction has sparked and assisted the formulation of treaties and international agreements. Much can be gained from concerted action. Since environmental degradation is everyone's problem, everyone needs to act. Only through concerted action will we be able to effectively address environmental degradation. Cooperation in the name of environmental protection also has the ability to bring states and peoples together who would not otherwise interact. Opening lines of communication through environmental cooperation may lead to cooperation on other issues.

International action, however, is not enough. Although international cooperation has produced many comprehensive and far-reaching global agreements, too often these efforts, though well intentioned, displace local efforts and ignore indigenous knowledge gained through centuries of living with and on the land. Additionally, international plans have suffered from a lack of effective and efficient implementation.[2] Successful implementation requires local involvement. The majority of international agreements fail to provide a supportive legal environment for local resource-dependent populations to conserve and manage their own environment.[3] The international community should now make effective implementation through an integrated approach its top priority.[4]

Although pollution is everyone's problem, most, if not all, has local roots. An integrated approach requires local action to complement international efforts. Localism is rooted in early political and social philosophy. The idea of community and community-based governance influenced our most respected political and social philosophers. At the local level, people are closer to the problem. They are also more aware of the problem. They experience its effects every day. Local communities must be involved and empowered if we are to devise workable and long-lasting solutions to environmental degradation.

Community programs to address environmental degradation are effectuating real change throughout the United States and abroad. When given the opportunity (and power) to devise local solutions to meet local environmental needs, communities have responded to the challenge. Local action brings the environment closer to the people, who in turn develop a special relationship with the land. No longer is the environment some amorphous entity controlled by centralized governments; rather, the environment is a valuable community resource to be protected and invested in for the future. But just as international action cannot solve the environmental problems by itself, local solutions need the support and resources provided by national and international actors.

An integrated approach pulls together both international and local actors to overcome the frailties of each and create a plan of attack that maximizes their respective strengths. Such a holistic approach recognizes environmental linkages. It provides local communities with the information and support to make local changes while it provides the international community with thousands of depositories of local information and plans of action. By utilizing a web of actors, environmental policy begins to better mirror the ecosystem, which is itself a vast body of interconnected entities that function as a whole.

Barriers still exist to an integrated approach. The North/South gap will remain a contentious issue, but one that an integrated approach is especially suited to overcome. Additionally, ethical obstacles, which prevent the environment from transcending our ethical and philosophical codes, must be overcome at the personal level. An international approach that imposes environmental protection in a top-down manner has only hindered efforts to change mores. On the other hand, solely local approaches have been unable to effectuate changes at the personal level through policy changes. An integrated approach, however, is able to transcend the personal level while enabling changes at the policy level. An integrated approach does more than just overcome barriers. It improves governance. It tempers the effects of uncontrolled economic growth. It empowers communities. In all, it improves society.

As the Roman Empire approached its demise, many citizens must have seen the end coming. Unfortunately, a combination of special interests, lingering skepticism, and lethargy stood in the way of devising an innovative approach to avoid the demise. Today, the signs of environmental degradation and impending collapse are all-too apparent. The stakes are higher than that of the Roman Empire; we face our own collapse.[5] Unfortunately, few are prepared to reexamine and undertake a new, thoughtful, and effective approach to environmental protection. This book does not offer a complete plan of action, but it does provide a framework for an integrated approach to environmental protection. Details need to be worked out. Research still needs to be done. But hopefully, the next century will be rewarded by a new approach to environmental protection that learns from both past human efforts as well as from the environment itself.

Notes

1. Thomas F. Homer-Dixon, "Environmental Scarcities and Violent Conflict: Evidence from Cases," *International Security* 19, no. 1 (summer 1994): 5.

2. U.S. General Accounting Office, GAO/RECD 92-43, *International Environment: International Agreements Are Not Well Monitored* (Washington, D.C.: U.S. General Accounting Office, 1992).

3. Gregory F. Maggio, "Recognizing the Vital Role of Local Communities in International Legal Instruments for Conserving Biodiversity," *UCLA Journal of Environmental Law and Policy* 16 (1997/1998): 179.

4. Edith Brown Weiss, "International Environmental Law: Contemporary Issues and the Emergence of a New World Order," *Georgetown Law Journal* 81 (March 1993): 675.

5. Milton Viorst, "The Coming Instability," *Washington Quarterly* 20, no. 4 (autumn 1997): 153.

Selected Bibliography

Adamson, David. *Defending the World: The Politics and Diplomacy of the Environment.* New York: I. B. Tauris & Co., 1990.
Alampay, Jose Gerardo. "Revisiting Environmental Security in the Philippines." *Journal of Environment and Development* 5, no. 3 (Sept. 1996).
Alpert, Peter. "Integrated Conservation and Development Projects: Examples from Africa." *BioScience* 46, no. 11 (Dec. 1996).
Anderson, Terry L., and Peter J. Hill, eds. *Environmental Federalism.* Lanham, Md.: Rowman & Littlefield, 1997.
Barber, Benjamin R. *Jihad vs. McWorld: How Globalism and Tribalism Are Reshaping the World.* New York: Ballantine Books, 1996.
Barber, Jeffrey. "The Sustainable Communities Movement." *Journal of Environment and Development* 5, no. 3 (Sept. 1996).
Beaumont, John R. "A New World Order and Managing the Environment." *Futures* (March 1993).
Benedick, Richard Elliot. *Ozone Diplomacy: New Dimensions in Safeguarding the Planet.* Cambridge: Harvard University Press, 1991.
Bowers, C. A. *Education, Cultural Myths, and the Ecological Crisis: Toward Deep Changes.* Albany: SUNY Press, 1993.
Brechin, Steven R., and Willett Kempton. "Global Environmentalism: A Challenge to the Postmaterialism Thesis?" *Social Science Quarterly* 72, no. 2 (June 1994).
Burby, Raymond J., ed. *Cooperating with Nature: Confronting Natural Hazards with Land-Use Planning for Sustainable Communities.* Washington, D.C.: Joseph Henry Press, 1998.
Caldwell, Lynton K. *International Environmental Policy: Emergence and Dimensions*, 2d ed. Durham, N.C.: Duke University Press, 1990.

Campiglio, Luigi et al., eds. *The Environment after Rio: International Law and Economics*. Boston: Graham & Trotman, 1994.

Clark, Ann Marie. "Non-Governmental Organizations and Their Influence on International Society." *Journal of International Affairs* 48, no. 2 (winter 1995).

DeWitt, John. *Civic Environmentalism: Alternatives to Regulation in States and Communities*. Washington, D.C.: Congressional Quarterly Press, 1994.

Di Leva, Charles E. "International Environmental Law and Development." *Georgetown International Environmental Law Review* 10 (winter 1998).

Dombeck, Michael P., Christopher A. Wood, and Jack E. Williams. "Focus: Restoring Watersheds, Rebuilding Communities." *American Forests* 103, no. 4 (Jan. 1, 1998).

Dryzek, John S. *Rational Ecology: Environment and Political Economy*. New York: Basil Blackwood, 1987.

Dunlap, R. E., G. H. Gallup, and A. M. Gallup. "Of Global Concern: Results of the Health of the Planet Survey." *Environment* 35, no. 9 (1993).

Emison, Gerald A. "From Compelling to Catalyzing: The Federal Government's Changing Role in Environmental Protection." *William and Mary Environmental Law and Policy Review* 20 (spring 1996).

French, Hillary F. "Partnership for the Planet: An Environmental Agenda for the United Nations." *World Watch Paper* 126 (July 1995).

Fry, Earl H. "State and Local Governments in the International Arena." *Annals of the American Academy of Political and Social Scientists* 509 (May 1990).

Fukuyama, Francis. *The End of History and the Last Man*. New York: Free Press, 1992.

Gallopin, Gliberto C., and Paul Raskin. "Windows on the Future: Global Scenarios and Sustainability." *Environment* 40, no. 3 (Apr. 1998).

Giampeitra, Mario, and Kozo Mayumi. "Another View of Development, Ecological Degradation, and North-South Trade." *Review of Social Economy* 56, no. 1 (Mar. 22, 1998).

Gleick, Peter H. "Water and Conflict: Fresh Water Resources and International Security." *International Security* 18, no. 1 (summer 1993).

Gunderson, Lance H., et al., eds. *Barriers and Bridges to the Renewal of Ecosystems and Institutions*. New York: Columbia University Press, 1995.

Grizzle, Raymond E. "Environmentalism Should Include Human Ecological Needs." *BioScience* 44, no. 4 (April 1994).

Henning, Daniel H., and William R. Mangum. *Managing the Environmental Crisis*. Durham: Duke University Press, 1989.

Hoffman, Scott. Introduction to *A New World Order: Can It Bring Security to the World's People*, ed. Walter Hoffman. Washington, D.C.: World Federalist Association, 1991.

Homer-Dixon, Thomas F. "On the Threshold: Environmental Changes As Causes of Acute Conflict." *International Security* 16, no. 2 (fall 1991).

———. "Environmental Scarcities and Violent Conflict: Evidence from Cases." *International Security* 19, no. 1 (summer 1994).

———. "The Ingenuity Gap: Can Poor Countries Adapt to Resource Scarcity?" *Population and Development Review* 21, no. 3 (Sept. 1995).

Huntington, Samuel P. *The Clash of Civilizations and the Remaking of World Order*. New York: Simon & Schuster, 1996.

Hurrell, Andrew, and Benedict Kingsbury, eds. *The International Politics of the Environment*. Oxford: Clarendon Press, 1992.

Kamieniecki, Sheldon. "Political Mobilization, Agenda Building, and International Environmental Policy." *Journal of International Affairs* 44, no. 2 (winter 1991).

———. "Emerging Forces in Global Environmental Politics." In *Environmental Politics in the International Arena: Movements, Parties, Organizations, and Policy*, ed. Sheldon Kamieniecki. Albany: SUNY Press, 1993.

Kaplan, Robert D. "The Coming Anarchy: How Scarcity, Crime, Overpopulation, Tribalism, and Disease Are Rapidly Destroying the Social Fabric of Our Planet." *The Atlantic Monthly* (Feb. 1994).

Kates, Robert W., and Ralph D. Torrie, "Global Changes in Local Places." *Environment* 40, no. 2 (March 1998).

Klötzli, Sefan. "The Water and Soil Crisis in Central Asia—A Source for Future Conflicts?" *ENCOP Occasional Paper No. 11* (Center for Security Policy and Conflict Research: Berne, May 1994). Available from http://www.fsk.ethz.ch/fsk/encop/11/en11-con.htm; Internet.

Lang, Christoph I. "Environmental Degradation in Kenya As a Cause of Political Conflict, Social Stress, and Ethnic Tensions." *ENCOP Occasional Paper No. 12* (Center for Security Policy and Conflict Research: Zurich, 1995). Available from http://www.fsk.ethz.ch/fsk/encop/12/en12-con.htm; Internet.

Last, John. "Redefining the Unacceptable." *The Lancet* 346, no. 8991 (December 23, 1995).

Lee, Shin-wha. "Not a One-Time Event. Environmental Change, Ethnic Rivalry, and Violent Conflict in the Third World." *Journal of Environment and Development* 6, no. 4 (Dec. 1997).

Leopold, Aldo. *A Sand County Almanac*. 1949; reprint, New York: Ballantine Books, 1966.

Libiszewski, Stephan. "What Is an Environmental Conflict?" *ENCOP Occasional Paper No. 1* (July 1992). Available from http://www.fsk.ethz.ch/encop/1/-libisz92.htm; Internet.

Lipschutz, Ronnie D., and Judith Mayer. *Global Civil Society and Global Environmental Governance*. Albany: State University of New York Press, 1996.

Maggio, Gregory F. "Recognizing the Vital Role of Local Communities in International Legal Instruments for Conserving Biodiversity." *UCLA Journal of Environmental Law and Policy* 16 (1997/1998).

Marietta, Don E., Jr. *For People and the Planet: Holism and Humanism in Environmental Ethics*. Philadelphia: Temple University Press, 1994.

McCallum, Scott. "Trade and the Environment: Local Action in a New World Order." *Environmental Law Review—Northwestern School of Law of Lewis and Clark College* 23 (winter 1992).

Mintzer, Irving M., and J. Amber Leonard, eds. *Negotiating Climate Change: The Inside Story of the Rio Convention*. Cambridge: Cambridge University Press, 1994.

Myers, Norma. "The Question of Linkages in Environment and Development." *BioScience* 43, no. 5 (May 1993).

Panjabi, Ranee K. L. *The Earth Summit at Rio: Politics, Economics, and the Environment*. Boston: Northeastern University Press, 1997.

Purser, Ronald E., et al. "Limits to Anthropocentrism: Toward an Ecocentric Organization Paradigm?" *Academy of Management Review* 20, no. 4 (Oct. 1995).

Robinson, Nicholas A., ed. *Agenda 21: Earth's Action Plan: Annotated*. New York: Oceana Publications, 1993.

Rosenau, James N. "Governance in the Twenty-first Century." *Global Governance* 1 (1995).

Sands, Philippe, ed. *Greening International Law*. New York: The New Press, 1994.

Santos, Miguel A. *Managing Planet Earth: Perspectives on Population, Ecology, and the Law*. New York: Bergrin & Garvey Publishers, 1990.

Shoenbrod, David. *Power without Responsibility: How Congress Abuses the People through Delegation*. New Haven: Yale University Press, 1993.

Shue, Henry. "Ethics, the Environmental and the Changing International Order." *International Affairs* 71, no. 3 (July 1995).

Singh, Jang B., and Emily F. Carasco. "Business Ethics, Economic Development, and Protection of the Environment in the New World Order." *Journal of Business Ethics* 15, no. 3 (Mar. 1996).

Teles, Steven. "Think Local, Act Local; Civic Environmentalism." *New Statesman* 126, no. 4348 (Aug. 22, 1997).

Thomas, Gerald B. "U.S. Environmental Security Policy: Broad Concern or Narrow Interests." *Journal of Environment and Development* 6, no. 4 (Dec. 1997).

Tocqueville, Alexis de. *Democracy in America*, ed. Richard D. Heffner. New York: Penguin Books, 1984.

Tolba, Mostafa K., and Iwona Rummel-Bulska. *Global Environmental Diplomacy: Negotiating Environmental Agreements for the World, 1973-1992*. Cambridge: MIT Press, 1998.

United Nations. *Report of the United Nations Conference on the Human Environment at Stockholm*, 11 I.L.M. 1416 (1972).

United Nations Conference on Environment and Development (UNCED). *The Rio Declaration*. New York: United Nations, 1992.

Viorst, Milton. "The Coming Instability." *Washington Quarterly* 20, no. 4 (autumn 1997).

Wapner, Paul. *Environmental Activism and World Civic Politics*. Albany: State University of New York Press, 1996.

Weiss, Edith Brown. "International Environmental Law: Contemporary Issues and the Emergence of a New World Order." *Georgetown Law Journal* 81 (March 1993).

Western, David, et al., eds. *Natural Connections: Perspectives on Community-Based Conservation*. Washington, D.C.: Island Press, 1994.

Young, Oran R. *International Governance: Protecting the Environment in a Stateless Society*. Ithaca: Cornell University Press, 1994.

Index

acid rain, 8, 50–52, 97–99, 128
Africa, 8, 26–31, 100, 142–50, 169, 172–73, 194–95
Agenda 21, 124, 181, 190
agriculture, 15, 17, 25, 28–32, 36, 50, 53, 63, 92, 144–50, 154, 172
Amu Darya River, 33
anarchy, 4, 9, 30
Annan, Kofi, 2, 62. *See also* United Nations
Antartica, 71, 75
anthropocentrism, 18, 57, 61, 64. *See also* ecocentrism
Aral Sea, 33–35
Arctic, 25, 53, 104, 110
ASEAN, 105
Asia, 32–40, 98–99, 101, 150–57

Baltic Sea, 101–3
Bangladesh, 25, 35–36, 100–101
Basel Convention on the Transboundary Movements of Hazardous Wastes and Their Disposal, 70, 104

biological diversity, 1, 48, 56, 63, 73, 117, 153, 173–74, 185, 187
bioregionalism, 103, 168–69
Bougainville, 16–17
Brazil, 73, 79
Brundtland Report, 8, 59, 121. *See also* World Commission on Environment and Development
Bush, George, 81–82, 85, 95, 106
business, relation to environmental degradation, 5–6, 72, 122, 128, 137, 155, 192

CAMPFIRE, 144, 148–49, 163
Canada, 22, 98, 103–4, 196
capitalism, 117
carbon dioxide, 51–52, 56, 176
carrying capacity, 18
Carson, Rachel, 186
Caspian Sea, 99–100
CDIs. *See* Community Development Initiatives
Center for Security Policy and Conflict Research, 34–35

Central Asia, 33–35, 150
Central Intelligence Agency, 10–11
centralization, 61, 115–17, 126, 136, 150, 188, 193, 206, 208–209
CFCs. *See* chlorofluorocarbons.
Chernobyl, 13
Chiapas, 31. *See also* Mexico
China, 17, 37, 39–40, 98–99, 154–56
Chipko movement, 151
chlorofluorocarbons, 85, 96, 141, 167
Christopher, Warren, 4
CIA. *See* Central Intelligence Agency
CITES. *See* Convention on International Trade in Endangered Species
climate change, 50–52, 91–96, 128, 141, 155, 174–76, 192
Climate Convention. *See* Framework Convention on Climate Change.
Clinton, William, 23, 95, 125, 172, 175, 193
Cold War, 3, 5–8, 25, 109, 113
common law, 193
communities, involvement in environmental protection, 3, 31, 38, 61, 69, 75–76, 91, 96–97, 115, 117–28, 135–57, 167–77, 185–98, 208–10
community-based conservation, 119, 127–28, 136–57, 164, 168–70, 173–74, 177, 181, 192–96
community-based democracy, 126, 143, 148, 164, 190, 192
community-based development initiatives, 126–27.

community-based forest management, 151
Conference on the Human Environment in Stockholm. *See* United Nations Conference on Human Environment in Stockholm.
Convention on International Trade in Endangered Species, 173, 180
cooperation, between adversaries, 40, 69, 80, 85, 186, 209. *See also* international cooperation; regional cooperation
Cuyahoga River, 140

dams, 12, 17, 38, 43, 151, 153. *See also* Three Gorges Dam
DDT, 102
decentralization, 57, 81, 117–18, 123, 126, 132, 189
deforestation, 4, 15, 27–28, 38–39, 50–51, 54, 151–52
democracy, 28, 58, 77, 116, 126, 143–44, 147–48, 192, 194–95
Department of State, 4, 10, 32, 85, 184. *See also* Christopher, Warren
dependency, resource, 8, 13–14, 16, 29, 43, 54, 69, 93, 143, 147, 192, 207, 209
desertification, 11, 26–27, 36, 117, 119, 145, 150, 172–73, 179
devolution, 116–17, 143, 188, 192
disease, 1, 25, 50, 187
dissemination of information, 63, 76, 96, 120, 141, 149, 153, 192. *See also* information
dual sovereignty, 118

"Dutch Campaign," 127

Earth Summit, 59, 73, 82, 94, 120, 124, 148, 171, 183, 185–86. *See also* U.N. Conference on Environment and Development; Rio Declaration
ecocentrism, 170
ecological marginalization. *See* marginalization, ecological
economic development, 2, 7, 15–16, 39, 72–74, 98, 138, 143, 186–87, 197
ecoregions, 168, 188
ecotourism. *See* tourism
education, 2, 75, 86, 93, 96, 103, 127, 137, 169, 171, 194–96
Egypt, 12, 21
elephant, 142–43, 145, 149–50
ENCOP. *See* Environment and Conflicts Project
endangered species. *See* species, endangered
Environment and Conflicts Project, 14
environmental activism, 3, 58, 61, 65, 121, 152
environmental conflict, 13–18, 25–27, 29–30, 35, 207; criticism of, 17–18
environmental cost pricing, 60. *See also* resource accounting
environmental crisis, 1, 5, 11, 61–62, 69, 80, 113
environmental degradation, 1, 3, 7–19, 25–39, 47–52, 91–105, 207–209
environmental ethics, 34, 57-58, 65, 130. *See also* land ethic
environmental law, 5, 70, 118, 135

environmental movement, 65, 80, 186
Environmental Protection Agency, 59, 140, 175, 192
environmental refugees, 9, 11, 18, 21, 26, 33, 35
environmental research, 9, 15, 17–18, 48, 50, 54–55, 76, 80, 100, 171, 174–75
environmental scarcity, 9, 14–16, 24–27, 29–30, 31, 33, 36–39, 94, 156
environmental security, 7–19, 26–27, 33–39, 47–49, 72, 74, 77–78, 87, 92–94, 113–14, 199
environmentalism, 58, 114, 116, 126–27, 144, 154, 170, 190, 200
EPA. *See* Environmental Protection Agency
ethical barriers, 184–86, 189, 210
ethics, 2, 56–58, 64, 123, 139, 184–86, 189, 210. *See also* environmental ethics; moral level
Euphrates River, 12–13, 103
Europe, 9, 13, 98–102
European Community, 39, 94, 96, 110, 196

Falk, Richard, 170, 195
federal government, 65, 117–19, 135, 137, 139–41, 181, 192–93, 197, 204
federal lands, 118, 137, 204
federalism, 141
fish farms, 39
fisheries, 1, 28, 50, 53–54, 100, 139, 155, 193
fishing conflicts, 22
flooding, 35, 39, 56, 153, 187
food chain, 50

food land. *See* agriculture
forest management, 54–56, 79, 137–38, 151–54, 203
fossil fuels, 14, 51, 56–57, 60, 92–93, 118
fragmentation: of markets, 199; of policy, 53, 56, 65, 116; of society, 30, 37
Framework Convention on Climate Change, 71, 75, 92–96, 174
free market, 5, 60, 117, 146. *See also* markets
future generations, 77, 80, 121–22, 169

Ganges River, 35, 100–101
genocide, 8, 24, 30
germ plasm, 63
global commons, 71, 77, 92, 96, 104
global frameworks, 61, 76, 83, 96, 99, 102, 120, 122, 128, 148–50, 154, 157, 168, 170, 189–96, 208
global governance, 115, 117, 126–27, 130, 143, 170, 190, 198–99
global institutions, 3, 115, 189, 191–93
global network of organizations, 121
Global Scenario Group, 47–48
global thinking, 123, 169, 191
global warming, 4, 12, 25, 50–53, 56, 63, 91–96, 119–20, 175–76
globalization, 49, 65, 115, 128, 189, 198
GNP. *See* Gross National Product
God, 184

grassroots: democracy, 143; efforts to protect environment, 86, 139, 152, 154; movements, 58, 127
Great Lakes, 103, 138–39
Green Peace, 71
Gross National Product, 17, 60
Gulf War, 13, 95

Habitat II, 11, 124–25, *See also* United Nations Conference on Human Settlements
habitats: conservation of, 138, 140, 146, 156, 185, 195; destruction of, 48, 51, 194
Haiti, 32
history, 11, 26, 70, 84, 92, 101, 103, 151
holism, doctrine of, 49
holistic approach to environmental protection, 3, 40, 53, 57, 59, 65, 105, 115, 133, 167, 209
Homer-Dixon, Thomas, 15, 23–24, 29–30, 36, 41, 54, 114, 121, 157
Horn of Africa, 30–31, 188
hyper-pluralism, 79, 123, 206

ICDP. *See* integrated conservation and development projects.
ICLEI. *See* International Council for Local Environmental Initiatives
India, 35–37, 97, 100–101, 151, 155, 164
Indian Ocean, 100
Indus River, 35
Indus Water Treaty, 101
information webs, 170

information: access to, 171–72, 174, 189, 194, 199, 209; dissemination, 63, 76, 96, 99, 120, 125, 149, 153, 192
ingenuity: local, 102, 121, 135, 140, 152, 157, 177–78; technical, 16, 54
institutional inertia, 3, 187–88, 190–91
integrated approach, 40, 53, 61, 82–83, 91–92, 102, 105, 116, 135, 142–48, 155–57, 167, 169–78, 183, 185–99, 208–210
integrated conservation and development projects, 144, 169
interconnectedness: of environmental issues, 3, 48–56, 63, 100, 115, 119, 167–68, 208; of environmental and economic issues, 28, 56, 59–60; of environmental and security issues, 7
interest groups, 2, 31, 76, 136–37, 139, 156, 169, 192, 194, 210
Intergovernmental Panel on Climate Change, 174
international agreements, 70–75, 78, 80–82, 95–104, 114, 171, 208–209
international conventions. *See* international agreements
international cooperation, 3, 61, 69–75, 80–81, 91–94, 98, 102, 104–105, 113–17, 135, 189, 196, 209
International Council for Local Environmental Initiatives, 119, 175-76
International Court of Justice, 71

international law, 2, 5, 70–81, 104, 115
international security, 2, 7–8, 22
inundation of land, 12, 14, 63, 92, 207. *See also* sea level rise; flooding
IPCC. *See* Intergovernmental Panel on Climate Change
Israel, 12, 32–33, 43

Japan, 98–99
Jordan River, 12, 43, 103

Kazakhstan, 34, 93, 99
Kenya, 27–29, 142, 144–46, 188
Kyoto Protocol to the Framework Convention on Climate Change, 93–96, 107

Lake Victoria, 28
lakes, degradation of, 51, 98–99, 103, 176. *See also* Great Lakes; Lake Victoria
land degradation, 9, 12, 15, 26–28, 39, 102, 128, 138–39, 142, 146, 154
land distribution, 31, 35–37, 49, 92, 142–45, 152, 194, 209
land ethic, 57, 139. *See also* environmental ethics
land use planning, 53, 120, 123, 175
landfills, 39, 75, 140
landownership, 138, 141, 195
Last, John, 8
Law of the Sea Convention, 71, 104
laws of ecology, 49
Leopold, Aldo, 57, 199. *See also* land ethic
Lesotho, 30

less-developed countries, 2, 40, 58, 72–75, 121, 126, 136, 189, 196
Linkage Paradigm, 48–50, 54–57, 59–61, 69, 76, 79, 82, 95, 115, 139, 151, 167–78, 185–86, 189, 208–209
linkages: between environment and development, 59–60, 62, 65, 148, 172; between environmental actors, 61, 105, 117, 124, 190; between environmental degradation and breakdown of political and social order, 15, 19, 29, 44; between environmental issues, 21, 29, 49–56, 58, 170, 209
local cooperation, 98, 197
local empowerment, 3, 40, 115, 127–28, 137, 146, 189–91
local environmental action/efforts, 3, 31, 61, 99, 116–28, 135–57, 169–77, 189–200, 209
local foreign policy, 196–97
local governments and political institutions, 49, 75–76, 115–18, 126–28, 135–56, 174–77, 189–98
local knowledge, 40, 102, 120–21, 135, 140, 174–75, 177, 209
local leaders, 38, 75–76, 125, 176
local pollution, 113, 209
local solutions, 76. *See also* local environmental action/efforts
localism movement, 117–20, 121, 130, 141
localism: roots, 116–17, 209; theory of, 48, 115–28, 137, 167–71, 191–99, 209

Lockean view of property, 184
logging companies, 204
logging, 39, 54, 56, 136, 139, 152–56

Malawi, 100, 146–47
marginalization, ecological, 15–17, 31, 36–37, 207
marketing of wildlife, 144
markets: in general, 12; world, 10, 144. *See also* free market
Mattole River, 139
Mediterranean Sea, 32, 102–3
Mexico, 31, 85, 197
Middle East, 12, 26, 32–33, 72, 85
mining, 118, 139, 151
monitoring: by global institutions, 3, 71, 192; of international treaties, 100; by nongovernmental organizations, 74–75
Montreal Protocol on Substances that Deplete the Stratospheric Ozone Layer, 11, 70, 96–97
moral level, 56–57, 121, 139, 151, 178, 184–86. *See also* personal level of linkage paradigm
Myers, Norma, 50, 53, 62–63, 167–68

Namibia, 100, 147
National League of Cities, 159
national security, 7, 10–11, 18, 77–78, 125, 188
NATO, 13, 17
natural law, 13
Nature Conservancy, 137–38, 140
NGOs. *See* nongovernmental organizations
Nile Delta, 12

Nile River, 12, 21, 29
Nile valley, 12
NIMBY ("Not In My Backyard"), 76
NLC. *See* National League of Cities
nongovernmental individuals, 103
nongovernmental organizations, 71, 74–77, 80, 102–4, 119, 121, 124, 137, 146, 153, 168, 173
nonstate actors, 82. *See* nongovernmental organizations
North/South: division between, 65, 97, 186–87; gap, 9, 72–74, 210; relations, 72–75, 104, 127, 189

oceans: degradation of, 1, 50, 52–53, 102, 104; and linkages, 52–53
OECD. *See* Organization for Economic Cooperation and Development
oil pollution, 33
oil scarcity/depletion, 14, 38
oil spills, 39, 60, 101
O'Neill, Tip, 113
Organization for Economic Cooperation and Development, 95
Ozone Layer. *See* Stratospheric Ozone Layer

Pakistan, 35–37, 101, 148, 152
PCSD. *See* President's Council on Sustainable Development
personal level of linkage paradigm, 3, 49, 56–58, 60–61, 69, 95, 139, 151, 185, 189, 193, 208, 210

Peru, 31
Philippines, 17, 39–40, 44–45, 152–53
phytoplankton, 50, 52
population growth, 12, 15, 25–32, 35–37, 39, 48–49, 63, 77, 126, 156, 184–85, 187, 195
poverty, 16, 36, 49, 73, 123, 143, 148, 172, 187
preferential purchasing, 126–27
President's Council on Sustainable Development, 122, 125
Project on Environment, Population, and Security, 15–16
protectionism, 142–43

radiation, 13. *See also* UV-B radiation
rain forests, 15, 38, 73, 79, 153
reforestation, 145, 150
regional cooperation, 12, 98–100, 103–4, 177. *See also* cooperation between adversaries; international cooperation
religion, 36, 64, 151, 184–85
resource accounting, 54, 60
resource capture, 16, 36
resource scarcity, 13–14, 37–38, 156–57.
Rio Declaration, 171, 185–86. *See also* U.N. Conference on Environment and Development
river basins, conflict within, 34–35, 43, 101, 177
Rosenau, James N., 197–98, 206
Rousseau, Jean-Jacques, 183
Rwanda, 8, 24, 30–31

Sahara region of Africa, 8, 144, 169
salinization, 32, 207
scarcity: in general, 10; politics of, 26, 31; water, 11–13, 15, 17, 33, 37–38, 42–43, 151; geopolitical, 14; socio-economic, 14; cropland, 36. *See also* environmental scarcity; resource scarcity
scientific uncertainty, effect on environmental protection efforts, 21, 63
sea level rise, 12, 21, 25, 53, 63, 92
seals, protection of, 53, 70, 101
Seattle, 119, 125, 157
Sierra Club, 71, 136–37, 203
Silent Spring. *See* Carson, Rachel
social justice movement, 122–23
soil loss/erosion, 15, 27, 31–32, 145, 187
Somalia, 30, 188
South Africa, 29–30, 147–48
South China Sea, 39–40
Southeast Asia, 37–40, 50, 108, 152–56
sovereignty, state, 69, 72, 76–82, 86, 188, 200
Soviet law, 33
species: foreign introduction of, 28; relation to humans, 57–59, 64, 151; endangered, 38, 55, 57–58, 61, 100, 105, 140, 149, 155, 173, 194–95. *See also* Convention on International Trade in Endangered Species
spill over, 19, 168
state, problems of, 72, 76–82, 86, 188–89

state-centric model, 78–79, 82, 188
statism, 187–90
Stockholm Declaration 1, 70, 76. *See also* United Nations Conference on Human Environment in Stockholm
Stratospheric Ozone Layer: depletion of, 11, 15, 51–52; effects of depletion, 25, 47, 50–52, 63, 77; efforts to protect, 11, 56, 61, 69–70, 73, 96–97, 141, 196
Sudan, 21, 27, 29, 144
sulfur dioxide, 51, 98–99
supercourt, 86
Supreme Court, 117–18, 141
sustainability 1, 17, 56, 79, 138–39, 143–45, 156, 170, 195, 199, 207
sustainable agriculture, 48
sustainable communities, 38, 40, 119–28, 132, 194
sustainable development, 93, 121–23, 125, 145–46, 150, 156, 159, 171
synergism, 5, 49–54, 61, 63, 79, 168–69, 208

Tajikistan, 33–34
technology, 23, 48, 92, 97, 156, 174–75, 189
technology transfers, 74, 93, 99
Three Gorges Dam, 38
Tigris River, 13
Tocqueville, Alexis de, 116, 143
tourism, 28, 101, 142–43, 145, 147, 149, 155, 195
treaty/convention method, 70
tribalism, 30, 142, 152–53, 198
tropospheric ozone, 51–52, 142
tyranny, private, 192

U.N. Habitat II. *See* United Nations Conference on Human Settlements
U.N. *See* United Nations
U.S. Agency for International Development, 142
U.S.A.I.D. *See* U.S. Agency for International Development
Uganda, 28, 73, 142, 146
UNCED. *See* United Nations Conference on Environment and Development
UNEP. *See* United Nations Environmental Program
UNESCO, 59, 150
United Nations, 2, 15, 28, 59, 62, 80, 145, 172, 175. *See also* Annan, Kofi
United Nations Charter, 70, 76
United Nations Conference on Environment and Development, 79, 81, 89, 106, 148. *See also* Earth Summit; Rio Declaration
United Nations Conference on the Human Environment in Stockholm, 1, 59, 70, 73
United Nations Conference on Human Settlements, 11, 124
United Nations Environmental Program, 26, 59, 70, 100, 102, 173
United Nations Population Fund, 59

UV-B radiation, 50–52, 54
Uzbekistan, 33–34

water wars, 15, 22, 26
web of life, 55, 61, 63, 167, 186
wetlands, 92, 139, 141, 154–55
wildlife, protection efforts, 54, 70, 137–53, 173, 194–95
wise use movement, 130, 136
women: role in environmental protection, 117, 145, 148–51, 164, 195–96; victimization of, 42, 65
World Bank, 102, 172, 176
World Commission on Environment and Development, 8, 121. *See also* Brundtland Report
world community, 20, 92, 178, 196, 199
world leaders, 2, 11, 56, 114
World Meteorological Organization, 102
world order, 3, 7–8, 74–75, 85, 95, 97, 200, 207
World Wildlife Fund, 149–50

Yellowstone National Park, 136, 194–95

Zambezi River, 100
Zimbabwe, 100, 148–49, 194

About the Author

Phillip F. Cramer is a John W. Wade Scholar at Vanderbilt University School of Law, where he is the senior articles editor of the *Vanderbilt Law Review*. He graduated summa cum laude from the University of Richmond with degrees in political science and speech communications. His first book, *Deep Environmental Politics*, examined how radical environmentalism influences American environmental policy. He is also the author of "Constructing Alternative Avenues of Jurisdictional Protection," published in the *Vanderbilt Law Review*.